CHARACTER AND MOURNING

CHARACTER AND MOURNING

WOOLF, FAULKNER, AND THE NOVEL
ELEGY OF THE FIRST WORLD WAR

Erin Penner

UNIVERSITY OF VIRGINIA PRESS

Charlottesville and London

UNIVERSITY OF VIRGINIA PRESS
© 2019 by the Rector and Visitors of the University of Virginia
All rights reserved
Printed in the United States of America on acid-free paper

First published 2019

1 3 5 7 9 8 6 4 2

LIBRARY OF CONGRESS CATALOGING-IN-PUBLICATION DATA
Names: Penner, Erin, 1983– author.
Title: Character and mourning : Woolf, Faulkner, and the
novel elegy of the First World War / Erin Penner.
Description: Charlottesville : University of Virginia Press, 2019. |
Includes bibliographical references and index.
Identifiers: LCCN 2019002902 | ISBN 9780813942964 (cloth : alk. paper) |
ISBN 9780813942971 (pbk. : alk. paper) | ISBN 9780813942988 (e-book)
Subjects: LCSH: Woolf, Virginia, 1882–1941—Criticism and interpretation. |
Faulkner, William, 1897–1962—Criticism and interpretation. | World War, 1914–1918—
In literature. | Grief in literature. | War in literature.
Classification: LCC PR6045.O72 Z8585 2019 | DDC 823/.912—dc23
LC record available at https://lccn.loc.gov/2019002902

Cover art: A British cavalryman in the First World War.
(National Library of Scotland/CC BY 4.0)

*First to my parents,
later to Katherine and Nathaniel,
and always to Sydney*

Contents

Acknowledgments ix

List of Abbreviations xi

Introduction 1

1 Multiplying Mourners in *The Sound and the Fury* 27

2 Competitive Elegy in *The Waves* 42

3 The Lively Response of the Dead in *As I Lay Dying* and *Jacob's Room* 78

4 "A Host of Others" in *Mrs. Dalloway* 115

5 "Unproductive" Grief in *Go Down, Moses* 146

Conclusion 189

Notes 191

Works Cited 209

Index 221

Acknowledgments

Critics of Woolf, Faulkner, modernism, and the interwar period have borne with various pieces of this project over the past decade, and I am grateful to fellow conference attendees for their questions and suggestions, particularly the hard ones. Beyond their significant material contributions to this project, I am thankful to those communities for proving so welcoming to a scholar who is still finding her footing.

My graduate advisor, Molly Hite, is an enthusiastic reader of both Faulkner and Woolf. She urged me to abandon my tidy arguments and go after the truly unruly: precisely the nudge I needed. My thanks also to Doug Mao, Roger Gilbert, and Kevin Attell for holding me accountable for my methods and materials. From the beginning of my project, all four advisors worked to make this a book worth reading, not merely a disciplinary exercise, and for that I am grateful.

An early version of chapter 2 first appeared as "The Order of a Smashed Window-Pane: Novel Elegy in Virginia Woolf's *The Waves*," in *Twentieth-Century Literature* 61.1 (2015): 63–91. Sections of chapter 5 also appeared as "Fighting for Black Grief: Exchanging the Civil War for Civil Rights in *Go Down, Moses*," in *Mississippi Quarterly* 67.3 (2014): 403–27. My thanks to the editors of both journals for permission to reprint, but even more to the anonymous readers who insisted that my material held greater significance than I had articulated and then patiently showed me how to find it. I am also grateful to the two anonymous readers for the University of Virginia Press, who provided detailed comments that take seriously what I am striving to accomplish. My thanks too to Eric Brandt for articulating what he found most promising in this project and, in identifying it, helping me to hold onto it through my revisions.

The *New Yorker* and the Artists Rights Society have kindly granted permission to reproduce Reginald Marsh's 1934 sketch *This Is Her First*

Lynching. I am grateful to the librarians at King's College, Cambridge, first for showcasing the archived sketches that caught my eye, and second for their patience in sending me scans of Frank Raphael Waley's full sketchbook. Not all of his sketches have made it into my book, but they continue to prod me to rethink the experience of university life a century ago, about which I spend so much time speaking, writing, and teaching. My particular thanks to Frank Waley's daughter, Joyce, for her gracious permission to use her father's sketches, and for filling in the arc of his life so that he has become far more fully realized to me, and nothing like Woolf's Jacob Flanders.

My students and colleagues at Asbury University have proven to be invaluable reminders of reality. They have intimated that spending so much time on literature of death can be hazardous, and yet they allow me to do it anyway. I am also grateful for two faculty research grants from Asbury that have helped tremendously in pulling together the materials for this book.

My final thanks are to my family, for their forbearance. This project has been a constant—and demanding—presence in my life for many years, and they gamely accepted the additional company. My parents maintained cheerful support of my academic endeavors from afar, swooping in to help when needed. Sydney balanced a philosopher's precision and a partner's tact in reading drafts and ensuring I would have a room of my own in which to work as first Katherine and then Nathaniel appeared. My thanks to these last two for obliging me to move continually between work and play, so that this project remains fresh and interesting to me yet. They also offered what no one else in my life could; they showed me what it is to regard writing as a permanent presence in one's life, since they have known nothing else.

Abbreviations

Works by Faulkner

AILD	*As I Lay Dying*
ESPL	*Essays, Speeches, and Public Letters* (ed. James B. Meriwether)
FU	*Faulkner in the University*
GDM	*Go Down, Moses*
LG	*Lion in the Garden*
SF	*The Sound and the Fury*
SL	*Selected Letters of William Faulkner* (ed. Joseph Blotner)

Works by Woolf

CSF	*Complete Shorter Fiction*
D	*The Diary of Virginia Woolf* (ed. Anne Olivier Bell, 5 vols.)
E	*The Essays of Virginia Woolf* (ed. Stuart Clarke and Andrew McNeillie, 6 vols.)
JR	*Jacob's Room*
L	*The Letters of Virginia Woolf* (ed. Nigel Nicolson and Joanne Trautmann, 6 vols.)
MOB	*Moments of Being*
MD	*Mrs. Dalloway*
TG	*Three Guineas*
TL	*To the Lighthouse*
TW	*The Waves*

Character and Mourning

Introduction

> Oh the dead! she murmured, one pitied them, one brushed them aside, one had even a little contempt for them. They are at our mercy.
> —Virginia Woolf, *To the Lighthouse*

A footnote in psychiatry's *Diagnostic and Statistical Manual* may prompt a cease-fire in the debate over grief—or fuel a dispute that erupted a century ago. The editors of the most recent *DSM* eliminated the "bereavement exemption" that in previous editions had ensured grief would not be regarded in the same light as clinical depression, despite similar symptoms. Advocates for the exemption protest that mourning is distinguished by its limited duration, but the new editors maintain that bereavement has no cutoff date and can "precipitate" a major depressive episode (American Psychiatric Association 811).[1] Amid outcries that they are medicalizing grief, the editors contend that the line between grief and illness is not as distinct as we have attempted to make it.

Sigmund Freud drew that line a century earlier in his essay "Mourning and Melancholia." There he characterized mourning as a normal process that restores the mourner's ego after loss; melancholia, on the other hand, he deemed a pathology. Although in later work he reconsiders those categories, Freud's original dichotomy has governed discussions of literature of mourning ever since. Peter Sacks first mapped the elegiac tradition from its classical origins to the beginning of the twentieth century; Jahan Ramazani has traced elegy through the century of poetry since then. Considered together, these scholars replicate Freud's distinction between productive mourning and pathological melancholia: Sacks sees traditional elegy as consolatory, whereas Ramazani claims the refusal to be consoled as the hallmark of twentieth-century elegy. Freud's diagnostic division now serves as a historical watershed, separating prewar mourning from postwar melancholia. The war literature at the center of this scholarly conflict has drawn considerable attention but little agreement. Paul Fussell argues that the First World War triggers a departure from tradition, but Jay Winter counters that the war compels a radical return to old religious and cultural forms of consolation. Winter's claim, in turn, faces criticism from Sandra Gilbert, who argues that such forms are "obliterated by the war" (183).

The novels of Virginia Woolf and William Faulkner sit at this fault line, their work a challenge to the Freudian dichotomy that has framed critical and popular discussions of mourning for a century. Culture, not psychoanalysis, the novelists argue, has the upper hand in determining how we assess manifestations of grief. Through a shift in literary form they challenge the culture of mourning that surrounds those who grieve. Both writers exchange poetic elegy, with its disciplined focus on the dead and the mourner, for novels that stage the interplay of psyche and society. Faulkner and Woolf would turn our attention not to the diagnostic categories of the current *DSM* but rather to its ancillary reminders to clinicians to exercise caution, since the "duration and expression of 'normal' bereavement vary considerably among different cultural groups" (American Psychiatric Association 717).

Although it may seem pedantic to begin a study of elegiac literature with a clinical manual, the *DSM* sets research agendas, brings conditions into the public eye, and determines insurance coverage for treatment. It both reflects and shapes public conceptions of reasonable human emotion. In shifting literature of mourning from poetry to prose, Woolf and Faulkner alter the schooled conventions of the elegy to capture such social aspects of mourning. The modern mind, Woolf observes in "The Narrow Bridge of Art," is "full of monstrous, hybrid, unmanageable emotions" that require prose to be used "for purposes for which prose has never been used before" (*E* 4:429, 435). In the wake of criticism that declares modernism too enraptured with aesthetic concerns, Patricia Rae has argued convincingly for the political efficacy of modernist literature of mourning, particularly when one looks beyond poetry to prose that intersects with public documents, institutions, and policies (15).[2] Sacks and Ramazani, the most prominent critics of elegy, limit their studies to poets, the latter claiming that literature of mourning is "more obviously suited to the inward torsions of poetry than to the psycho-social emplotments of fiction" ("Afterword" 287). And yet Ramazani names Virginia Woolf first in a list of novelists whose work pushes against the "generic paradigm" (287). Both she and Faulkner insist that the "psycho-social," as Ramazani calls it, is essential to a full understanding of mourning.

These authors' novels of mourning implicate the community in judging, circumscribing, or alienating those who grieve. Drawing attention to the cultural conditions of mourning also has surprising effects on the elegiac subject. By challenging the role of the dead in public and national identity narratives, Woolf and Faulkner reclaim the elegiac subject from eulogy—which strips him or her of individuality—and from neglect, when his or her death merely serves as the occasion for others' reflections. Woolf and Faulkner champion the significance of the dead, reconstructing the stories that link the dead to the world of the living.

Hugh Kenner once deemed both Faulkner and Woolf "provincial" (57), but Jessica Berman and Rebecca Walkowitz have routed such efforts to cast Woolf's scrutiny of a particular culture as lack of ambition. Even Faulkner has been liberated from country-bumpkin caricature by critics such as Jolene Hubbs. Current criticism emphasizes both authors' cognizance of world events, argues for their place in the roster of cosmopolitan modernists, and reads their work as both politically and socially engaged. This project participates in that line of inquiry, emphasizing Woolf's and Faulkner's attention to the social influences that deem some mourners elegists and others merely sentimental. As Doug Mao and Rebecca Walkowitz observed a decade ago, the new modernist studies both expands the stable of modernist writers and attends to the many material and social influences at work in modernism. Scholarship of the elegy has followed a similar arc; recent feminist scholars argue not only for recognition of female and underrepresented writers within the elegiac tradition but also for an expanded definition of elegy that accounts for experiments in form and subject. Faulkner and Woolf, though high modernists, are interlopers in the elegiac canon. In conceiving of them not primarily as fixtures of modernism but rather at the forefront of a reimagined elegy, this project identifies new motivations for the formal experimentation for which Woolf and Faulkner are famous.

Looming large in both Woolf's and Faulkner's creative process is their concern that the First World War has narrowed the ways in which the dead are perceived and mourned. In direct contrast to the homogenizing culture around them, they offer readers a variety of narrative perspectives as they engage in ongoing formal experimentation throughout their careers. Critics have tended, however, to view their experiments only in terms of aesthetics; Malcolm Cowley wrote rather dramatically of Faulkner, "It was writing another book by the same formula—something he never did—that would have been a sin against the religion of art" (*Faulkner-Cowley File* 157). Woolf and Faulkner experimented with several genres, including poetry, biography, memoir, drama, and essay, but more significantly, both worked to blend existing forms. Faulkner's *Requiem for a Nun* infuses drama with fiction, and Woolf's *The Pargiters* oscillates between essay and fiction. Her description of *The Waves* as a "playpoem" captures her desire to create new literary categories out of old ones (*D* 3:203).

Woolf's and Faulkner's formal variety only highlights their recurring interest in central characters who are absent or dead, a theme that has not gone unnoticed by critics. The Faulkner discussion echoes larger critical trends in shifting from thematic to psychoanalytic to deconstructionist readings of grief. Whereas André Bleikasten regards *The Sound and the Fury* as a work "*about* lack and loss" (*Ink* 47), Gail Mortimer goes further, arguing for Faulkner's novels as substitutes for what has been lost (89). John T. Matthews links the theme of mourning to Faulkner's style, employing Derrida to argue for "Faulkner's belief that writing is a kind of mourning" (10). Similar discussions of Woolf's work are focused by comments that Woolf herself made on the subject. Her famous diary remark, "I have an idea that I will invent a new name for my books to supplant 'novel.' A new — by Virginia Woolf. But what? Elegy?" has opened the door to readings of Woolf's novels as elegiac (*D* 3:34). "Elegiac," however, is ambiguous, suggesting either the adjectival form of "elegy" (e.g., "elegiac tradition") or a mode of literature that in either affect or theme exhibits the qualities of mourning.[3] Although critics are happy to grant fiction writers an elegiac gloss if the term is applied loosely, most have not taken seriously Woolf's and Faulkner's direct engagement with the elegiac tradition.

In his provocatively titled *Virginia Woolf's Quarrel with Grieving*, Mark Spilka responds to Woolf's generic proposal, offering instead the term "abortive elegies for our time," "since she refuses in these books to deal with death and grieving in any direct or open way, and her elegiac impulse—by which writer and reader alike may normally work out grief through formal measures—is delayed, disguised, or thwarted—at best only partially appeased" (15–16). Spilka forgoes a lengthier consideration of Woolf's elegies on grounds that pursuing it "would be to dwell on the evasions of a writer who is not wholly engaged with her inmost problems" (10). Rebecca Walkowitz has recently argued that such "evasions" form the core of Woolf's most acute social engagement ("Virginia Woolf's Evasion"). Thus it seems that in these elegiac evasions, these "abortive elegies," lie some of her most fertile literary and critical work. Recent monographs by Tammy Clewell and Christine Froula have given sustained attention to Woolf's elegy, evidence of renewed interest in the role of elegy in the shaping of her oeuvre.

Too often, however, studies of Woolf's or Faulkner's elegy remain focused on the authors' psychology, though their engagement with elegy is less personal than historical. Biographical and psychoanalytic studies of their work abound, and Woolf is happy to comply with such readings. She saw herself as being singled out for Greek tragedy after losing her mother, half sister, father, and brother in quick succession (Lee 169). She addresses the deaths of her parents directly in *To the Lighthouse,* the 1927 novel that has prompted the most work on Woolf and mourning.[4] Faulkner also emphasizes personal losses in his introduction to *The Sound and the Fury:* "I, who had never had a sister and was fated to lose my daughter in infancy, set out to make myself a beautiful and tragic little girl" (252).[5] But Faulkner had confessed earlier that he had no plan when he began writing the novel. John T. Matthews concludes that Faulkner's writing "*precedes* any sense of loss. . . . Writing does not respond to loss, it initiates it" (19). Faulkner's decision to rewrite the facts of his life to suit his work—four years after his novel's publication—calls into question critical attempts to identify personal loss as the impetus of elegiac novels.

One of the striking features of Woolf's and Faulkner's work is that they emphasize the need for multiple perspectives even though their elegiac reforms are solitary undertakings. One aim of this book is to test the critical merits of the method that both authors exemplify within their work: a social approach to mourning that circumvents mass memorialization. How might a comparison of two elegists who share a high regard for cultural specificity help us skirt the Scylla and Charybdis of overgeneralization of the modernist elegy and excessive attribution to individual biography or psychology? Could a comparative analysis make it easier to see Woolf's and Faulkner's projects as complementary, her crisp cultural critique borne out by his visions of culture fraying and straining at alternative modes of mourning? The fruitfulness of such a partnership does not rely on the authors having collaborated, just as the mourning they illustrate in their novels does not rely on their characters' cooperation with one another. It is, in fact, important that each character and writer bear the full effort of mourning, even as each voice contributes to a greater understanding of grief. Mass commemorative ceremonies, such as the ones that punctuated public life after the First World War, reinforce the belief that there is one way to grieve. That is precisely what Woolf and Faulkner deny.

Faulkner and Woolf not only did not collaborate with one another, there is no evidence that they so much as owned each other's books.[6] What may be the only acknowledgment by one author of the other is recounted by Carvel Collins in the introduction to Faulkner's poems, *"Helen: A Courtship"* and *"Mississippi Poems"*: "Faulkner's grandaunt, Mrs. Walter B. McLean, said in August, 1951, that once when she was reading Virginia Woolf's *Orlando* and told Faulkner she was finding it difficult, he urged her to put it aside because there was no reason to struggle over difficult reading, that some works are for some people and others for others" (102). Collins notes the oddness of this remark, since Faulkner was prone to recite Shakespeare's *The Phoenix and the Turtle* when others lauded the clarity of modern poetry (70). *Orlando* is also perhaps the least likely of Woolf's works to be rejected on grounds of difficulty.[7]

Critical conversation has not done much to pave the way for a consideration of Woolf's and Faulkner's work together. Toni Morrison's 1955 master's thesis on Faulkner and Woolf remains the only critical work to explore the two writers' connections in detail, and even there Morrison argues that Faulkner's approach to alienation is the "antithesis" of Woolf's ("Virginia Woolf's and William Faulkner's" 4). Yet the biographical, cultural, and critical gap between Faulkner and Woolf only amplifies the significance of their solitary efforts to assume the mantle of the modern elegist in the wake of the First World War. Their pairing here is grounded not in the familiar dynamics of literary influence, or even of professional rivalry, but rather in each author's determination to create, alone, the foundation for a novel form of elegy. Each mounts a sustained engagement with the conventions of mourning—in literature and in public life—that spans the length of his or her writing career.

Setting Woolf alongside Faulkner illuminates one aspect of their biographies that plays a significant role in their approach to elegy: they share a striking wariness of the university-educated elite. Both authors exhibit a tendency that Peter Sacks claims is characteristic of American elegists: being "explicitly on the margins, dislocated, vagrant, or expelled," reflecting "a marked distance from the comforts of community" (313).[8] Though critics argue over Woolf's and Faulkner's relative privilege and canonicity, it is significant that both authors regarded themselves as outside the literary and educational elite.[9] When Faulkner felt cornered by questions about literature in interviews, he repeatedly asserted that he was not a literary man but simply a farmer (*LG* 169). As he sums up in a letter to his publishers, "All my writing life I have been a poet without education" (*SL* 188). For all his late association with the University of Virginia, Faulkner remained wary of universities, critics, and contemporary writers. Woolf turned her lack of a university degree to her advantage, articulating the benefits of an "outsider" position when the English education system seemed to lead straight to war. Although she speaks directly to these concerns in the essays of *A Room of One's Own* and *Three Guineas,* her most powerful argument for the outsider lies in her fiction, particularly the novel *Jacob's Room.* There she contrasts her female narrator's inability to attend the Cambridge she haunts with Jacob's unwillingness to consider life outside his dormitory window. His loss, Woolf suggests, is the greater.

In part because of what they perceive to be their outsider positions, Woolf and Faulkner stand to gain by taking part in the elegiac tradition. As one of literature's most distinguished genres, elegy can establish one's place in literature without requiring a university degree. The contributors to *The New Princeton Encyclopedia of Poetry and Poetics,* of which Peter Sacks is one, carefully note that, as much as theme or form, elegy is defined by its literary capital: "The elegy has been a favored form not only for mourning deceased poets but also for formulating ambitions and shaping poetic genealogies. As such it is a genre deeply implicated in the making of literary history" (Brogan et al. 324). Since Milton's *Lycidas,* elegy in English has been aligned with the pastoral, replete with classical deities and catalogs of flowers and mourners, but elegy's definition has shifted over the centuries, slipping easily between mode and motive (322). Woolf and Faulkner argue that the social aspects of mourning are an integral part of the nature of mourning and thus cannot be a casualty of the poetry/prose divide.

Even as they benefit from elegy's status in the hierarchies of literature, Woolf's and Faulkner's perception of themselves as outsiders prompts them to criticize the elegy, one of the most formal and allusive strains of literature, as the product of a closed educational and cultural system that prizes legacy over culture. As they extend elegy's reach to include more perspectives and forms, Woolf and Faulkner pursue the larger goal of revealing how much of elegy's existing conventions rely on culture. In "The Mark on the Wall," Woolf calls attention to the "military sound" of the word "generalisation" (86). Rebecca Walkowitz argues that, in this small gesture, Woolf shows, "by speaking abstractly and theoretically about genre, that all rhetorical terms have social contexts" (*Cosmopolitan* 87). And yet one literary form in particular comes under Woolf's fire. Shortly after linking generalization to militarism, Woolf's narrator reflects, "Generalizations bring back somehow ... ways of speaking of the dead, clothes, and habits" ("The Mark on the Wall" 86). Elegy and the public conventions of mourning are soiled by their proximity to "generalisation," marred by the "military sound" that conveys the violence emanating from such rigid conventions. If the war has made elegy—the genre that offers a way of "speaking of the dead"—rigid in its conventions and habits, it has not yet stripped elegy of the cultural significance that gives Woolf a powerful platform for her criticisms of the very form she employs.

Woolf's elegiac rewriting enables her to cast a judicious eye on the role the literary subject has come to play in supporting the institutions that suppress critical thinking and lead to a militarized society. She disapproves of both the novelistic hero and the eulogized subject in elegy, and her work does much to extricate literature from its reliance on heroes and the poets who sing their praises. Faulkner, for his part, uses the elegy to illuminate the harm of preserving an idealized image of a character at the cost of his or her voice. Faulkner's work thus aligns the frail beauty of white southern womanhood and the impenetrable faces of black servants in his contemporary Mississippi as he poses significant challenges to the South's discomfort with intimacy, whether sexual or racial. Woolf is the more articulate critic of elegy and culture, but Faulkner illustrates the fruits of those critiques; whereas she insists on the need for changes to mourning conventions, he is bolder in illustrating those cultural changes through his fiction. Though their projects arise independently, as powerful critiques of their respective cultures of mourning, together they argue for a much greater transformation: that elegy knit together the prewar and postwar worlds and acknowledge the continuity of social life across that chasm without lapsing into either nostalgia or pathology.

War-Stricken Freud

Freud's psychoanalytic categories have not prevailed in the field of psychology, but the explanatory force of "Mourning and Melancholia" (1917) has proven persuasive for critics of literary mourning. Peter Sacks looks to Freud to motivate the elegist's project: the poem serves as a substitute for the loved one who was lost, and completing the poem enables the elegist to conclude the process of mourning (4–7). Setting aside concerns about the efficacy of such substitutions, at the heart of Sacks's formulation lies a problem that he inherits from Freud: substitutive mourning places the well-being of the mourner above other considerations. Perhaps unsurprisingly, the chief criticism of Freud's "Mourning and Melancholia" is that successful mourning is predicated on narcissism, since in Freud's analysis mourning ends when the subject's ego is fully restored. As Tammy Clewell notes, "Mourning and Melancholia" was written shortly after Freud's early work on narcissism; by the time of *The Ego and the Id* (1923), she argues, Freud had developed a more sophisticated theory of mourning ("Mourning beyond Melancholia" 47).[10] Significantly, the change in Freud's theory occurs during the First World War, which shapes the elegiac work of both Faulkner and Woolf. Sacks and other scholars of elegy, however, seem to attend only to Freud's early work. Such scholarship thus perpetuates Freud's initial focus on the mourner's psychology, when it should take into account the complex relations among the dead, the mourner, and the culture that even Freud begins to acknowledge after the overwhelming losses of the First World War.

Though Jahan Ramazani considers elegy and mourning through a wider historical and social lens, his argument remains wedded to Sacks's psychoanalytic framework.[11] Ramazani advocates for anticompensatory elegy because such elegists "hold open a cultural space for a complex experience that contravenes social and economic norms of getting-over and getting-on" ("Afterword" 290). In an era of social activism, it is easy to see how not stifling the fires of grief could encourage one to stoke them for social change. Still, as both Diana Fuss and Greg Forter have argued, replacing mourning with melancholia only begets new problems. Fuss argues that the current emphasis on melancholic, resistant mourning is the result of critical tendencies to "fetishize resistance; it assumes that only acts of melancholic refusal are ethical, while acts of hopeful reparation are not. But is reparation always an act of forgetting? And is refusal always an act of remembering? Can resistance, for resistance's sake, guarantee ethics?" (108). Freud warned against melancholia in part because the affect of melancholia is self-loathing and disconnection—hardly the conditions for engendering a social revolution (Forter 139).

David Eng and David Kazanjian rightly point out that Freud casts doubt on the distinction between mourning and melancholia even within "Mourning and Melancholia": "It is really only because we know so well how to explain [mourning] that this attitude does not seem to us pathological" (3). They take this to mean that "were one to understand melancholia better . . . one would no longer insist on its pathological nature" (3). Faulkner's and Woolf's work, however, encourages a different reading: the behaviors of both mourning and melancholia are weird, but the former is made palatable through storytelling. Tradition renders familiar a wild and untamable thing, revealing society's significant role in deeming particular behavior either civilized or pathological. Woolf and Faulkner put the onus on society to manifest a supportive environment for grief before they inquire into any individual's manifestation of it. We cannot, they suggest, make sense of the latter without first acknowledging the influence of the former.

Situating Faulkner's and Woolf's contributions to the study of literary mourning requires that one set aside Freud's "Mourning and Melancholia," and even *The Ego and the Id,* and look to the essays Freud wrote six months after the outbreak of the First World War, collectively known as "Thoughts for the Times on War and Death."[12] Precursors to his well-known work *Civilization and Its Discontents,* the essays capture a key moment in Freud's changing understanding of the relationship between the individual and society. He dwells on the widespread disillusionment of those who had believed Europe to be increasing in civility, and he suggests that by avoiding discussing death, society leaves individuals ill-prepared to face the horrors of the war.

Freud may be best known for his psychoanalysis, but it is as a keen observer of the intersection of psychology and social change that he best captures the dynamics of modern mourning. In his expansive characterization of prewar civilization, Freud seems to be performing the work of mourning for lost ideals, revisiting each of the memories that bind society to them. But in declaring civilization an "illusion" and arguing that "there are very many more cultural hypocrites than truly civilized men" ("Thoughts for the Times" 284), he turns against the lost object, attacking it, much as, in his earlier work, he portrays the melancholic doing. Though Freud acknowledges that "probably . . . our sense of these immediate evils is disproportionately strong," he notes that "we cannot but feel that no event has ever destroyed so much that is precious in the common possessions of humanity" (275). He may remind his readers that the current war is "like every other war" in forcing on individuals an "altered attitude towards death," but he cannot help but speak to "the disillusionment which *this* war has evoked" (275; emphasis mine). Seemingly despite himself, he emphasizes the elements that make the First World War an incomparable event and the catalyst for shifting cultural ground.

Freud's attempts to marry objective assessment and the inclination to see this war as unique speak to the difficulty of the noncombatant's perspective. If the combatant is, in Freud's words, "a cog in the gigantic machine of war" (275), the noncombatant's task is to situate the war within a larger cultural framework. And yet his or her experience shares a great deal with the combatant's: "Not only is it more bloody and more destructive than any war of other days. . . . It disregards all the restrictions known as International Law, which in peace-time the states had bound themselves to observe; it ignores the prerogatives of the wounded and the medical service, the distinction between civil and military sections of the population, the claims of private property. It tramples in blind fury on all that comes in its way, as though there were to be no future and no peace among men after it is over" (279). Freud's inability to maintain distinctions shakes his objectivity, showing the war's reach beyond the front and beyond the present, threatening to overwhelm clinical diagnoses and hope for treatment. "Thoughts for the Times" is Freud's chance to redress the first flaw he acknowledges in "Mourning and Melancholia," that is, a lack of empirical evidence for the theories that follow. In his reflections on the war, psychoanalysis meets historical reality, and the subsequent reconsiderations prove far more significant as a map of modern mourning than those early hypotheses.

Following his reflections on cultural disillusionment, Freud offers an unusual characterization of public attitudes toward death both before and after the war. He argues that prewar "sensitiveness," in which individuals avoid thinking of or discussing death, has terrible effects: "Life is impoverished, it loses in interest, when the highest stake in the game of living, life itself, may not be risked" (290). Freud sees as "an inevitable result" of this impoverishment that

> we should seek in the world of fiction, in literature and in the theatre compensation for what has been lost in life. There we still find people who know how to die—who, indeed, even manage to kill someone else. There alone too the condition can be fulfilled which makes it possible for us to reconcile ourselves with death: namely, that behind all the vicissitudes of life we should still be able to preserve a life intact. For it is really too sad that in life it should be as it is in chess, where one false move may force us to resign the game, but with the difference that we can start no second game, no return-match. In the realm of fiction we find the plurality of lives which we need. We die with the hero with whom we have identified ourselves; yet we survive him, and are ready to die again just as safely with another hero. (291)

The compensation Freud describes is quite different from the compensatory elegy Sacks imagines. Here, the inability to discuss death leads individuals to seek portrayals of death in art. Even there, the death that a reader seeks can be faced only when he or she is assured a plurality of lives. Freud's sketch of the prewar role of literature is a common one, but he dares to consider how the balance has shifted when life is altered by war: "Death will no longer be denied; we are forced to believe in it. People really die; and no longer one by one, but many, often tens of thousands, in a single day. And death is no longer a chance event. To be sure, it still seems a matter of chance whether a bullet hits this man or that; but a second bullet may well hit the survivor; and the accumulation of deaths puts an end to the impression of chance. Life has, indeed, become interesting again; it has recovered its full content" (291). Freud depicts a nightmare in which the diverting perils of literature now encroach on life, as the profusion of fictional deaths becomes a mass of real casualties. But he leaves his reader to ask whether literature offers more than nightmare in a war-stricken world. Has fiction simply been replaced by a life lived in "full content," or might it yet make a contribution in a world in which "we are unable to maintain our former attitude towards death, and have not yet found a new one" (292)? If prewar literature extend the limits of a life lived cautiously, postwar literature addresses the new fears of those who face loss that is not only proliferate but real.

In reading Faulkner's and Woolf's texts, we continue to find "the plurality of lives we need" (Freud, "Thoughts for the Times" 291), but now, rather than identifying with the heroes, we find our place among the bereaved. Caddy Compson's brothers, Percival's friends: Woolf's and Faulkner's characters surround the absent individual as mourners gathered at a funeral. Losses occur early and often unexpectedly, leaving the surviving characters to find their way through the broken world that remains. Like Freud, who speaks from the position of the noncombatant rather than the soldier—whose psychology he acknowledges as "interesting, no doubt... but I know too little about it" (291)—Faulkner and Woolf position their civilian speakers around the dead, a formal arrangement that reflects a social shift in who speaks for the dead.

Walter Benjamin suggests that it is not the veterans who speak for war casualties but rather others who must elegize: "Was it not noticeable at the end of the war that men returned from the battlefield grown silent—not richer, but poorer in communicable experience?" (84). Although Freud ultimately concludes that the war "compels us once more to be heroes who cannot believe in their own death" ("Thoughts for the Times" 299), Woolf and Faulkner contest a return to a world of make-believe. Leaving heroes aside, they trust the future to the role that Freud describes earlier in the same essay: "It is indeed impossible to imagine our own death; and whenever we attempt to do so we can perceive that we are in fact still present as spectators" (289). Although Freud dismisses spectatorship as a failed imagination of death, Faulkner and Woolf recognize that imagining life after the war falls to those who will stand perennially graveside.

Freud's characterization is a common one: the spectator "only" stands at the sidelines of the defining event. Woolf and Faulkner, however, argue that the spectator balances death and culture in a vision of the future that is only inhibited by romanticized heroes. Woolf draws a straight line between the idealization of the individual and war: "The reason why it is easy to kill another person must be that one's imagination is too sluggish to conceive what his life means to him—the infinite possibilities of a succession of days which are furled in him, & have already been spent" (*D* 1:186).[13] As she notes in comparing her memoirs with the fictional lives she creates: "A real life has no crisis. . . . It must lack centre. It must amble on" (*D* 5:335). This, then, lies behind Woolf's desire to see the ordinariness in others that heroism—and, I would add, eulogy—can only obscure.

In both her fiction and her criticism, Woolf's compulsion to reflect a world changed by war is palpable. Faulkner's, however, has been largely eclipsed by his attention to the earlier war that marks him as a product of the American South. But the First World War prepares the broken landscape through which Faulkner can sympathetically engage with the Civil War experiences of earlier generations. The First World War provides the footing for his fiction, from his first novel, *Soldiers' Pay* (1926), which follows a wounded veteran's return to the United States, to the work Faulkner considered his magnum opus, *A Fable* (1954), in which he endeavors to write "an indictment of war" set at the French front in 1918 (*SL* 178). Decades after he toured Europe as a young man, he recalls his feeling of kinship with the French upon seeing in the French countryside the same topography as his war-torn American South. In his letters to his mother during that 1925 tour, Faulkner speaks of his own country of citizenship with the distance of one who identifies primarily as a Mississippian, and for whom "America" is composed of the northern states: "It looks as if a cyclone had passed over the whole world at about 6 feet from the ground. Stubs of trees, and along the main roads are piles of shell cases and unexploded shells and wire and bones that the farmers dig up. Poor France! And now America is going to hold their noses to the grindstone" (*SL* 28).[14] Faulkner's attention to the war and to the literature that spilled from it is evident in five stories he collected under the title "The Wasteland," after T. S. Eliot's poem, and which share Eliot's emphasis on soldiers' disillusionment.

In an unpublished essay from 1924 or 1925, "Literature and War," Faulkner places himself in conversation with the war poets Siegfried Sassoon and Rupert Brooke and the war novelists Henri Barbusse and R. H. Mottram. Michael Millgate notes that Faulkner was particularly attuned to Mottram's ability to approach war indirectly, a tactic Faulkner adopts in *Soldiers' Pay* and later work (390). Faulkner's indirection was perhaps a necessity; he was still training in Toronto with the Canadian Royal Air Force when the war ended, though he styled himself as a veteran afterward. As if wary of repeating the mistakes of critics who read in Faulkner's early fiction the sentiments of a soldier (Kohler 119), recent scholars have focused instead on Faulkner's ties to the Civil War, removing him from the global stage in the process. But though he writes most often of an American South broken by the Civil War, the First World War was, as Millgate notes, "the one event of his own lifetime commensurate with that Civil War which had been the crucial event in the history of his own region and his own people" (392).

The First World War foundations of Faulkner's reinventive elegy are evident even in the texts that seem far removed from the event. One of the most widely quoted Faulknerian lines on mourning appears late in *If I Forget Thee, Jerusalem* (first published as *The Wild Palms*), when the protagonist eschews suicide and declares, "*Between grief and nothing, I will take grief*" (715; italics in original). Harry Wilbourne's avowal that he will remain and remember after his lover is gone affirms not only the significance of elegiac work but also the role of the "wheezing entrails" (715), the physical and social body, that would house and give expression to memory. Though elegists tend to emphasize transcendence of the physical body, Faulkner concludes Harry's story by affirming the significance of the human body in a direct repudiation of both elegiac precedent and the recent war's reminder of the body's fragility. The latter is a surprising intrusion in a love story. Even as Harry laments the waste incurred by death, he acknowledges, "*There is always plenty of meat. They found that out twenty years ago preserving nations and justifying mottoes*" (709; italics in original). He will not use Charlotte's dead body to attest to her significance, since he saw too clearly how the war was justified in part through its body count: young men must not die in vain, and thus more young men must die to justify the others' deaths. But Harry can, with his own living body, continue to mourn Charlotte. *If I Forget Thee, Jerusalem* is not a war novel, and yet the war, in Faulkner's formulation, forced society to acknowledge how much it justifies itself over the bodies of the dead. The section of the Psalms from which Faulkner takes his title makes a slightly different point: if I should forget thee, Jerusalem, let my right hand falter. Failing to preserve memory will bring down a curse on the body. Though his publishers chose a different title for the novel's publication, Faulkner's original choice identifies the war as the catalyst for modern mourners' desperation to prove themselves through new means.

Faulkner may have invented a public identity of war hero and fighter pilot, but in his fiction he, like Woolf, assumes the perspective of the mourning spectator who will contribute to visions of a postwar future. Neither soldier nor civilian is immune from the illusions of war; as one of Faulkner's characters comments in *Soldiers' Pay*, "You know how it was: all soldiers talking of dying gloriously in battle without really believing it or knowing very much about it, and how women kind of got the same idea, like the 'flu—that what you did today would not matter tomorrow, that there really wasn't a tomorrow at all" (128). That Faulkner's and Woolf's novels concern themselves precisely with that unforeseen "tomorrow" is indicative of the ways in which they, the spectators, stand apart from those who, whether soldier or civilian, see only the war in front of them.

Novel Elegy

Theories of melancholia have a rich literary pedigree (Eng and Kazanjian 2–3), but elegy was originally defined by its form rather than its content. It only became allied with mourning in the sixteenth century (Sacks 3). Woolf and Faulkner retain elegy's original emphasis on form, but they have a new purpose in mind: What literary form could offer a model for mourning in postwar society? Jahan Ramazani cites Woolf as evidence of "a popular myth of the modern" that "posits that in 1900 or 1910 or 1916 literature broke free from ... the chains of generic affiliation" (*Poetry* 23–24). Both Woolf and Faulkner, however, prove powerful champions of Ramazani's larger claim, that "genre analysis helps to focus both departures and inheritances" (24–25).[15] Faulkner's and Woolf's deviations from both elegiac and novel conventions reflect their recognition of the hazards of each genre. The authors' innovations thus serve as a map of their critical reading of the literary tradition and their attentiveness to the needs of their era.

In "The Narrow Bridge of Art," Woolf celebrates the modern novel's indirection, the "sweeps and circles" with which it will dominate the literary world: "So, then, this unnamed variety of the novel will be written standing back from life ... prose thus treated will show itself capable of rising high from the ground, not in one dart, but in sweeps and circles" (*E* 4:438).

Robert Penn Warren describes Faulkner's work in a similar manner: "His movement has not been linear, but spiral, passing over the same point again and again, but at different altitudes" (257). Warren's description seems apt when one recalls that Faulkner once claimed he would like to be reincarnated as a buzzard (*LG* 243). His choice captures what Woolf desires—an observer "standing back from life"—but he introduces an unsavory note into the discussion by allying those traits with an animal that preys on the dead. Elegists have long been accused of opportunism, particularly if they take part in the compensatory mourning that Peter Sacks allies with traditional elegy. Tammy Clewell offers a sharp criticism of this model of substituting poetry for the dead: "That the traditional elegy transforms the lost other into the writer's own aesthetic gain raises certain political and ethical suspicions" ("Mourning beyond Melancholia" 50). Faulkner and Woolf both confront this dark undercurrent in the elegiac tradition. Ambitious elegists dog the first half of this study: in Faulkner's *The Sound and the Fury*, Caddy's brother Quentin engages in extreme imaginative flights in order to make of her a pure elegiac subject, whereas Bernard of Woolf's *The Waves* slowly smothers the other elegiac speakers with his endless words. Faulkner even recasts abstract literary benefits in commercial terms in *As I Lay Dying*, when the Bundren family members exchange their matriarch's corpse for false teeth and bananas from town.

Both authors suggest that the baldly ambitious elegist can be tempered with literary forms that encourage multiple perspectives. The heteroglossic structure of their novels enables the authors to explore the "division between or within mourning voices" that Peter Sacks identifies as a key trope in the elegiac tradition (34–35). The antiphonal choruses in the *Iliad* and the *Odyssey* find their counterpart in the call and response of a grief-stricken black woman and her brother in the titular story of Faulkner's *Go Down, Moses*. The vacillations of the mourning poet in Tennyson's *In Memoriam* reappear in the thoughts of the war veteran Septimus Smith in Woolf's *Mrs. Dalloway*. Sacks explains the preponderance of divided mourning voices in elegy as "the necessarily dialectical movement of the work of mourning" (36), a protection against the individual's inclination to deny death. Woolf and Faulkner take the dialogue further, using the novel's community of characters to grapple with the complications that arise when divided voices are considered as social as well as psychological data. The call and response of "Go Down, Moses" is narrated through the eyes of a white lawyer whose elite education leaves him ill-prepared to understand the mourning tradition he witnesses. Septimus's elegiac burden is buried under the medical diagnosis of shell shock, and his narrative is reduced to a brief news item batted about among professionals in London. Faulkner makes the heteroglossic stakes of the novel elegy clearest in *The Sound and the Fury,* when the elegy is staged four times, each incomplete; the novel ends after four versions, not because the story is accomplished but because by then Faulkner has trained his reader to expect that each new perspective will not weave more than it unravels.

In Bakhtinian language, Woolf and Faulkner write "novelized" elegy, elegies that contain "an indeterminacy, a certain semantic openendedness, a living contact with unfinished, still-evolving contemporary reality" (7). Such "openendedness" favors historical specificity over storytelling resolution and aids Faulkner in unmooring the South from its antebellum mystique, "all magnolias and crinoline and Grecian portals and things like that" (*FU* 131). Although Mikhail Bakhtin's heteroglossic dialogue occurs at the level of the narrator, in many Faulkner and Woolf novels the characters take on the narrator's role, most visibly in *The Sound and the Fury, The Waves,* and *As I Lay Dying.* Neither narrator nor elegist is given a privileged position; instead, both authors invest in character as a means of reestablishing the significance of social and historical context. The dialogic interactions that shape elegy are composed of friends, family, and lovers, and that social network helps to make space for the dead within the world of such connections. Bakhtin reflects established beliefs when he claims, "The dead are loved in a different way. They are removed from the sphere of contact, one can and indeed must speak of them in a different style" (20). Yet Woolf and Faulkner make accurate representation of the dead a point of competition among elegiac speakers. Rather than assume a different plane of conversation when speaking of the dead, their elegists hold each other accountable for bridging the two worlds and thus return the dead to "the sphere of contact." When Woolf writes of her mother's death, it is the distancing, the making "unreal" of the dead, that she finds most disturbing: "The tragedy of her death was not that it made one, now and then and very intensely, unhappy. It was that it made her unreal; and us solemn, and self-conscious. . . . It obscured, it dulled" (*MOB* 95). The challenge, then, for both Woolf and Faulkner, is to unmake the fiction created by death. The novel offers a way of repersonalizing or recharacterizing the elegiac subject so that only the loved one is lost and not also the bereaved's understanding of who that person once was.

Because character, rather than psychology, is central to Woolf's and Faulkner's novel elegy, Freud proves less useful as a guide for this project than narrative theorist Alex Woloch, who offers a system for interpreting how and why an author negotiates social and narrative space for each character. In *The One vs. the Many: Minor Characters and the Space of the Protagonist in the Novel,* Woloch considers the suite of characters in nineteenth-century novels in terms of "character-space," which he defines as "the *intersection* of an implied human personality ... with the definitively circumscribed form of a narrative" (13; italics in original). These character-spaces are, in turn, considered as parts of a "character-system," "the arrangement of multiple and differentiated character-spaces ... into a unified narrative structure" (14). Woloch's theory offers a vocabulary for Faulkner's and Woolf's efforts to redistribute the elegiac role among a wide variety of characters, which they achieve by manipulating the relationship between a character's significance to the story and his or her voice within the narrative. Even more significantly, as the characters jockey for space and voice within a narrative, attention to character-space helps us articulate the means by which the dead remain significant in a fictional world—and, by extension, the real one.

The strength of Woloch's theory lies in his attention to the relationship between the individual character's significance to the story and the extent to which the narrative lingers on or passes over the character. Moving between story and discourse, Woloch argues that "narrative meaning takes shape in the dynamic flux of attention and neglect toward the various characters who are locked within the same story but have radically different positions within the narrative" (2). This analysis of a formal dialectic has a social dimension, as well: "All character-spaces inevitably point us toward the character-system. ... The space of a particular character emerges only vis-à-vis the other characters who crowd him out or potentially revolve around him. It is precisely here that the social dimension of form emerges" (18). In his analysis of nineteenth-century novels, Woloch attends to the bursting out of minor characters within narrative limitations. Faulkner and

Woolf, however, challenge the significance of the central figure's position, particularly in the elegy, when the elegiac subject's centrality to the "story" of mourning is subsumed under the elegist's discourse.

Faulkner and Woolf use the novel's focus on character to demand that their readers conceive of elegiac subjects as characters, so that even when they die, readers maintain social and ethical relations to them—relations that tend to be either obscured or exaggerated in other literary forms. The authors' work is particularly important because in the past century the dead have garnered less and less of a place in the social spaces of real life. Anticipating Philippe Ariès's famous study of death, Walter Benjamin laments that the dead have been pushed to the margins of society: "There used to be no house, hardly a room, in which someone had not once died. . . . Today people live in rooms that have never been touched by death, dry dwellers of eternity, and when their end approaches they are stowed away in sanatoria or hospitals by their heirs" (93–94). There is a significant body of work on narrative imagination that supports drawing a line from the fictional world to reality, particularly if the former can improve the latter. Clifton Spargo argues that in mourning we create a narrative in which we could have prevented the other's death—useless for saving that individual but resulting in a heightened sensitivity and commitment to preserving others. Spargo speaks to the possibility of using fictions, both literary and psychological, to effect ethical action.

Mourning is currently treated as a matter of psychology, but Woolf and Faulkner insist that we understand it narratively. The authors can only do so by maintaining the "openendedness" Bakhtin celebrates, resisting conventions that cater to the allure of the end in the novel's story arc. Faulkner and Woolf refract their story through multiple perspectives, place death and other major events early in the novel, and encourage recursive reading habits. They resist Frank Kermode's famous "sense of an ending" as the logical arc of the narrative. They undermine, through their form, the alliance of narrative ends and death, knowing that such narratives are cold comfort for the survivors of the First World War, who must create a story that extends beyond the death of those they loved.

Although the correspondence between Faulkner's work and Woolf's is formal in nature, they themselves might protest so much emphasis on form. In response to interview questions that focused on form or style, Faulkner responded that he was too busy "writing about men and women, human beings, the human heart in conflict with itself, with its fellows, or with its environment" to attend to such matters (*FU* 88): "Whenever my imaginaton [*sic*] and the bounds of that pattern conflicted, it was the pattern that bulged ... that gave. When something had to give it wasn't the imagination, the pattern shifted and gave. That may be the reason that man has to rewrite and rewrite—to reconcile the imagination and pattern" (51–52). Faulkner wrote and spoke in terms of characters rather than in finished books. When he was confronted about discrepancies of dates and details between the publication of *The Sound and the Fury* and the "Compson Appendix," he argued, "At the age of 30 I did not know these people as at 45 I now do; that I was even wrong now and then in the very conclusions I drew from watching them, and the information in which I once believed" (*SL* 222). He rejected the term "appendix" for his additions to *The Sound and the Fury*, arguing, "It's really an obituary, not a segregation" (*SL* 237).

Woolf was sensitive to criticisms that her novels lacked well-rounded characters, particularly since those criticisms came from friendly readers as well as antagonistic ones; Woolf's own husband referred to her characters as "ghosts" after reading *Jacob's Room* (*D* 2:186). In his 1941 Rede Lecture on Woolf at Cambridge, itself a study in elegy, E. M. Forster echoes contemporary criticisms of Woolf's style even as he admires her daring: "What wraiths, apart from their context, are the wind-sextet from *The Waves*, or Jacob away from *Jacob's Room*! They speak no more to us or to one another as soon the page is turned. And this is her great difficulty. Holding on with one hand to poetry, she stretches and stretches to grasp things which are best gained by letting go of poetry. She would not let go, and I think she was quite right, though critics who like a novel to be a novel will disagree" (258). He offers in sum, "So that is her problem. She is a poet, who wants to write something as near to a novel as possible" (259).

In her introduction to *Mrs. Dalloway*, which I consider further in chapter 4, Woolf confronts those critics who accuse her of prioritizing form over character. She also makes clear, in her attack on Arnold Bennett, that she agrees with him on the importance of characters before critiquing the way he builds his: "I believe that all novels ... deal with character, and that it is to express character—not to preach doctrines, sing songs, or celebrate the glories of the British Empire, that the form of the novel, so clumsy, verbose, and undramatic, so rich, elastic, and alive, has been evolved" (*E* 3:425). A key element in both Faulkner's and Woolf's work is the craft of character making, and it is in their emphasis on character, the lyric "I" of poetry giving way to a cast of characters, that they offer their most significant challenges to elegiac precedent. The profusion of spectral saints and heroes in their novels is a nod to the social and literary convention of speaking of the dead in unreal terms, and it calls into question the wisdom of such detachment.

Psychoanalytic theories of mourning and traditional elegy emphasize the elegist's voice and the restorative work accomplished by speaking of the dead: repeating his or her name, creating a volume of words to mark and replace that lost one, and, in some versions, crafting a prayer in which the elegist offers up the dead to the care of a deity. There is, however, little attention to the lost voice of the elegiac subject, particularly in Freudian readings that rely on a narcissistic view of the bereaved that ignores the subjectivity of the dead. Faulkner's and Woolf's concern with character makes them sensitive to the ways in which such practices limit the range of elegiac attitudes and fail to acknowledge the subjectivity of the lost individual. In their novels they restore the voices of the elegist and the elegiac subject, using the novel as a means of renegotiating the character-space of what was originally a poetic relationship between mourner and the dead.

This study traces three distinct stages in the process of elegiac reinvention, pairing novels from Faulkner and Woolf at each step. Although they articulate the foundation for their endeavor at different points in their writing careers, Woolf and Faulkner begin by multiplying the elegists in their work, creating a contest of mourning voices that draws attention to the stakes of the elegist's position, as well as the difficulty of knowing the dead through others' stories. The complexities of such multiplicity are the focus of the first two chapters of this project. Faulkner acknowledges the compensatory and melancholic mourning conventions through some of his characters but insists that grief not be isolated by such forms. He favors the inquiries of children as a means of reassessing the conventions of mourning, a method Woolf also employs. Like *The Sound and the Fury*, which revels in the distinct voices of its four elegists, Woolf's *The Waves* explores both the harmony and the dissonance in the mourning hymn of its six speaking characters. The competition between mourning voices is acute in Woolf's novel, and there is more pathos than satisfaction in the final pages when only a single mourner speaks and readers "hear" the silence of the other voices. Faulkner and Woolf facilitate storytelling in which the protagonist does not take the lion's share of discursive and story space. Instead, by creating an absent center in their novels, an elegiac figure who is both significant and silenced, Woolf and Faulkner retain the form of the novel while renegotiating the role of peripheral figures, establishing a dialectical relationship between the absent figures at the center and the peripheral figures who attempt to speak for them.

Woolf and Faulkner do not linger on the elegist, however. In the second stage of their elegiac reinvention they offer the voices of the dead, raising questions about the truth of the elegist's story and also, intriguingly, about the elegiac subject's own ability to represent him- or herself to the reader. Fittingly, the voices of the dead in *Jacob's Room* and *As I Lay Dying* irrupt in the middle chapter of this project, refuting the eulogies offered by the other characters and insisting on their individuality. Here, too, there is a poetic parallel, what Diana Fuss has called the "corpse poem," in which the dead speak for themselves, a genre I explore further in chapter 3. Fuss argues that "speaking in the voices of the dead provides a way for poetry to make present a certain kind of absence. Corpse poems, unlike elegies, strive to reconstitute death, not to compensate for it" (71). She sees the corpse poem as a means of breaking through the dichotomy of mourning and melancholia, consolation and resistance. Fuss's work provides a useful set of terms for considering the novels in which Woolf's and Faulkner's elegiac subjects break out of their silent roles, challenging the stories that are being told about them.

Recent critics have argued that decaying corpses, animals, and plant matter should tilt interpretation toward context over character, as literary studies embraces a posthumanist lens.[16] But this study reflects Woolf's and Faulkner's wariness of reading a corpse without the social sphere that shapes the reading of the person who inhabited it; indeed, they use formal experimentation to revivify the corpse, reinvesting it with the traits of the character. Such wariness stems from seeing ill bodies and black bodies stripped of subjectivity, a practice Woolf and Faulkner are keen not to replicate in their own writing. Through the unpredictable, often disagreeable voice of the dead, character appears as the primary tool of Woolf's and Faulkner's reinvention. Although in reality the dead will not return to chastise the living, such fantastical appearances in Woolf's and Faulkner's novels are useful embodiments of the feelings of the living, who strive to conceive of their own place in the world after death. Literary treatment of the dead could seem of limited use, were it not for the fact that the living see something of their value to society in how we treat our dead.

In their final stage of reinvention, Faulkner and Woolf revisit the goal of mourning, undermining the "grief work" that is at the core of psychoanalytically inflected readings of elegy. Freud attributes successful mourning to the "grief work" (*Trauerarbeit*) that restores the mourner's ego by distancing the living from the dead,[17] but mourning is insistently incomplete in Faulkner's and Woolf's novels, as they reject the "grief work" that would evaluate success by diminishing another. The respective elegiac subjects of *Mrs. Dalloway* and *Go Down, Moses*, Septimus Smith and Rider, challenge the expectations of productive mourning and are the focus of this book's final two chapters. Woolf uses Septimus's persistent grief to explore the fissure between veterans and noncombatants, as the latter use diagnoses of mental illness to silence the poetic voices of those who witnessed the war on the front. Faulkner's character, Rider, refuses to engage in the socially acceptable mourning that would perpetuate the linking of black bodies with labor, a stain from the days of slavery. Like Benjy Compson, of *The Sound and the Fury*, who knows neither past nor future but only an unrelenting present, these characters insist on loss as a current matter. They are silenced only by death, which results from the tension between their expressions of grief and the communities around them. In this final pairing, Woolf and Faulkner acknowledge the social pressure on mourners who attempt social change but are asked simply to play the role society has shaped for them. One character performs the expected role, committing suicide after returning from the war with shell shock. The other seizes his public role for other purposes, making lynching an act of political protest and showing that mourning can kindle a bold new form of social criticism.

Freud regards the destruction of the self as the result of failed mourning, but these characters reclaim a larger historical picture by invoking cultural networks of grief and calls for justice. Septimus and Rider are both broken protagonists, individuals incapable of bearing the weight of their grief or their story alone, but that is precisely what makes the collaborative elegy of Faulkner's and Woolf's novels so compelling. In a recent discussion of the state of modernist studies, Paul Saint-Amour argues that scholars' investment in an existing conceptual framework "keeps us in a field-formation that it might be time to think about dissolving and reconstituting around some other term or concept," since it suggests "we're travelers trying to warm our hands at a fire that's gone out, as fires do, and that we'd all be better off moving on" (455). But in laying claim to the power of "weak modernism," Saint-Amour reconsiders the significance of that image: "Maybe the fire was never the point, the dwindling having been the real occasion for the gathering" (456). Elegy, like the study of modernism, can be rebuilt only by making more of the company gathered at the scene. Unlike a traditional elegy, in which death provides the occasion for literary production, Woolf's and Faulkner's works make the failure of traditional elegy itself the occasion for writing. Death, they suggest, is already on the scene in the years after the war. Freud may consider the spectator's perspective a sign of imaginative failure, but Faulkner and Woolf use such marginality to insist on the multiplicity of voices singing elegy, voices that, in turn, insist on their own limitations and those of the dead.

This project is chiastic in nature: Faulkner begins it and ends it, but Woolf forms its core. Most significantly, the arrangement shifts attention from chronology to what we might think of as three stages of elegy making. Faulkner and Woolf first transform elegy from a solitary to a multivoiced song, in a critique of generic conventions and the social forces that determine who sings the hymn of mourning. They then revive the voice of the elegiac subject, defying Freud and his insistence on extricating oneself from a relationship with the dead. Finally, Woolf and Faulkner defy the terms of successful mourning by tightening the bonds between the elegist and the elegiac subject. Their mourners are a testament to the events of the first half of the twentieth century that make death and mourning ever present. Faulkner and Woolf register grief in incomplete stories and corporate mourning as they strive to remember marginalized figures of loss. Although there may still be "people who know how to die" in fiction, as Freud put it, the reader stays behind, standing with the characters who live to grieve.

I

MULTIPLYING MOURNERS IN
The Sound and the Fury

> Grief, when it comes, is nothing we expect it to be. . . . Grief has no distance. Grief comes in waves, paroxysms, sudden apprehensions that weaken the knees and blind the eyes and obliterate the dailiness of life. Virtually everyone who has ever experienced grief mentions this phenomenon of "waves."
> —Joan Didion, *The Year of Magical Thinking*

Woolf's and Faulkner's canonical novels attest to the centrality of elegy to their work. The authors' similarities are more conspicuous, however, if we set aside the order in which the works appeared. For both writers, elegiac reinvention unfolds over three distinct stages, but Woolf and Faulkner contribute to those stages at different phases of their careers. *The Sound and the Fury* (1929) offered Faulkner his first success, whereas *The Waves* (1931) appeared well after Woolf had established a reputation with critics and reviewers. And yet both novels expose the solitary voice of the traditional elegy as inadequate either for representing the dead or for consoling the living. In the initial stage of their reinvented elegy, Woolf and Faulkner flout traditional elegy's monologic structure, insisting on the need for—and challenges of—a dialogic model for grappling with death and representation.

Faulkner seizes the opportunity to expand elegy's form by separating his novel into four sections, each guided by a different speaker. His critique of the monologic elegy is oblique, as he presents readers first with Benjy's narrative and then Quentin's and Jason's and a third-person account that focuses on the character of Dilsey. Woolf's critique is more direct. She employs six speakers whose integrated narratives underscore the competition for space in which to elegize. Faulkner foregrounds each character's distinct experience of mourning, demonstrating what a multifaceted elegy could offer, but Woolf removes the artificial boundaries of such conventions so that each character flinches, hesitates, or blusters in the society of others. Eric Sundquist interprets Faulkner's method as one designed to "sequester modes of consciousness and formally depict them as incapable of responsive interaction" (10), but Faulkner makes possible a range of elegiac narratives that may not survive competition in a shared space. His narrative facilitates multiplicity, even as Woolf's, appearing much later in her elegiac revisions, warns that the competition among speakers can lead too easily to a fight for dominance—and the silencing of those other speakers.

Faulkner's lectures on the craft of writing are littered with language that links mortality, artistic success, and genre. He explains his famously protracted sentences as the result of "the compulsion to say everything in one sentence because you may not live long enough to have two sentences" (*LG* 141). Rather than embrace his success as a novelist, he styles himself as a "failed poet," inscribing in his successful prose a lament for the lost "fire" of poetry: "35–45 is the best age for writing novels, fire not used up, author knows more. This type of writing is slower, the fire lasts longer. 17–26 is the best age for writing poetry. Writing poetry is like a sky rocket—all the fire condensed in one rocket. Most outstanding poetry is written by young men" (56). But Faulkner does not relinquish all claims to poetry. In another interview he declares, "My prose is really poetry" (56), indicating that he has not, as Freud encourages mourners to do, severed all ties with the lost object. Faulkner makes no explicit claim to elegy, but even as his posture of "failure" links his work to southern identity after the Civil War, it acknowledges that he writes of loss in a form that emerges out of the failure of an older one.

When Woolf and Faulkner take up the elegy in a new form, they depict loss and mourning through their novels' characters rather than through a poetic speaker or narrator. As a result, they create an opportunity to consider elegiac work in context, as their elegiac characters are influenced by other characters and their broader cultural environment. Faulkner sets diverse modes of mourning alongside one another; his roster of grieving characters includes several melancholics, particularly Harry Wilbourne of *If I Forget Thee, Jerusalem* and Quentin Compson of both *Absalom, Absalom!* and *The Sound and the Fury*. To echo Elizabeth Bishop, no elegist loses farther or faster than Quentin Compson, the central character in what John B. Vickery calls Faulkner's "elegies of patrimony," novels in which Faulkner considers the legacy of the Civil War in the American South (129). Faulkner has proven himself more than capable of representing the melancholia of southern gentility. But in *The Sound and the Fury*, even as he acknowledges the fascination of such headlong mourning, he emphasizes its horrors. *The Sound and the Fury* breaks on the division between nostalgic melancholia and Faulkner's emerging articulation of modern mourning. To be more precise, the character Quentin is broken on that division. Jahan Ramazani argues that melancholic elegy is the hallmark of the twentieth century (*Poetry* xi), but though Faulkner records Quentin's desire to be reunited with his sister in death, Quentin's elegy does not set the parameters of mourning in *The Sound and the Fury*.

Although in *Absalom, Absalom!* Faulkner will return to examine the cultural footing for Quentin's elegiac struggles, Faulkner's earlier novel frames Quentin's grief through more modern sensibilities that point forward rather than back. Through Benjy's opening narrative, Faulkner insists on "presentness" rather than nostalgia. He also initiates an ongoing search for further narratives because Benjy's elegiac perspective is acknowledged as incomplete. In *The Sound and the Fury*, Faulkner shifts attention to the role of mourning in a contemporary culture of which the Civil War is not the only explanatory event. Reinventing mourning requires a radical departure from gothic melancholia, and Faulkner indicates that the materials for reinvention are already at hand. For alternative versions of mourning, he turns to female, African American, and disabled characters, figures who have traditionally remained outside the elegiac tradition, and who, in Faulkner's rendering, resist melancholic despair. As a result, this study focuses on the ways in which he both calls attention to such characters' marginalization and returns to them a voice in the elegiac tradition that they help to redefine.

Benjy's Elegy of Dependence

Faulkner's first stage of elegiac revision is closely tied to the character Benjy, in part because, with Benjy, Faulkner commences a lifelong narrative of artistic failure: "I wrote the Benjy part first. That wasn't good enough so I wrote the Quentin part. That still wasn't good enough. I let Jason try it. That still wasn't enough. I let Faulkner try it and that still wasn't enough, and so about twenty years afterward I wrote an appendix still trying to make that book what—match the dream" (*FU* 84). Although Faulkner goes on to identify failure in each successive narrative, by beginning with Benjy, a character he deems "incapable of relevancy" (63), Faulkner detaches narrative from implicit expectations about a speaker's ability to put all the pieces together. Benjy's rotating cast of caretakers signals his dependence on others; in opening with his voice, Faulkner trains readers to recognize the narrative inadequacy of the other speakers who, despite their lack of disability, also offer fragmented attention and perspective.

Dismissive as Faulkner's description of Benjy may seem, it captures one of Benjy's most valuable contributions to the role of the modern elegist: his lack of distinction between events of the past and those of the present. Rather than curate the image of the lost loved one at a much later point in time—the balancing act that most elegists undertake—Benjy offers a series of impressions of the individual as relived in an endless present. There is no nostalgia in Benjy's narrative. In fact, as Michael Bérubé argues, Benjy's ability to link "spatial and emotional associations" across time makes him "an ideal narrator for a novel whose characters are obsessed with the past" (575). The risk, of course, as Bérubé notes, is that the narrative will fall into the tradition of rendering disability "as exceptionality and thereby redeemed" (569). In *The Sound and the Fury*, *As I Lay Dying*, and *Go Down, Moses*, Faulkner relies on creative license to articulate new mourning; in Benjy's "exceptionality" one might read the cost of Faulkner's manipulation of narrative form.

Through Benjy, Faulkner gestures toward the traditional roles of the elegist. Benjy holds a flower on the drive to the cemetery, in an echo of elegiac flower catalogs. They are vestiges of the funeral rites and ceremonies that are being trimmed at the beginning of the century even as, Jahan Ramazani argues, the elegy is on the rise (*Poetry* 11). Although Benjy's mother banishes the name of his sister, Caddy, in an attempt to erase her daughter from memory, Benjy demonstrates the elegist's attachment to the name of the lost one (Sacks 25), moaning any time it is uttered. But Benjy is most significant as a revisionary figure. The first time Faulkner shows Benjy moaning, it is in response to the word "caddie," uttered by golfers. Faulkner shifts attention from the lost Caddy to her slipper, the smell of trees, and the sound of her name. As Faulkner indicates, "Those things were flashes that were reflected on her as in a mirror. He didn't know what they meant" (*FU* 63). Those objects may be flashes that are reflected on Caddy, but Caddy herself remains out of reach, and the objects in Benjy's narrative remain "flashes" of a grief that will never be formulated as a whole. Knitting together past and present through memories that are stripped of nostalgia, Faulkner uses Benjy's perspective to introduce new episodic ways of speaking of absent figures.

Benjy does not experience grief in waves, paroxysms, or sudden apprehensions, as Joan Didion describes, but rather in abrupt, intrusive images that share with others who grieve a lack of control over when and how the feelings and images appear. Faulkner's rendering of Benjy's grief challenges the reader to acknowledge how much of the elegist's role is defined by a measure of control. Although Benjy's narrative is influenced by his own experience, it relinquishes the elegist's role in actively shaping a portrait of the one who is lost. His emphasis on Caddy's role as caretaker draws out the implications of acquisition and control that so often shape the elegist's attempts to "capture" the absent figure. In this tension between new technique and old narrative habits, Faulkner kindles in his reader a desire for further perspectives, since any one will be marked by the speaker's limitations. The reader's appetite, however, speaks to his or her belief in the ability to stitch a coherent whole from the fragmented narratives. In his novel's sweep, Faulkner juxtaposes the stories offered by a mentally disabled man incapable of speech, a melancholic unable to bear the weight of solitude, and an unsentimental capitalist of contemporary Mississippi. In no approach does Faulkner deem himself successful in rendering Caddy visible to the reader, and yet in his failure he succeeds in revealing such an elegiac goal as inherently flawed. Benjy's narrative inculcates in the reader a yearning for more than one elegist, and in creating this initial dynamic, Faulkner reconceives of the conditions of elegy such that no subsequent elegy is sufficient for the stated goal, whether in his novel or in the elegiac work of any author. The quest, then, turns outward, to an examination of the elegists, as well as the community that surrounds them.

Benjy bellows relentlessly throughout *The Sound and the Fury*, triggered by Caddy's name or others' expressions of sorrow. His lack of "relevancy," in Faulkner's phrasing, reflects Joan Didion's sense that "grief has no distance" (27). Benjy's insistence on Caddy's loss is more visible but not more out of time than Quentin's obsessive melancholia or Jason's resentful tallying of all that Caddy has cost him. Jason's desire to wring restitution from Caddy, one cashed check at a time, parodies the compensatory model of elegy, in which poets create what Peter Sacks terms "consoling substitutes" for what is lost (4). Critic John Matthews rightly draws attention to Faulkner's character Versh, who jokes that Jason will grow up to be a rich man, since he keeps his hands in his pockets as he cries: "Versh's joke, like so much else in Benjy's section, accurately forecasts the intimate connection between crying and pocket filling, between grief and reimbursement" (94). In Quentin's narrative too, other characters attempt to interpret Quentin's actions, though their attempts reveal the difficulty of reading grief through social cues. Quentin's smart suit prompts his Canadian roommate, Shreve, to ask, "Is it a wedding or a wake?" (54). Shreve's inability to tell the difference should give readers pause. As Shreve becomes increasingly concerned, he more accurately identifies the reason for Quentin's attire, but only by crossing cultures and gender roles: "Say, what're you doing today, anyhow? All dressed up and mooning around like the prologue to a suttee" (67). The language of marriage is Shreve's only means of articulating—however unwittingly—the bond between Quentin and the lost Caddy, but its appearance is jarring and points to the absence of contemporary terms by which to understand Quentin's elegiac attachment to his sister. In assuming the elegist's role, Quentin has made himself archaic. Even as Faulkner deprives readers of his stated goal to represent Caddy, he uses secondary characters' varied voices to capture the difficulty of understanding not only the mourned subject but also the mourners themselves.

More than any narrative device in the novel, Benjy's moans foreground the ways in which others in his culture respond to those who insist on the presence of sorrow. As critics have noted, the other characters draw attention to Benjy's moans through frequent expressions of frustration and chastisement. But what have gone unnoticed are the many attempts to pay off Benjy's mourning through treats and tricks. Those exchanges reflect the widespread impatience that is extended not only to the outbursts of the disabled but also to mourners who carry their grief when others would have it subside. Benjy's moan on the first page of the novel is merely the first of many that will punctuate the novel. But in his response, Benjy's caretaker, Luster, also sets a precedent: "Listen at you, now. . . . Aint you something, thirty three years old, going on that way. After I done went all the way to town to buy you that cake. Hush up that moaning. Aint you going to help me find that quarter so I can go to the show tonight" (3). Only a few lines later, Luster turns from shaming Benjy to threatening him: "If you dont hush up, mammy aint going to have no birthday for you. If you dont hush, you know what I going to do. I going to eat that cake all up. Eat them candles, too. Eat all them thirty three candles. Come on, les go down to the branch. I got to find my quarter" (3). Luster's admonishments fill the first page of the novel, setting mourning alongside entertainment. He attempts to buy contentment with cake. Luster then turns quickly to his own desire for entertainment as he searches for a lost quarter with which to go out in the evening. If the birthday cake seems an inadequate bribe for silence when one has lost a sister, we might wonder for what, precisely, Luster is being paid off with the prospect of a show that night. The frustrations of chaperoning Benjy are readily apparent to the reader. When Benjy notes that "my shadow was higher than Luster's on the fence" (3), the reader remembers, abruptly, that a grown man is being shepherded by someone half his age and smaller in stature.

Through intrusions such as those of Luster, Versh, and Shreve, Faulkner draws on the novel's complex character relations to erode the elegy's emphasis on a single speaker and a single relationship. Although each Compson brother maintains a narrative shaped by his own priorities, the piling on of narratives and the contributions of secondary characters insist on a sociable scene. Quentin's repetition of the word "sister" reflects his own obsession, but it also underscores relationality. Even Caddy defends Benjy only by articulating his relationship to her: "You're not a poor baby. Are you. Are you. You've got your Caddy. Haven't you got your Caddy" (6). Caddy emphasizes relationship over individuality, encouraging Benjy's tendency to see his world shaped by her presence in it.

The Question of Caddy's Courage

Caddy's reassurance is extended both to Benjy and to the reader. As the elegiac center of the novel, her rebellion against southern mores serves as the genesis for Faulkner's novel. But Faulkner begins his foray into elegiac reinvention with an elegiac subject who seeks connection to her family well after she leaves home. Such overtures do not seem to affect her brothers' mourning, a fact that underscores elegy's tendency to prioritize the speaker's experience of loss over the actual state of the elegiac subject. Despite the cool reception, as articulated in Benjy's narrative, Caddy insists on a relationship with her family members and with the narrative from which she is largely excluded. She is the "empty center" of *The Sound and the Fury*,[1] "the beautiful one," Faulkner's "heart's darling," and his most enduring figure of loss (*FU* 6). But much remains unclear in that formulation: Is a "figure of loss," as so many Faulkner critics put it, more or less than a character?

When asked why Caddy was not one of the novel's narrators, Faulkner responded, "The explanation of the whole book is in that. . . . Caddy was still to me too beautiful and too moving to reduce her to telling what was going on" (*FU* 1). Faulkner's treatment of Caddy reflects his general policy of withholding information when something significant is at stake. When asked in an interview to describe his ideal woman, he hedges:

> Well, I couldn't describe her by color of hair, color of eyes, because once she is described, then somehow she vanishes. That the ideal woman which is in every man's mind is evoked by a word or phrase or the shape of her wrist, her hand. Just like the most beautiful description of anyone, a woman, since we are speaking of women, is by understatement. Remember, all Tolstoy said about Anna Karenina was that she was beautiful and could see in the dark like a cat. That's all he ever said to describe her. And every man has a different idea of what's beautiful. And it's best to take the gesture, the shadow of the branch, and let the mind create the tree. (*LG* 127–28)

Faulkner's fear that hearing from Caddy would mean only further loss reflects a broader cultural investment in the ideals that the dead represent for those who survive. And yet, as Woolf indicates in her short story "The Mark on the Wall," both the individual and the ideals she bears can become warped through idealization: "It is curious how instinctively one protects the image of oneself from idolatry or any other handling that could make it ridiculous, or too unlike the original to be believed in any longer" (85). Caddy Compson may be lost to Faulkner's reader not because she is not a narrator but rather because both her brothers and her author emphasize beauty over intimacy. Faulkner's emphasis on beauty surprises, since it is not beauty but rather muddy drawers that readers associate with the young Caddy early in *The Sound and the Fury,* drawers that indicate the rebellious streak that will fill her brothers with sorrow and drive her from home. After removing her dress so that she will not get it dirty, Caddy plays in the muddy creek and then climbs a tree. Her brothers, the novel's speakers, all look up, which is why her muddy drawers loom large in their memories and in the text. And yet the scene yields an important caution that is not about Caddy's future but about the limitation of what her brothers see: her brothers observe only muddy drawers, but Caddy sees much more.

André Bleikasten's reading of *The Sound and the Fury* as an elegy has defined decades of Faulkner criticism. He reads Caddy as a traditional elegiac subject and Faulkner's work as a traditional elegiac enterprise that engages in Freud's *Trauerarbeit,* or work of mourning, in which "literature functions as a substitute" (*Ink* 47). Bleikasten does express ambivalence, arguing that Caddy is "both more and less than a 'character': she is at once the focal and the vanishing point" (49). And yet Caddy is not simply "a pure and poignant figure of *absence,*" an "empty signifier," but also a figure who possesses an "uncanny power," as Bleikasten and others argue (49–51; italics in original). Defining that power will require a recharacterization of elegy, since Faulkner does more to reclaim the elegiac subject than one could see from either his rhetoric of loss or the elegiac tradition.

Even as he tucks Faulkner's novel into a Freudian narrative of compensatory mourning, Bleikasten observes that the "seminal" image of the novel focuses on the children's grandmother's death and their interest in that event (*Ink* 47). That, I argue, is where Faulkner leaves behind the traditional elegiac project, and even the modern melancholic one. In their stead, Faulkner inculcates in his readers the same sense of curiosity and multiplicity that his characters exhibit in their "childish games" on the day of their grandmother's funeral (*LG* 146). In his descriptions of the scene, Faulkner does not hesitate to set death and the conventions of grief alongside child's play: "That began as a short story, it was a story without plot, of some children being sent away from the house during the grandmother's funeral. They were too young to be told what was going on and they saw things only incidentally to the childish games they were playing, which was the lugubrious matter of removing the corpse from the house" (*LG* 146). Repeatedly, Faulkner explains his original interest in terms that foreground childlike curiosity: "It struck me that it would be interesting to imagine the thoughts of a group of children . . . their curiosity about the activity in the house, their efforts to find out what was going on, and the notions that would come into their minds" (qtd. in Bleikasten, *Ink* 47). Faulkner situates the modern mourner not at the funeral but rather speculating and lingering outside the house, with a child's freedom from convention.

In the glimpses of Caddy afforded by Benjy's narrative, she becomes not only the elegiac subject but also one in search of the meaning behind the conventions of mourning. At the same time as she embraces free, even defiant, exploration of the adult world, she struggles when her independence and her control over others fail under unfamiliar conditions. This pairing is not coincidental: if one wonders why outmoded conventions of mourning cannot be thrown off and better ones adopted, one need only look to Caddy to see the anxiety that blossoms when old rules are abandoned. Hers is a narrative of the loss of control over mourning and the desperate desire for possession of such control.

Caddy, in a show of bravado, suggests that she sit in her grandmother's chair, not knowing that her grandmother has just died. Caddy defiantly declares, "I'd sit in Damuddy's chair. . . . She eats in bed" (16). Although Caddy does not have a chance to make good on her boast, she does take her grandmother's place in other ways, assuming a narrative position marked by absence, and delimiting it through her presumption of authority over the rest of the family. Damuddy's funeral appears as the immediate occasion for elegy within the fiction, just as Caddy's climbing of the tree in order to observe that same funeral serves as the occasion for Faulkner's novel. Caddy's own family may have wished to align her with death in order to dismiss her, but Faulkner aligns her with death in order to give her a seat at the table.

Not all, however, read Caddy as a character, much less a significant voice in the narrative. Eric Sundquist argues that Caddy is not a character but rather "an idea" (10). Paul Lilly sees in Caddy an embodiment of Faulkner's investment in silence over speech: "What she sees through the window cannot be conveyed in words" (173). He argues that Caddy "imparts . . . a center of pure silence around which radiate the voices of those speakers further down on the pyramid, less fortunate with words" (173). And yet Caddy not only speaks but is prompted by what she sees to hush her brothers, the narrators of most of the novel. Although Caddy is often described as speechless, aligning her with Benjy, through Faulkner's literary play they both have the opportunity to indicate all that they cannot say. When Caddy's suitor, Charlie, attempts to embrace her in front of Benjy, noting, "He cant talk," Caddy rightly points out, "He can see. Dont" (32). Caddy is not only the subject of her brothers' mourning but also an observer of grief whose inability to articulate what she sees reflects the difficulty of reconciling her observations with the terms of mourning in her culture. Her silence reflects the tension between personal experience and a society that has made mourning unrecognizable to those who are unschooled in its rituals.

Though he is reluctant to lose the idealized Caddy by making her a narrator, Faulkner uses her position, as she sees without recognizing, to reconsider standard characterizations of mourning, grief, and loss. He may have begun his career by setting beauty and intimacy at odds with one another, but this project attends to the many ways in which he closed the gap between the two, bringing the voice of the subject back to elegiac literature. When recounting the origin of *The Sound and the Fury,* Faulkner emphasizes that "her brothers ... didn't have the courage to climb the tree" (*FU* 1):

> The girl was the only one that was brave enough to climb that tree to look in the forbidden window to see what was going on. And that's what the book—and it took the rest of the four hundred pages to explain why she was brave enough to climb the tree to look in the window. It was an image, a picture to me, a very moving one, which was symbolized by the muddy bottom of her drawers as her brothers looked up into the apple tree that she had climbed to look in the window. (31)

In this explanation, nearly thirty years after the book's publication, Faulkner rewrites his rationale to align with the Genesis narrative that is suggested by the snake that slithers from beneath the house as the children approach: a "forbidden" tree of knowledge, traditionally bearing apples, becomes a "forbidden window" (*SF* 25). Faulkner invites the reader to gauge whether he fulfills the traditional elegiac project: whether he is able "to draw the picture of Caddy" (*FU* 6). And yet, looking in that window, watching outsiders process the conventions that have become all too familiar to adults, becomes Faulkner's true project.

Caddy's view at the window makes strange to the reader the conventions of mourning. The reader has, before this point in the novel, endured endless rounds of caretakers telling Benjy to "hush," as his laments punctuate the narrative. At the scene of Damuddy's death, Caddy and the other children are told to "hush" by their father. The special circumstances that prompt his command are dulled, however, by the fact that this is the seventeenth time "hush" has appeared in the pages leading up to the scene. "Hush" is more than the behavior of an occasion; it has become a way of life. In fact, because "hush" appears so many times before the grandmother's funeral in the narrative, one is inclined to, with Caddy, resist such niceties and demand that shared discourse trump the codes of respect. Why is respect for the dead aligned with silence? The children are only quiet without hushing in the moment that their mother's cries of grief reach them as they eat in the kitchen (*SF* 17).

When the reader hears from Caddy in Benjy's narrative, Faulkner takes the opportunity not to reveal Caddy's character, as would be expected, but rather to criticize the methods of elegiac revelation. Caddy approaches the event of her grandmother's death and funeral through what could be read as a child's version of the elegist's desire for cogency and control. She would, without understanding the significance of a funeral, "walk right in the parlor where they are," adding, "I'll walk right in the parlor. I'll walk right in the dining room and eat supper.... I'd sit in Damuddy's chair" (*SF* 16). Even as she reflects the ugliness of an elegist's attempts to fill the void of a loss with words, Caddy unwittingly charts her own role in following her grandmother in a series of losses that will devastate her family. And yet she is more than, as John T. Matthews argues, a "'little girl' 'manufactured' by the text" who "never achieves the presence or substance of a 'real' character" (21). For Matthews, Caddy's status is defined by Faulkner's origin story; as Matthews notes, Faulkner's narrative of the genesis of *The Sound and the Fury* gives the scene a greater prominence than is evident in the novel itself, which implies that Caddy's character remained stunted in its development. Eric Sundquist echoes Matthews's misgivings, noting that the finished novel seems to have "little to do with its own genetic myth, the image of Caddy in the pear tree" (19). Yet such readings assume that the development of Caddy's role in the narrative entails revelation of her character, which is the very thing she thwarts.

As Caddy, in the muddy drawers that signal her own misbehavior, offers to take the place of another in her family, she both enacts compensatory mourning and challenges her future erasure from the family records. But as one who, over the course of the scene, becomes acculturated to the conventions of mourning, she also embodies a prior desire to seize control that is then accomplished through elegiac work. She insists on being put in charge while the adults are preoccupied, taking advantage of another kind of absence as the usual authority figures are away: "Let them mind me tonight, Father" (*SF* 16). Caddy's sense of control slowly fails, however. Caddy hushes Benjy when they hear their mother's cries, "But I didn't hush," he reports (17). Quentin insists, "That was Mother. . . . She was crying," to which Caddy responds, "It was somebody singing. . . . I told you it was a party" (17). She unconsciously echoes Woolf's character Clarissa Dalloway, who throws a party into which death intrudes. In that novel, the party continues, and death is merely the subject of conversation. In Faulkner's novel, however, Quentin refuses to finish his meal even though Caddy makes a show of ordering him to do so. Even Jason, seemingly so removed from the emotional center of the family, finishes eating but then begins to cry (18). As each brother's attention is arrested, the reader sees a microcosm of the novel that will unfold: first Benjy, so attuned to stimuli but pacified by a rearrangement of the pieces; then Quentin, whose cogitations do not ease when the noise stops, challenging his sister with "How can they have a party when Damuddy's sick" (18); and finally Jason, who first satisfies his appetite but then turns to acknowledge what is missing. Faulkner's novel may be a "failed" rendering of Caddy's character, but it is an apt depiction of Caddy's failure to control her brothers.

Caddy's obstinate fight for control is a humorous counterpoint to the funeral happenings elsewhere in the house, but through her Faulkner does not simply replicate the failed attempts at control that mark the elegiac tradition. Instead, he revels in her unschooled assessment as she defamiliarizes the funeral, using its superficial resemblance to a party to challenge the way in which grief is expressed in her culture. When the older girl Frony introduces the term "funeral," Caddy is perplexed, but she responds vehemently when Frony explains that funerals are "where they moans": "That's niggers.

White folks dont have funerals" (22). Caddy's color consciousness prompts her to articulate the lack of emotion that she associates with her white world. Having dispatched "funeral" from her world, she also rejects Frony's reminder that "white folks dies too. Your grandmammy dead as any nigger can get" (22). Caddy widens the gap between her world and death with a turn to animals: "Dogs are dead. . . . Nancy fell in the ditch and Roskus shot her and the buzzards came and undressed her" (23). Death as Caddy has seen it is limited to animals, because it is linked to a cruelty she only dares consider in reference to them. Caddy reasserts that she is witnessing "a party" (24) and sets out to prove it, so that she does not have to admit Frony's superior—and devastating—knowledge.

Bleikasten attends to the sight of Caddy looking in the window, as she occupies an "intermediary position, suspended as she is between her brothers and the intriguing scene of death" (*Ink* 48). He goes on to read Caddy as an example of the "mythic mediating function of woman through whom, for man, passes all knowledge about the origins, all knowledge about the twin enigmas of life and death"; for Bleikasten, her relationship with her brothers is marked by the threat of castration that follows a boy's seeing a woman's sexual organs (as Caddy's brothers look at her muddy drawers) (*Ink* 48). The link between sexuality and death is certainly present, but in reaching for that psychoanalytic connection, Bleikasten loses the story that is both original to and touted in the novel: hushing, being hushed, but fighting to see.

Although Faulkner attributes courage to Caddy as she scales the tree to peer into the house, her act seems to be motivated at least in part by fear and the need to gather evidence that will silence Frony. Thus it is poignant that Caddy's thrashing in the tree suddenly halts and she shushes all those who are below, both quelling the criticism from those who cannot see and perhaps also newly hushed by what she sees. What she sees is not moaning, but it is also no party: "They're not doing anything in there. . . . Just sitting in chairs and looking" (31). What Caddy conveys is not satisfying either to her or to the reader, who waits with Caddy's brothers below. But that is because Faulkner's attention is caught by the children rather than the adults in this scene. If funeral traditions are not legible to the children, their own power dynamics become a vivid way to see and understand grief, rather than the "nothing" framed by the upstairs window. The rituals of grief occur in the kitchen, when each child lays claim to his or her own method of grief and denial, rather than in the parlor, where the adults sit. Caddy's denial of grief may explain her lack of a narrative more than her gender. Thadious Davis argues that Caddy later demonstrates a "lack of historical consciousness" (246), and there is something of that in Caddy's childhood rejection of death, which cuts her off from her family narrative.

To capture the ways in which grief is socially conditioned, both Woolf and Faulkner render it as confusion: mistaken impressions of scenes that are glimpsed through trees and windows. Making grief unrecognizable proves fruitful for dismantling social conventions and the literary forms that support and are shaped by them. Mourning for Damuddy is not rendered through a scene in the parlor because it has been most eloquently captured by Caddy's horror at the thought of allying her grandmother with the cruel deaths of livestock. Caddy's "childish" boldness in rejecting categories and labels that do not reflect what she witnesses may well be the source of the courage Faulkner admires in his character (*LG* 156). Her curiosity about the adults' secretive behavior transforms her discovery of the funeral into a child's game. These games, like the hide-and-seek played by Woolf's characters in *The Waves*, render the cultural shape of mourning suddenly visible because one sees it only incidentally. Woolf and Faulkner ensure that the reader will see grief and mourning through the eyes of those who are too young either to understand or to disguise the cultural codes that hush grief when it appears in "unacceptable" forms.

2

COMPETITIVE ELEGY IN *The Waves*

> The dysphoria in grief is likely to decrease in intensity over days to weeks and occurs in waves, the so-called pangs of grief.
> —American Psychiatric Association, *The Diagnostic and Statistical Manual of Mental Disorders*, 5th edition

As early as 1925, Virginia Woolf's diary entries show her casting about for an adequate description of her work: "I have an idea that I will invent a new name for my books to supplant 'novel.' A new — by Virginia Woolf. But what? Elegy?" (*D* 3:34). Woolf scholarship frequently opens with this quotation before launching into discussions of her experimental form and the many family deaths that haunt her writing career.[1] *To the Lighthouse* (1927) makes for a poignant textual complement, since there Woolf explores the role of mourning in her own life. Although a biographical account of her style is compelling, Woolf's question demands a different line of inquiry if critics are to see how she ensures that the genre speaks to losses beyond her own. Though elegy sets the tone of novels such as *Jacob's Room* (1922), *Mrs. Dalloway* (1925), and *To the Lighthouse*, elegy itself becomes Woolf's object of study when she writes *The Waves* (1931).[2] The elegy leaves its mark on much of her work, in form or tone, but it does not do so uncontested. In

The Waves, she dramatizes her challenges to elegiac tradition, giving voice and character to the criticisms that generate her elegiac reinvention in other novels.

Faulkner's *The Sound and the Fury* focuses on familial grief, but Woolf widens her scope in *The Waves* as she argues that nostalgia has warped the grief of the entire postwar British public. Woolf's book reviews for the *Times Literary Supplement* impress on her both the volume and the popularity of fiction that imitates prewar life (Lee 372), a nostalgia that seems both at odds with modern culture and inherently dangerous. Though others harken back to schoolyard games before the war, Woolf insists that the militarism of England's traditional public school system is a catalyst of the war. As she illustrates in *The Waves,* the emphasis on order in English public school and university education seeps into the form of the elegy, so that there too, order reigns supreme. In *The Sound and the Fury,* Caddy Compson seizes on the disarray of her grandmother's funeral to claim authority over her siblings and servants, and Woolf echoes Faulkner's disquieting connection between mourning and the desire for control. But her parade of schoolboys, who "march, two by two . . . orderly, processional, into chapel" (*TW* 23), ties the schoolyard to the battlefield, a connection that calls into question the place of order and control in the elegiac tradition. Her reconception of elegy in *The Waves* draws on elegiac precedent but is at odds with the cultural emphasis on order and control that has so limited elegy's scope. The elegy in *The Waves* reveals the genre's flaws: the voices of other mourners are lost, the dead are manipulated for the poet's benefit, and other, perhaps worthier, subjects and speakers of elegy are ignored—all in order to fit the demands of a genre that is circumscribed by the traditions of British schoolboy life.

Woolf not only recognizes that contemporary elegy retains much of its prewar ethos, but she also demands that the public see it too. *The Waves* educates her readers in the ways that elegy and mourning reflect cultural rather than natural or moral concerns. That shift transforms mourning from a personal struggle, one shielded from scrutiny by the "respect" of others, to a social endeavor that admits its susceptibility to bias and can be criticized for it. Woolf enacts this transformation by replicating prewar sensibilities within a novel whose experimental aesthetics make such prewar sentiments seem out of place. Rather than, as others have done, allow readers to escape modern life into literature whose aesthetics support an idealized view of the

Edwardian or Victorian era, Woolf uses aesthetics to ground her readers in the present, demanding that they assess the ideological pipeline of schoolboy to soldier with the brokenness of the modern era in full view.

As "an educated man's daughter" (*TG* 17), Woolf stands to inherit elegiac traditions, though, inasmuch as being a daughter and not a son kept her from formal education, she also remains outside them. Since the elegy is as concerned with inheritance as it is with mourning, Woolf's treatment of the elegy makes visible her social negotiations as a major player in modernist reinvention who is also the daughter of Leslie Stephen, a prominent Victorian intellectual. Playing with genre is, for her, a form of intellectual engagement that does not require a university degree. In claiming the elegy she leverages its rich tradition against the oppressive weight of the nineteenth-century novel, using the former to wrench her fiction away from the triple-decker novels of the preceding century.

In Jahan Ramazani's estimation, the pursuit of mourning is only half of the modern elegist's work; the other half is his or her contention with the mantle of the elegiac tradition (*Poetry* 2). Although the question Woolf poses in her 1925 diary entry, whether or not to call her work "elegy," appears to be casual speculation, by 1931, with the publication of *The Waves*, Woolf makes elegy the backbone of her work. She uses her six speaking characters' search for order to echo—and critique—her own search for novelistic form.[3] In the end, elegy dominates the scene, with the lamentations of the elegist, Bernard, drowning out the voices of the other characters. But the novel begins with six speakers rather than one. She uses a cast of characters one might expect in a nineteenth-century realist novel to diffuse the responsibility of the narrative throughout a wider range of views and voices than in traditional elegy. When, by the end of the novel, there is only one speaker remaining, Woolf draws on the elegiac milieu to prod her reader to seek out what has been lost. Bernard's concluding soliloquy carries traces of the five other voices and, through them, Woolf's critique of the traditional elegist's monopoly on mourning. Her exploration of order is political, ethical, and generic, as she rewrites the terms of the genre to make visible the mourners and subjects that traditional elegy erases.

Inherited Forms

The private grief of the characters in *The Waves* stands in sharp contrast to the public mourning rituals of Woolf's Victorian childhood. Woolf's comments on her mother's death make clear that not only are the dead made "unreal" through such conventions, but the mourners too are divorced from grief: "We were made to act parts that we did not feel; to fumble for words that we did not know. It obscured, it dulled. It made one hypocritical and immeshed in the conventions of sorrow" (*MOB* 95). Woolf's resentment makes its way into *The Years* (1937), in which she charts the shift from Victorian to modern society through several generations of the Pargiter family. *The Years* opens with the death of the matriarch and the steady march of Victorian funeral rites that follow. At each stage of the mourning process, however, Woolf undermines communal rituals. The shades of the neighbor's house are drawn with respect, "but a servant peeped" (84). Men on the street remove their hats, "but by the time [the second] carriage passed, the hats were on again. The men walked briskly and unconcernedly along the pavement" (84). Observers fulfill their roles, "but" something occurs to expose these actions qua roles, thereby mitigating the consolation that such public solidarity offers the bereaved. Although Woolf abandoned her initial plan to pair chapters of the story in *The Years* with essays of social criticism, the published novel clearly retains elements of her critique.[4]

Through the Pargiters, Woolf exposes to her reader the strain of maintaining a public posture of grief. For mourning to be successful, all must act in concert. Woolf's character Delia, however, is out of step. Rather than be soothed by the contributions of the community, the young girl's grief is fanned into rage by the choreography of mourning. She feels emotions stirring as her mother's coffin is being covered, but her thoughts are promptly interrupted by the minister: "What a lie! she cried to herself. What a damnable lie! He had robbed her of the one feeling that was genuine; he had spoilt her one moment of understanding" (87). "None of us feel anything at all," she concludes, "we're all pretending" (87). Even when they are alone together the family members adopt a near-silent formality, "as if they were already taking part in the ceremony" (84). The performance of grief invades every setting.

Woolf's dissatisfaction with Victorian mourning speaks to a larger cultural shift. The massive war losses and the increasing turn to hospitals in one's final hours prompted many to look to poetry in search of a "cultural space" for mourning (Ramazani, *Poetry* 1). Elegy is a more flexible vessel than Victorian mourning rituals, but in Woolf's estimation it must be revised to permit diverse feelings and perspectives—the opposite of monolithic Victorian mourning. Woolf's elegy is distinctive not primarily in her use of prose but rather in her attention to the relationships that take place among mourners instead of the one that links the speaker to the dead. Her reluctance to abandon the elegy and her care in disentangling it from its ideological trappings result in a work that combines critical and creative components, much like the early drafts of *The Years,* which she began shortly after finishing *The Waves.*[5] *The Waves* offers a double focus: Woolf criticizes the elegy as an instrument of Bernard's narrative and social control but then sets forth alternative strategies of elegiac work through the characters of Jinny and Rhoda. Even as she frames the writing of elegy as an extension of the male characters' experience of order and authority, Woolf uses her novel to create new terms of order.

Woolf was well positioned to appreciate formal education's ties to elegy. What became known as the Bloomsbury Group, of which Woolf was a member, began as a gathering of Thoby Stephen's Cambridge friends, at which his sisters, Vanessa and Virginia, were often quiet observers. As Leonard Woolf remembers of the group: "Our roots and the roots of our friendship were in the University of Cambridge.... Three are women and ten men; of the ten men nine had been at Cambridge, and all of us, except Roger, had been more or less contemporaries at Trinity and King's" (*Beginning* 23). The majority of the male members of the Bloomsbury Group were also members of the Apostles, the famous Cambridge society whose history is entwined with that of English elegy.[6] Two young Apostles ensured that Shelley's "Adonais" was published in England, and, in turn, one of those two Shelley admirers, Arthur Hallam, became the subject of Tennyson's *In Memoriam* when Hallam died at the age of twenty-two (Sacks 166). By bringing his Cambridge friends in contact with his sisters, Thoby Stephen extended to Virginia a peculiar intimacy with the English elegiac tradition.

As elegy extends into Woolf's own era, however, conspicuous tensions develop between its conventions and the postwar world. The same year that *The Waves* is published, the Bloomsbury Group member Desmond MacCarthy produces *Portraits,* which includes a prose elegy to J. K. Stephen,

Virginia Woolf's cousin. MacCarthy suggests that Stephen replace Thomas Gray, a poet best known for his "Elegy Written in a Country Churchyard," as the school bard of Eton. In the final lines of his portrait MacCarthy argues that "the Byron group had their Matthews . . . the Tennyson group, their Hallam. . . . J. K. S. belongs to those dim, romantic figures, who have loomed much greater in intimacy than in performance" (254). Jane Marcus argues that J. K. Stephen may lie in the background of *The Waves,* and she criticizes him as a man of violence, elegized as a hero, who perpetuated the imperial myths of England (137, 142). But Stephen contributes to Woolf's novel in quite another way: it is his lack of an established public persona that makes him a useful elegiac figure, since he enables MacCarthy to dwell on youth and Eton. When MacCarthy argues for Stephen's institution as the poet of Eton, he does so on the grounds that "when he wrote about the school, he recalled the scenes and places which already rose in our minds in absence, places we knew would be some day remembered more poignantly" (251). Woolf could not have missed how MacCarthy's elegy hollows out the figure who is ostensibly at the center of elegiac attention, much less how grounding elegy in the schoolyard excludes those who, like Woolf herself, could not take part in such experiences. In MacCarthy's portrayal, Stephen is worthy of elegy because he links the living to a place and to a time that cannot be recovered, notably one that preceded the First World War.

Woolf was not immune to the temptation of accessing other places and experiences through the dead. Quentin Bell, Virginia Woolf's nephew and biographer, argues that Thoby Stephen's death helped the Bloomsbury Group re-form around loss, rather than "their" years at Cambridge (118),[7] but it also deepened Woolf's curiosity about Thoby's Cambridge life. Upon his death Woolf attempted to acquire a written record of him from those who knew him best, and she asked several of his Cambridge friends, all of whom found the task beyond them (Bell 117). Bell surmises, "That unknown part of Thoby was important to her partly . . . [for] an amused yet resentful curiosity about the privileged masculine society of Cambridge" (117). As Woolf's favorite brother, Thoby Stephen makes for an obvious source of inspiration for Percival, the subject of Bernard's elegy in *The Waves.* Upon writing the last words of the novel on February 7, 1931, Woolf considers dedicating the book to Thoby, but then refrains.[8] His contribution to

Woolf's work extends beyond the outline of Percival, however, to his role in awakening Woolf's interest in elegy and other forms of literary mourning.

Thoby's death brings Cambridge to his sisters even as it unites the Bloomsbury Group beyond school affiliations. His death also deepens his sister's investment in elegy, though whether because Woolf desired insight into Thoby's school experience or into him remains unclear. It is this double possibility on which the elegy in *The Waves* breaks, as Woolf considers the elegiac subject both as a portal to schoolboy nostalgia and as an individual who demands the elegist's full attention. If the fact that elegy is taught in schools contributes to a tendency toward the former reading, Woolf's elegy, outside the educational system, might well restore interest in the latter.

Woolf's writing reflects competing interpretations of England's investment in the public school system. The view that dominates her work is nicely summed up by her husband: "The public school was the nursery of British philistinism. To work, to use the mind, to be a 'swot' . . . was to be an untouchable (except for the purposes of bullying) in the hierarchy of the public school caste system" (*Sowing* 88).[9] Virginia Woolf was disdainful of public school's propensity for limiting an individual's promise and overinflating the egos of young men. When several male members of the Bloomsbury Group produced a collection of poetry in 1905 under the title *Euphrosyne,* she wrote a scathing commentary on the work which began: "There is much to be said surely for that respectable custom which allows the daughter to educate herself at home, while the son is educated by others abroad. At least I am fain to think that system beneficial which preserves her from the omniscience, the early satiety, the melancholy self satisfaction which a training at either of our great universities produces in her brothers" (qtd. in Q. Bell 212). These sentiments are given their fullest expression much later in *Three Guineas,* when Woolf calls on women to make the most of their "outsider" position by keeping themselves free from "unreal loyalties" such as the "pride of nationality," followed by "college pride, school pride," and so on (80). The link between school and nation makes her criticism of the elegy, a genre so closely tied to the institutions of English education, a highly political one even without overt references to the war. Although MacCarthy's elegy inclines to nostalgia, Woolf uses the public school setting of *The Waves* to call up the postwar association of the public school with the efforts of the First World War. Contemporary readers of both MacCarthy's and Woolf's work would have been all too aware of the public schools' propensity to "melt the boys down and run them all out of the same mould like bullets" (Parker 17), which tied the schools irrevocably to both the glory and the horror of wartime. Although the deaths in *The Waves* are not, as in *Jacob's Room*, explicitly tied to the First World War, Woolf's invocation of elegy in *The Waves* provides an equally powerful and pointed criticism of the costs of a culture so deeply driven by school pride and national feeling. Creeds such as the one John Galsworthy penned both echo and supersede public professions of religious faith: "I believe that we have made the country, and shall keep the country what it is. And I believe in the Public Schools, especially the Public School I was at" (Parker 19). If the modern elegy has distanced itself from the religious transcendence that marked elegies of earlier times, Woolf is just as eager to separate it from the public school ideals that take religion's place.

And yet Woolf's work includes a countercurrent to this derision of the male school culture. After mocking the Bloomsbury men for their high-minded poetry, she claims the name of their volume for the boat on which Rachel Vinrace sails away in *The Voyage Out*, her first novel. As Christine Froula argues, this might be taken as a sign that Woolf was "putting on the writer's mantle her beloved brother had laid down" after his unexpected death (*Virginia Woolf* 21). In some of Woolf's more thoughtful reflections on education, she admits to a longing for the social opportunities of formal education, as much as she does the access to professors and vocations: "But then think how I was brought up! No school; mooning about alone among my father's books; never any chance to pick up all that goes on in schools—throwing balls; ragging: slang; vulgarity; scenes; jealousies" (*L* 3:247).[10] Given Woolf's delight at the gatherings of Thoby's friends at their house in Bloomsbury, gatherings in which she was able to glimpse the social, as well as intellectual, fruits of Cambridge, it would be rash to characterize her as a woman violently opposed to the masculine enclaves of university life. In *The Waves*, Woolf has the means with which to express her criticisms of the narrowness of the elegiac tradition, as it is handed down through the male education system. But she also conveys the warmth and familiarity that such a system provides in a modern world that seems to lack such shared institutional experiences—or the perception of shared experiences when one sees them, as Woolf did, from the outside.

She is unusual among modernist writers for emphasizing the social and not simply the aesthetic dimensions of elegiac literature. Woolf uses elegy to reveal, rather than dictate, the terms of modern mourning, and in doing so she joins a long tradition of elegists who, as Laura Cowan argues, exploit the elegy's potential for public protest: "Theocritus, for example, protested the negligence of the nymphs who allowed Daphnis to die. Milton takes the occasion of the death of Edward King to attack the corrupted clergy.... In 'Adonais,' Shelley attacks the cruel reviewers whom he blamed for Keats' death.... Modernist writers exploited this elegiac convention to attack imperialism, materialism, the bourgeois, the capitalists, the older generation—all that they felt responsible for the war and the death of civilization" (46–47). The cultural associations among religion, public school, patriotism, and the war led, as one would expect, to pressure on elegists of Woolf's time to recuperate losses, to attest to the fact that "the youth we have lost in these dread years has not perished in vain" (qtd. in Parker 24). At the same time, as Melissa Zeiger notes, "elegiac pastoralism has been increasingly implicated in the political deception that led to World War I" (14). Jahan Ramazani characterizes the modern elegist as engaging in an act of mourning that encompasses not only the individual dead or even unenumerated war casualties but also "the diminished efficacy and legitimacy of poetic mourning" (*Poetry* 8). As a result, Ramazani argues, "the genre develops by feeding off a multitude of new deaths, including the body of its own traditions" (8).

It is this ravenous modern elegy that Woolf lets loose in *The Waves*, as the character Bernard moves capriciously from the death of his friend to the losses of the other mourners and on to his own artistic failures. Mourning becomes indiscriminate. But Woolf's critique of elegy moves beyond the modern elegy's appetite for loss. In unfolding Bernard's elegy within her novel, Woolf does not indicate that modern elegy is aesthetically inadequate for representing mourning, the line that many war poets took, and upon which Ramazani's argument rests. Nor is it defined in terms of health and pathology, success and failure, as Sacks argues by leaning on Freud's analysis of mourning and melancholia. Louise O. Fradenburg, speaking for many feminist scholars of elegy, argues, "When 'health' is defined as submission to the rule of law ... then we need a political reading of the elegy, of theories of the elegy, and of elegiac theory" (qtd. in Zeiger 4). Zeiger takes Fradenburg's point further: "The need for political consciousness in this arena becomes even more apparent when criteria of success and failure are invoked: of 'successful' mourning in the first place, but then of cultural 'success' as its reward and counterpart" (4). By indicating that elegy is infused with the ideology of order and control that flourishes in public school and prepares officers for war, Woolf indicates that the writers who seem the most obvious sources for the modern elegy—well-educated and well-connected young men—produce a form of elegy that is too politically compromised to render an adequate process of mourning.

Order and Ego

The speaking characters of *The Waves* divide neatly along gender lines: three boys, three girls. While they are children, the six share games and fears, speaking in voices that weave seamlessly together. But as they grow, differences emerge between the two genders as the boys and girls attend single-sex schools. Given Woolf's customary concern for social dynamics, *The Waves* is notable in that she excludes the characters' families and other friends from the novel, as well as much of their cultural milieu. As Robin Hackett notes, Woolf's approach is in direct contrast with the Victorian realist tradition and her own father's efforts in the *Dictionary of National Biography*. Hackett rightly argues that Woolf's approach reflects her turn from the realist tradition, "to eliminate what she calls the 'waste' of the 'appalling narrative business of the realist'" (Hacket 62; she quotes *D* 3:209). But the effects of Woolf's pared-down narrative point to additional motives. In a novel with so little contextual information, the differences in the children's education looms large, a fact that has not garnered sufficient critical attention. James Phelan argues that the interludes of natural scenery that interrupt the narratives—scenes rich with waves, birds, and the arc of the sun over the course of a day—lend the characters a sense of artlessness, as if they are merely following "natural laws that are governing their movement from childhood to death" (40). And yet the prominence of the children's education in the narrative points to institutional rather than natural causes for the differences that emerge between the male and female characters.

Percival dies halfway through the novel, an event that gives shape to the seemingly endless succession of character monologues and underscores the elegist's role as an organizing agent who carves narrative out of the mess of ordinary life. But order and control, first in the educational institutions and then in the characters' adult perspectives, emerge as stifling components of contemporary mourning. Woolf's attention to elegy begins well before Percival, with the educational differences that prompt male elegists to see the world in terms of the form and content of classical texts. Through early indications of the way that educational differences generate interest in different systems of order, Woolf charts not only her characters' lives from childhood to death but also a sea change in the culture at large, as the Edwardian public school commitment to order and social function comes up against the complexities of postwar life.

In the half century before Woolf's novel appeared, England's educational priorities changed. Following the lead of the elite public schools, grammar schools throughout the country adopted policies that emphasized "cohesion, control and status" (Mangan 313). Woolf's male characters reflect these values, seeking them in their schools as they leave home for their education. Bernard is relieved to end the "ceremony" of leaving his family for school (*TW* 20), Neville notes that "a noble Roman air hangs over these austere quadrangles" (21), and Louis observes, "I like the orderly progress" (23). All three regard their education as a means of coming into their cultural inheritance, and it is clear that they will take that legacy with them when they leave school. As Louis intones, "Life will divide us. But we have formed certain ties. Our boyish, our irresponsible years are over. But we have forged certain links. Above all, we have inherited traditions" (41).

To find their place in the world, the male characters of *The Waves* must rewrite it, using the language they learned in their schoolboy days. The female characters, by contrast, have no scholarly framework with which to map their world, and thus their monologues form a counterpoint to those of the male characters. Although Rhoda, Jinny, and Susan attend a school for girls, they chafe under the assimilation that comes with it. Rhoda says, "Here I am nobody. I have no face. This great company, all dressed in brown serge, has robbed me of my identity" (22). Susan tears the days off the calendar as they pass, hating that "they have made all the days of June ... shiny and orderly, with gongs, with lessons, with orders to wash, to change, to eat" (28). And even Jinny protests the ugly frocks and looks forward to the day when she "shall leave school and wear long skirts" (38). For each of them, school is merely to be endured, and it leaves little impression on them after they are permitted to move on.

The difference in schooling between the two sets of children affects their sense of life's order for the rest of the book. Taught to embrace the tradition they inherit, the three boys seek to make sense of their subsequent lives through the terms of their education. Although Bernard contrasts Neville's desire for order with his own "Byronic untidiness" (64), they share not only a desire for order but also a common perception of where it might be found. When the rest of the world presses in too closely, Louis recalls the words of dead poets, Neville reaches for his scholarly credentials, and Bernard flirts with biography and novel writing—all as a means of reordering the world so that they are at its center.

Bernard's prominence in the text is difficult to ignore, given that his voice opens seven of the nine sections of the novel, and in the final section his is the only voice one hears. Space speaks loudly in a novel, and Bernard is given far more than his share. But much of that space is devoted to his insecurities about language and design: "I have made up thousands of stories; I have filled innumerable notebooks with phrases to be used when I have found the true story, the one story to which all these phrases refer. But I have never yet found that story. And I begin to ask, Are there stories? . . . Why impose my arbitrary design? Why stress this and shape that and twist up little figures like the toys men sell in trays in the street? Why select this, out of all that,—one detail?" (136–37). This passage appears late in the novel, when the promise that Bernard shows, his "fertility" of description and his gift of conversation, have become merely unrealized talent (85). He has admitted that he cannot guide the reader through the story that he is in or any story of which he is the teller. But in his dominance of the page, with his ruminations on phrases and references to his elusive novel, Bernard keeps readers' attention on the relationship between language and control throughout the novel.

Bernard's anxiety about mastering language and concern for "arbitrary design" heighten one's attention to the other characters' abilities to control themselves and others. The other male characters tie their identity and their continuing search for order directly to their education. Neville turns to books to prove his worth to the world: "I am merely 'Neville' to you, who see the narrow limits of my life and the line it cannot pass. But to myself I am immeasurable. . . . I detect, I perceive. Beneath my eyes opens—a book; I see to the bottom; the heart—I see to the depths" (157). And yet these sentiments form a sharp contrast to Neville's speech just prior to this section, as he nervously feels for "my credentials—what I carry to prove my superiority" (155). Neville's identity wavers between his acuity and the paper that he carries to attest to it, and neither stands up to the fierce stare of Susan, leaving Neville to ask, "What then remains, when I cannot pull out my papers and make you believe by reading aloud my credentials that I have passed?" (155). Both Neville and Louis cling not just to words but also to books, contracts, maps, and credentials in their attempts to order their world, even though such means prove inadequate to allay their anxieties.

As the male characters venture out into life beyond the quadrangle, they retain the lens of their education even when it no longer seems to fit the busy city rhythms in which they find themselves. When he observes the bustle and clatter of customers and waitresses in an eating house, Louis is moved to some of his most poetic speech: "Here is the central rhythm; here the common mainspring. I watch it expand, contract; and then expand again. Yet I am not included" (67). He pulls back, unable to sustain a connection to this riotous scene, and brandishes his classicist credentials:

> I will reduce you to order. . . . What the dead poet said, you have forgotten. And I cannot translate it to you so that its binding power ropes you in, and makes it clear to you that you are aimless; and the rhythm is cheap and worthless. . . . To translate that poem so that it is easily read is to be my endeavor. . . . I will not submit to this aimless passing of billycock hats and Homburg hats and all the plumed and variegated head-dresses of women. . . . I will reduce you to order. (67–68)

Although Louis initially characterizes the scene as one of "perpetual disorder" that he will "reduce" to order (67), at other times he acknowledges, "I feel, too, the rhythm of the eating-house. It is like a waltz tune, eddying in and out, round and round" (67). The shifting terms of Louis's assessment reflect his need not merely to find order everywhere but to find an arrangement in which he plays a central role. Because he feels "I am not included" (67) in the eating-house waltz, he positions himself as "the companion of Plato, of Virgil" (68), determined to reshape the system to fit his needs. To find his place in the world he must rewrite what he sees, using the language he learned in school.

When Louis later tries to impose order, he exchanges poetry for international trade and colonialism, affirming his role as one who sets the order for others through the signature he affixes to contracts: "I have helped by my assiduity and decision to score those lines on the map there by which the different parts of the world are laced together" (121). "Those" lines on the map "there" are a visual affirmation that this Australian son is making his mark on the world. Louis's enthusiasm cannot hide the shift that has occurred in his conception of success. The map on the wall and the papers to sign are the new, affirming texts in Louis's life. Plato and literature, his old tools for changing the world, are now pushed aside: "If we blink or look aside, or turn back to finger what Plato said or remember Napoleon and his conquests, we inflict on the world the injury of some obliquity" (122). Such affirmations of his self-importance take on a bitter tone as he acknowledges how they have circumscribed his future: "The weight of the world is on our shoulders. This is life. If I press on, I shall inherit a chair and a rug; a place in Surrey with glass houses, and some rare conifer, melon, or flowering tree which other merchants will envy" (123). Rather than transform the rhythm of the ordinary world, Louis has become ensnared by the splendors of colonialism. As he is himself a colonial, such fruits can only come at a cost to his personal identity, even as they offer evidence of his new social position. Although his new textual order offers him success, it is of a very limited, and limiting, kind.

Drawing on Adorno, Ramazani argues that one of the most significant challenges for modern elegists is "the impossibility of preserving a pristine space apart, of grieving for the dead amid the speed and pressure of modern life" (*Poetry* 14). In Woolf's novel, the flat repetition of Louis's insistence that he "will reduce you to order" contrasts unfavorably with the eating-house crowds that "dive and plunge like guillemots whose feathers are slippery with oil" (67). In the interplay of these lines the writer who elsewhere calls for a room of one's own challenges the need for "a pristine space apart" for the modern writer. Louis's insistence on books and order lead him to struggle, since they accustom him to accept only systems of order that place him at the center rather than allow him to be a player in the scene around him.

Without the guidance of a narrator or even what Molly Hite calls tonal cues, Woolf's readers have few resources with which to gauge the relationship between her narrative and the male characters' systems of order. One would not be left with such a sizable interpretive task if Woolf took a more Victorian approach. When George Eliot describes a character's system of order in *Middlemarch,* her narrator leaves little doubt as to how the scene should be interpreted:

> An eminent philosopher among my friends, who can dignify even your ugly furniture by lifting it into the serene light of science, has shown me this pregnant little fact. Your pier-glass of extensive surface of polished steel made to be rubbed by a housemaid, will be minutely and multitudinously scratched in all directions; but place now against it a lighted candle as a center of illumination, and lo! the scratches will seem to arrange themselves in a fine series of concentric circles round that little sun. It is demonstrable that the scratches are going everywhere impartially, and it is only your candle which produces the flattering illusion of a concentric arrangement, its light falling with an exclusive optical selection. These things are a parable. The scratches are events, and the candle is the egoism of any person now absent—of Miss Vincy, for example. (248)[11]

Eliot's unflattering description of egoism calls to mind Louis's experience in the eating house in *The Waves,* as he strives to replace the hustle and bustle with a scene of instruction that would place him at the center as translator and sage. Eliot's narrator steps between the philosopher and her reader to make the connection to—and evaluation of—her character, but in Woolf's novel the character himself introduces criticism of his perspective, in a curious mixture of self-knowledge and self-blinding. He acknowledges that there is already a rhythm in the world around him, albeit not one of his choosing, and he dwells on his inability to join in. His fantasy of class-based hierarchies and schoolboy schemes of order is entirely inadequate to the adult world of modern urban life. Although Woolf does not employ an imposing Victorian narrator, she does reveal the internal thoughts of her three male characters. Glimpses into their insecurities enable the reader to adopt a more sympathetic view toward them than that of Eliot's narrator,[12] but it also just as effectively undermines the sense of order that they attempt to fashion for themselves.

Not all systems of order that place an individual at the center are suspect, however. Susan's characterization of Jinny as the latter enters a restaurant echoes Eliot's pier-glass description, but without the moralizing at the end: "'There is Jinny,' said Susan. 'She stands in the door. Everything seems stayed. The waiter stops. The diners at the table by the door look. She seems to centre everything; round her tables, lines of doors, windows, ceilings, ray themselves, like rays round the star in the middle of a smashed windowpane. She brings things to a point, to order'" (87). Jinny in the restaurant stands in striking contrast to Louis in the diner. Rather than engage in an intellectual battle motivated by feelings of inferiority, she offers her body as an aesthetic object, facilitating a fluid order that neither Neville nor Louis can match: "Now she sees us, and moves, and all the rays ripple and flow and waver over us, bringing in new tides of sensation" (87). Neville demeans his observers, asserting his superiority over them, but Jinny's system rewards her viewers for their attention. Her body is an instrument, the center of a system that relies not on dictation but on attraction. When she recounts the scene later on, she notes: "When I came in just now everything stood still in a pattern. . . . I can imagine nothing beyond the circle cast by my body. My body goes before me, like a lantern down a dark lane, bringing one thing after another out of darkness into a ring of light. I dazzle you; I make you believe that this is all" (93). Whether viewed externally, through Susan's description, or through her own narration, Jinny exhibits none of the self-doubt that plagues Louis in the eating house, and yet she maintains a measure of distance from the scene that staves off accusations of egoism like those of Eliot's narrator. She is successful because she seems to see herself from the outside, handing off agency to "my body" and what it achieves as it "goes before" her. She, like Susan, is an observer in the scene, and she focuses her attention not on ordering the universe but on making a momentary effect on the scene around her.

 Here is a tantalizing figure for order. One cannot, however, overlook the violence of the image: Jinny is at the center of the smashed windowpane. She is the point of impact. As such, the order she provides is a temporary one: "Beauty must be broken daily to remain beautiful," she observes (126). When she reappears later, a glass once again brings all to a halt for her. Standing in the Tube station, she catches sight of herself in a looking glass and is surprised: "How solitary, how shrunk, how aged!" (141). She chastises herself for quailing at the sight, assuring herself that she responded only because she was "catching sight of myself before I had time to prepare myself as I always prepare myself for the sight of myself" (141).

 Jinny's recovery from the shock is as important as the shock itself. She regains her confidence by thinking of "the superb omnibuses, red and yellow, stopping and starting, punctually in order" (141). When her own power to create order fails, she turns to the order of civilization, of city life: "This [omnibuses, cars, and men and women] is the triumphant procession; this is the army of victory with banners and brass eagles and heads crowned with laurel-leaves won in battle" (141). Woolf here deftly links fashion, urban life, and military victory in indicating all that can be achieved—and lost—by emphasizing control above all else. The effect Jinny creates at the dinner party is one for which only her own powers are required. Later, she must reach out to signs of British order and progress to regain the sense of control she desires. She is not, then, an enduring figure of order, but that is precisely the point. For a moment, and a moment only, Jinny reveals an image of order in the novel that is outside the order of the schoolyard and its emphasis on enduring traditions, pointing one toward a new kind of order in *The Waves*. Although Jinny may seem merely a pleasant distraction from the scuffles for narrative control in the novel, she is in fact a powerful means of redefining the reader's priorities. Readers of a novel may demand a hero or a protagonist, but Jinny reveals both the weight of expectation of that role and also, paradoxically, that all that is really required is an image that will provide momentary order. Jinny is more alert to the flimsiness of control, and to the relationship between control and loss, than Woolf's other characters. The elegy is a means of separating voice from agency, since the elegiac subject is the focus of the genre, and yet another character controls the image of that lost one. In her moment of "drawing together," Jinny anticipates the role of broken gathering that death will play in the novel, drawing the reader's eye to it as a formal device well before it enters the novel as a function of Woolf's plot. Here Woolf's critical study of the elegy is most apparent, as Jinny's attention to style teases out the costs of a formal arrangement before it can be employed.

Phantom Character

Although Jinny does not go on to develop the order she imposes in the scene at the restaurant, another character does take up the trope. At the center of the novel lies the elusive and silent figure of Percival. His role is quite different from those of the six characters whose narratives collaboratively form the novel, but he creates an effect that is felt by all: "He flicks his hand to the back of his neck.... Dalton, Jones, Edgar and Bateman flick their hands to the backs of their necks likewise. But they do not succeed" (24). Because Percival is peerless, he imposes an order on those around him. All six friends rest secure in the knowledge of their appropriate roles in relation to Percival and to each other precisely because they cannot hope to unseat him. As Bernard wittily observes: "The little boys trooped after him across the playing-fields. They blew their noses as he blew his nose, but unsuccessfully, for he is Percival.... We who yelped like jackals biting at each other's heels now assume the sober and confident air of soldiers in the presence of their captain" (89). Percival's presence offers a security and a stability of identity for those around him that surpasses anything they can create on their own.

But Percival's position is also, largely, an empty one. He slides easily into the novel and out again, leaving behind a yearning for his presence but no clear conception of what qualities, precisely, one longs for. Since Percival does not speak, the others are free to interpret him as they choose: "His blue, and oddly inexpressive eyes, are fixed with pagan indifference upon the pillar opposite. He would make an admirable churchwarden. He should have a birch and beat little boys for misdemeanours. He is allied with the Latin phrases on the memorial brasses. He sees nothing; he hears nothing. He is remote from us all in a pagan universe" (24). Neville struggles to keep a bead on the figure in front of him; first pagan and then churchwarden, Percival fails to impose any limit on the other's representation. In the difference between those two descriptions one begins to see the potential that this figure represents to those around him, since his is a personality upon which much can be mapped. The image of the churchwarden beating little boys with a birch switch lingers long after Neville returns to describing the blank gaze of the boy in front of him, the former far more suggestive than the latter. Neville uses Percival to bridge the gap between the current world, with all of the elements that make Neville feel judged, and the world of his books: history and literature, Greek and Latin. Neville's description suggests that, when aligned with the Latin phrases on memorial brasses, Percival can breathe new life into the schoolboy language that Louis and Neville have abandoned in favor of contracts and credentials. One need not even be bound to a single, coherent interpretation.

Such uses of Percival undercut what R. Clifton Spargo identifies as one of the chief ethical components of the elegy. Even as he acknowledges the "unrealistic" aspects of mourning, since nothing the mourner does can aid the person who is dead, Spargo asks: "Might not the mourner's wishful re-visioning of the past, through which she unrealistically sustains relationship, also signify profoundly an ethical openness to the other? . . . How does a vulnerability to the other, an imaginative proximity to her suffering and death, also define what it means to be ethical?" (9). Spargo explores a range of ethical relations in the process of mourning, including the elegiac tendency to idealize the dead to counteract the elegist's own "sense of vulnerability, which results from being in relation to that which is absolutely other and therefore impossible to desire" (130). In Woolf's novel, the other characters' idealizations of Percival veer into self-interested exploitation. Like Desmond MacCarthy's celebration of J. K. Stephen, that "dim, romantic" figure, whether he is pagan or churchwarden, the blank canvas that is Percival can hold it all (MacCarthy 254).

Rather than fight for an order that places them at the center, the other characters find in Percival's presence a more comfortable place on the perimeter. It is ultimately Percival, in a sustained version of Jinny's smashed-windowpane effect, who offers the strongest ordering schema of the novel. But unlike the mutable Jinny, who is "volatile for one, rigid for another, angular as an icicle in silver, or voluptuous as a candle flame in gold" (162–63), Percival remains unaffected by audience. Jinny's image relied on Susan's observation, but what about Percival's? Though all six friends, particularly the love-stricken Neville, contribute to Percival's eulogy, Bernard takes up Percival's system of order and carries it through to the final pages of the novel. In shaping Percival's effect on the reader, Bernard finds a logic for drawing together those scraps of language that he jotted down in his notebooks. He may fail to write his autobiography, but Bernard finds his role in the writing of an elegy.

Bernard's engagement with Percival's elegy is the final step in a lifelong rivalry. Bernard struggles to hold his friends' attention with his storytelling, while Percival attracts it merely with his charisma. In an early scene, Percival yawns and breaks the spell of Bernard's voice: "Yes, the appalling moment has come when Bernard's power fails him and there is no longer any sequence and he sags and twiddles a bit of string and falls silent, gaping as if about to burst into tears" (26). Percival, we are told, "is always the first to detect insincerity" (26), a charge that undermines Bernard's storytelling authority in such a way that he never fully recovers. Were it not for Percival, we are given to understand, Bernard might have held the attention of his peers.

Watching Bernard arrive at a gathering, Neville remarks that, "if it were not for Percival, who turns all this to vapour, one would feel, as the others already feel: Now is our festival; now we are together. But without Percival there is no solidity. We are silhouettes, hollow phantoms moving mistily without a background" (88). One sees what Bernard's role might have been had Percival not existed. The dinner, a send-off for Percival as he goes to India to uphold England's empire, is echoed by a second dinner in which his friends gather to lament his death from a fall. As Percival's elegist at the second dinner, Bernard effectively reworks the dynamics of their rivalry, containing it within a record of which he is the sole author, and thus gaining the upper hand in his contest with Percival. Peter Sacks notes that the elegy has a long-standing tradition of uniting mourning and competition: "In Greece the right to mourn was from earliest times legally connected to the right to inherit. . . . The heir apparent must demonstrate a greater strength or proximity to the dead than any rival may claim, but he must also wrest his inheritance *from* the dead" (37; italics in original). In Bernard's narrative, Percival is repeatedly represented in spatial terms: "He sat there in the centre. Now I go to that spot no longer. The place is empty" (110). Making Percival the absent center of the narrative makes it easier for Bernard to maintain Percival's place in the narrative schema well after he dies, and to lay claim to his structural, but not personal, significance. Bernard purports to regard elegy as unsuitable to the modern cultural moment, claiming that "we have no ceremonies, only private dirges and no conclusions, only violent sensations, each separate. Nothing that has been said meets our case" (113). And yet in Bernard's final speech, even as he begins with the audacious "Now to sum up," he asks his listener to enter into the "illusion . . . that something adheres for a moment, has roundness, weight, depth, is completed" (176). This illusion is the order that Percival created while still alive and that Bernard now revives for his own purposes.

Through his elegy to his friend, Bernard maintains Percival's place at the center of attention and positions himself as one of the many mourners who surround the absent Percival, in an echo of the "spider's web" with "beads of water on it, drops of white light" that Bernard describes in the novel's opening pages (4). Such positioning makes possible the kind of identity ambiguities that proliferate in Bernard's final speech: "When I meet an unknown person, and try to break off, here at this table, what I call 'my life,' it is no one life that I look back upon; I am not one person; I am many people; I do not altogether know who I am—Jinny, Susan, Neville, Rhoda, or Louis: or how to distinguish my life from theirs" (205). Bernard repeats this sentiment just a few pages later in gendered terms: "For this is not one life; nor do I always know if I am man or woman, Bernard or Neville, Louis, Susan, Jinny or Rhoda—so strange is the contact of one with another" (208). As Percival's elegist, Bernard enjoys the radiance of that central position in which he speaks for the dead as well as for the other figures that surround Percival.

But though Bernard claims their narrative space in the novel, he does not use his expanded role to give voice to the other characters' grief. Instead, his monologue returns again and again to his own interests. In what Bakhtin would have condemned as monologism, Bernard's concluding elegy unifies the novel at the cost of the other mourners' voices. In silencing the heteroglossic mourning that filled the earlier pages of *The Waves* he makes the reader feel the loss of such variety.[13] The ethics of literary mourning, as a single speaker seizes the opportunity to speak for a community of mourners, remains outside critical discussions of traditional elegy but plays a significant role in Woolf's novel. By shifting the elegizing voice from a lyric "I" to a cast of characters of whom Bernard is merely the most prominent, Woolf casts the elegy as a literary form that is far from a universal cry of mourning. In departing from the multigenerational familial relations that are at the heart of novels such as *The Years* and *To the Lighthouse*, Woolf emphasizes the ties formed by words and not by blood, those in which comparison and competition form a continual undercurrent of the characters' interactions with one another. When Percival dies, an opportunity arises for a reshuffling of the hierarchy, and it is no surprise that Bernard, the persuasive one, rewrites the relations to his advantage.

Studies of the elegy offer insight into the negotiations of legacy—both material and poetic—at play in the act of mourning, but they do little to address the jockeying among peers that occurs before a winner claims his place in the poetic tradition. Much of the conversation in elegy and elegiac study takes place among generations of poets, a continuous line through history, rather than concurrently, as in Woolf's novel. Prose and its accompanying criticism, however, is accustomed to emphasizing contemporaneous relations. E. M. Forster identified poetry as the defining feature of Woolf's oeuvre, but in her essays and diary entries she envisions a modern convergence of styles in which poetry gives ground before prose, even as prose becomes more liltingly poetic. In the essay "Poetry, Fiction and the Future" (1927), better known as "The Narrow Bridge of Art," she predicts the course of literature, a prediction that prefigures the turn her own writing will take in subsequent years:

> We may guess that we are going in the direction of prose and that in ten or fifteen years' time prose will be used for purposes for which prose has never been used before. That cannibal, the novel, which has devoured so many forms of art will by then have devoured even more. We shall be forced to invent new names for the different books which masquerade under this one heading. And it is possible that there will be among the so-called novels one which we shall scarcely know how to christen. It will be written in prose, but in prose which has many of the characteristics of poetry. It will have something of the exaltation of poetry, but much of the ordinariness of prose. It will be dramatic, and yet not a play. It will be read, not acted. By what name we are to call it is not a matter of very great importance. What is important is that this book which we see on the horizon may serve to express some of those feelings which seem at the moment to be balked by poetry pure and simple and to find the drama equally inhospitable to them. (*E* 4:434–35)

A form that expresses what poetry and plays no longer can: one year later she calls *The Waves* her "playpoem" (*D* 3:203) and writes, "I will never write a novel again. Little bits of rhyme come in" (*D* 3:177). Although in "The Narrow Bridge of Art" Woolf ostensibly forecasts a change in the literary future, she conveniently makes the catalog of genres more hospitable to the writing she is already producing. If Woolf chafes at the limitations of the available genres, one also hears a note of exultation at the opportunities to be had when poetry will be, as Bakhtin might call it, "novelized."[14]

What Woolf calls poetry's tendency to "balk" before the mess of the modern world makes it seem as though the elegy would be a part of the poetic world that modern writing has left behind. But in "The Narrow Bridge of Art" she confesses to a longing for the beauty of that world, suggesting that she has not fully abandoned it: "But can prose... chant the elegy?... I think not. This is the penalty it pays for having dispensed with the incantation and the mystery, with rhyme and metre.... One has always a feeling of discomfort in the presence of the purple patch of the prose poem. The objection to the purple patch, however, is not that it is purple but that it is a patch" (*E* 4:436–37). In making elegizing an act of narrative concern in *The Waves*, Woolf makes room for the beauty of poetry and the elegiac tradition in her modern and experimental prose work. But the critical distance she achieves in making Bernard the elegist allows her to fault the elegy for encouraging one to "take refuge in the past" (*E* 4:434).

Woolf's claim that "it is not a matter of very great importance" what the new work is called flies in the face of her interest, expressed elsewhere, in finding a name for her work that links it to traditional forms. In her diaries she repeatedly demonstrates a desire to place her work in its literary context, even as she remains concerned that making it fit will inhibit the more experimental aspects of her writing. In a 1929 entry, speaking of what will later become *The Waves*, she writes: "But there must be more unity between each scene than I can find at present. Autobiography it might be called. How am I to make one lap, or act . . . more intense than another; if there are only scenes? One must get the sense that this is the beginning; this the middle; that the climax" (*D* 3:229). Generic conventions offer a formal restraint that Woolf finds necessary to her work—"Everything in a work of art should be mastered and ordered" (*E* 4:439)—even as she struggles to find the form that will fit her own vision.

Alex Woloch's theory of character has as its focus the realist novel of the nineteenth century, but he describes a system that is germane to Woolf, a writer who is in conversation as much with George Eliot as with T. S. Eliot. Woloch makes the case that "narrative meaning takes shape in the dynamic flux of attention and neglect toward the various characters who are locked within the same story but have radically different positions within the narrative. . . . With so many narratives, this arrangement of characters is structured around the relationship between one central individual who dominates the story and a host of subordinate figures who jostle for, and within, the limited space that remains" (2). Woloch's title, *The One vs. the Many*, captures the tension between the novel's narrative focus on a single protagonist and the attention allotted to a host of minor characters. He explores what he calls character-space, "the *intersection* of an implied human personality . . . with the definitely circumscribed form of a narrative" (13; italics in original), and character-system, the arrangement of character-spaces into a unified narrative (14). Woloch's theory provides a way of assessing the competition among speakers in *The Waves,* as each maneuvers for narrative space within the limits of the novel.

In Woloch's study of the *Iliad,* Achilles's temporary departure prompts the sudden emergence of a "disruptive" minor character, masses of nameless soldiers and ships, and a carefully defined group of elite who maintain the narrative space during Achilles's absence. These vacillations in narrative scope and attention are the effect of a creative burst that occurs only when Achilles is away, "since his exalted status and distinctive superiority renders comparative judgments . . . obsolete" (6). In the absence of a leader the narrative eye wanders, whether that leader is Achilles or Percival. In Bernard, Woolf creates a character who seizes on such opportunity. No character in Woloch's study so methodically or comprehensively eliminates competitors for discursive space. But rather than inherit Percival's role, Bernard creates a complex schema for control that relies on Percival's shadow to create order. One wonders why he does not strike out with a more aggressive approach that would place him unquestionably at the center of the novel. After all, he is invigorated by attention: "I need eyes on me to draw out these frills and furbelows. To be myself (I note) I need the illumination of other people's eyes, and therefore cannot be entirely sure what is my self" (83). Bernard's reluctance to lay claim to Percival's position speaks to his own insecurities; he remembers, perhaps, how easily Percival dissipated his storytelling magic in childhood. It also distinguishes Woolf's modernist novel from those of her predecessors. In evacuating the protagonist's position in the novel, Woolf recenters narrative on the creative disruption Woloch describes, making her story not a heroic quest but rather an undefined space in which the minor characters are at perpetual play on the edges of the hero's influence.

Such peripheral positions are a refuge. In a 1937 letter, Woolf observed, "I think action generally unreal. Its the thing we do in the dark that is more real; the thing we do because people's eyes are on us seems to me histrionic, small boyish" (*L* 6:122). Her characters in *The Waves* seek positions that shield them from observation, beginning in childhood. Though he is bright, Louis hides his Latin knowledge from the others: "I do not wish to come to the top and live in the light of this great clock" (12). Even the sociable

Jinny desires a place "out of this sun, into this shadow" (6). As the novel opens, the reader's first view of the characters is of them playing children's games, hiding and seeking one another, each dismayed when found. As he hides from the others, Louis says: "But they cannot see me.... Oh, Lord, let them pass.... Let me be unseen.... Now something pink passes the eyehole. Now an eyebeam is slid through the chink. Its beam strikes me. I am a boy in a grey flannel suit. She has found me.... All is shattered" (6–7). He is a boy in a flannel suit only when seen, forming a fixed identity only as a response. The game of hiding and seeking, seeing and being seen, continues as Susan sees Jinny kiss Louis, and then she herself runs away to hide, but Bernard finds her. These diversions are not simply reminders of the characters' youth but rather the beginning moves of the game that occupies them for the rest of the novel. This is not, as Robin Hackett argues, play at imperialism and its requisite desire to conquer (67) but rather an opportunity to become accustomed to the loss of "all," as Louis describes it, through repetition. If seen, the children must interpose something, usually a text, between themselves and the rest of the world. Echoing Louis, Bernard cries, "Now the awful portals of the station gape; 'the moon-faced clock regards me.' I must make phrases and phrases and so interpose something hard between myself and the stare of housemaids, the stare of clocks, staring faces, indifferent faces" (20). The lurking dread of the central position occupies nearly all of the characters. Jinny, the notable exception, interposes her body between herself and the world; she merely "follows" it. She maintains a fluid relationship with her public self, using the body to draw the looks that order the world.

In being made the occasion for elegy, the subject must "[bring] things to a point," as Jinny does. Given the characters' fear of the central position, the violence of her smashed windowpane deserves further consideration. Woolf describes the prevailing sound of the modern age as "smashing and crashing," "the sound of breaking and falling, crashing and destruction" as old literary forms are thrown out (E 3:433–34). Descriptions of the rift between pre- and postwar life echo Jinny's smashed windowpane and explain, at least in part, the sudden need for new forms. In Freud's "Thoughts for the Times on War and Death," after he writes eloquently of one's "disappointment" in the state and the wartime abandonment of civilization, he draws up suddenly, noting that there is a sense of betrayal only because one has invested, emotionally, in things that have been exposed as illusions: "We must not complain, then, if now and again they come into collision with some portion of reality, and are shattered against it" (280). Woolf echoes this vision in her critique of postwar novels that reflect only prewar society. As Hermione Lee notes in her biography, Woolf felt that such works were "reflecting a world which 'the war had done nothing to change'; but those mirrors had been 'smashed to pieces'" (372).

Such images of violence evoke the casualties of the war, both human and ideal, but they also facilitate the re-creation of character in modernist fiction. Toni Morrison, an author whose debt to Woolf is just as strong as that to Faulkner, describes her use of memory for character creation in terms of fragmented pieces: "That's not much, I know: half-closed eyes, an absence of hostility, skin powdered in lilac dust. But it was more than enough to evoke a character—in fact, any more detail would have prevented (for me) the emergence of a fictional character at all" ("Memory" 214). Like Morrison, the speakers of Woolf's novel select particular traits from Percival in making him the center of their story, fragmenting him for their own purposes. Storytelling and ordering thus rely on the splintering of an individual; the fragment is extracted, mused over, remembered and relived, and the integrity of the individual is sacrificed for the birth of the story. But in fragmentation there comes an opportunity for rewriting the individual so that he is more like a globe than a mirror, to paraphrase Woolf's comments on Proust, with "one side . . . always hidden" (E 5:68). Writers who seize such an opportunity liberate character in both poetry and prose from its pretense of capturing the individual in his or her entirety.

The violence done to character both reflects the violence of the war and develops out of it a new approach to the role of the protagonist in fiction, one that relies on fragmentation and characters made up of glimpses and shadows. In what might be read as a play on "remember" and "re-member," Morrison speaks of turning "pieces" of memory into "parts" through the creative process ("Memory" 214): "I then tried to distinguish between a piece and a part—in the sense that a piece of a human body is different from a part of a human body" (216). But she never fully reconstitutes the body that forms the center of her narrative. Only by being shattered or dismembered can the central character hold all together. This is a practice Bernard seems to recognize in Woolf's novel: "It is the shattering and piecing together—this is the daily battle, defeat or victory, the absorbing pursuit" (200).

H. Porter Abbott has drawn attention to Woolf's fear of "character," which she understands to be an assigned shape that precedes one and that is wielded by others; for Woolf, "personality" indicates something emanating from within, something so powerful that it seems to need the presence of others to keep it in bounds. Woolf, like Faulkner, gives new form to literature of mourning through literary character, largely by substituting a narrative character for what in elegy remained a disembodied lyric "I," but the novelists do so only by first underscoring that character is a negotiation between the individual and the fictional structure in which it is deemed "useful." In Woolf's view, layer upon layer of "character" can be created while leaving "personality" untouched. Variety of perspectives does not ensure that one's identity, or one's perception of oneself, will be uncovered. At the beginning of her attack on Arnold Bennett in "Character in Fiction," better known as "Mr. Bennett and Mrs. Brown," Woolf acknowledges that "men and women write novels because they are lured on to create some character which has thus imposed itself upon them . . . spending the best years of their lives in the pursuit. . . . Few catch the phantom; most have to be content with a scrap of her dress or a wisp of her hair" (E 3:421). Character is a phantom rather than the thing itself. If Woolf's character Neville claims that, without Percival, "we are silhouettes, hollow phantoms moving mistily without a background" (87–88), her elegy serves as a formal recognition of the personality that remains beyond the grasp of fiction. Although Bernard boldly attempts to pin down Percival's character by asserting, "He is a hero. Oh yes, that is not to be denied" (89), Bernard quickly slides into metaphors that disturb the heroic image. Thus the yelping jackals that are transformed into soldiers and the birds that now manifest love toward each other. Each image is uprooted by the one that precedes it, manifesting Percival's utility as a fragment with which the other characters' imaginations might play.

To the standard images of modernist fracture Woolf adds the hide-and-seek of those in the war's aftermath. Although her characters' attempts to shield themselves from attention may seem childish, Bernard's desire for something outside the central role speaks to the contemporary associations of such a position with the violence of the war and its claim on those whose service was rewarded with death and testimonies of heroism. His elegy complicates the terrain that Woloch outlines in the novel tradition, since Bernard seizes on the central role as a point of access to the other characters and their voices. He does not hope to don the mantle of protagonist. He is a figure on the margins who yet speaks for the rest, and it is in this turn outward, an egoism that exhibits itself most fully when purporting to be most altruistic, that a more complex but equally terrifying vision of order emerges for postwar society. Woolf's characters' desire to avoid the fragmentation of the central position competes with their desire for attention, an acknowledgment of the pull of those prewar ideals. She does not simply dismiss the nostalgic allure of the public schools, of poetry, and all of the other institutions of prewar life; instead, she leaves room for such things in her elegiac novel, engaging them critically through the characters' overlapping dialogues and competition for speech. Unlike the war poets, whose rejection of elegy was often abrupt and brutal, Woolf allows elegiac elements to retain their centrality, even as she calls that very centrality into question by suggesting other perspectives and inscribing in her text the costs of such ideals. The defining role in the postwar elegiac novel is that of the mourner on the periphery of the central character's influence rather than the traditional hero or protagonist. The hole left by Percival goes unfilled. In making a place for the war in her novel, however implicitly, by refusing to identify a successor for Percival, Woolf marks a rift in the tradition of elegiac succession, one that leaves scars on the structure of elegy and of novel form.

An Elegy of Borrowed Books

Woolf fights rigid definitions of character in *Jacob's Room,* published nine years earlier than *The Waves,* but here, in a novel that offers far fewer explicit ties to the First World War, she more thoroughly explores its effects on literature of mourning. It is not only fear that keeps Bernard from claiming the protagonist's position; the role he occupies, that of chief mourner, has grown in significance. In turning the reader's attention from the hero to the one who speaks for the dead, Woolf encourages her reader to cast a critical eye on that newly powerful voice. If the elegist might be criticized for skewing toward the conventional military hero for his choice of subject, so too the elegist might come under fire for his own brushes with conventionality through his years in institutional education. Conventionality is a trait prized by both public schools and military training: "In some ways the [war] training *was* a hideous parody of a public-school upbringing, in which the individual became subservient to and subsumed by the institution.... They were stripped of their possessions, separated from their families and forced into a communal existence from which privacy was totally eliminated" (Parker 37). This description echoes the limitations that Woolf herself imposes on her characters in *The Waves,* though her experiment has as its notable variation the incorporation of women.

Melissa Zeiger argues, "Mourning has been women's work since at least classical antiquity" (12). And yet, as Ramazani observes, participation in the elegiac tradition has been particularly difficult for women, since mourning is "'masculine' as an elite literary form yet 'feminine' as a popular cultural form" (*Poetry* 21). The highly allusive elegiac tradition is learned in school, a literary form that enables men to articulate their grief in writing; women, on the other hand, traditionally manifest mourning in their person (dress, posture, emotional expression) and in writing that is dismissed as sentimental. For any female writer who desires to engage the former literature, the latter always exists in the background as a genre to be resisted.

Although Woolf devotes the majority of *The Waves* to cultivating Bernard's elegy, she also offers the beginnings of an alternative elegy, using the novel's scope to suggest abler subjects and speakers of elegiac lament. Her attempt to show life beyond the public school of Percival and the male narrators of *The Waves* re-creates what Woloch describes as the effect of changing social norms on literary structure: "As the logic of social inclusiveness becomes increasingly central to the novel's form ... the novel gets infused with an awareness of its potential to *shift* the narrative focus away from an established center, toward minor characters" (19). As is evident in his study of character-systems, the minor character makes readers aware of the narrative's construction, the "generative tension between story and discourse" (40). It is precisely because the hints of Rhoda are so promising in *The Waves,* and yet her narrative position so circumscribed, that she is of particular interest as an elegiac figure, both speaker and subject. Feminist scholarship on elegy has criticized women's exclusion from traditional elegy, but Woolf's contribution to the field, as both critic and writer, is notable in that it largely reproduces the marginalization of which the feminist critics complain.[15] She even draws on imperialist language to make Rhoda appear distinct from the other characters, an approach for which Woolf has been roundly criticized by Robin Hackett (73). Woolf works with and through the elegiac tradition even as she suggests ways in which a female elegist could evade the emphasis on order that has become suspect in the years following the war.

Bernard's elegy is an inadequate substitute for the voices of the five other characters, but so too is Percival an inadequate elegiac subject who sends the reader looking for a better one. Louis says of Percival, "I adore his magnificence... I despise his slovenly accents." Percival is "heavy," "walks clumsily down the field" (25), he "blunders off" (27), and even love-struck Neville acknowledges that "I could not live with him and suffer his stupidity" (33). What is upheld as a model of greatness and promise is not a poet, but rather a figure with the "magnificence... of some mediaeval commander" (25) who will ride a "flea-bitten mare" and solve the "Oriental problem" with "the violent language that is natural to him" (98). And for that he will be considered "a God" (98).[16] Although Rhoda's tone is perfectly bare of irony, her description of Percival's role reveals that England's poets will get their hands dirty in attempting to elegize figures such as this: "We see muddy roads, twisted jungle, swarms of men, and the vulture that feeds on some bloated carcass as within our scope, part of our proud and splendid province, since Percival, riding alone on a flea-bitten mare, advances down a solitary path, has his camp pitched among desolate trees, and sits alone, looking at the enormous mountains" (99). She takes up Bernard's language, Percival riding a flea-bitten mare and not a gallant steed, and exposes the desolation of the gain to be had by sending the "hero" out alone. The repeated indications of his isolation suggest a medieval quest, but the proximity of the vulture to "our proud and splendid province" suggests that what is gained is closer to a carcass than a promising treasure. If this is the modern elegiac subject, the elegy must undergo serious revision before it can be useful to Woolf.

Percival is not a burgeoning poet, unlike many traditional figures of elegy. Bernard describes him as "conventional; he is a hero" (88). Rhoda, though steeped in Shelley, dies with little fanfare, a potential elegiac subject that Bernard largely ignores. If, as Rhoda suggests, Percival expands their world by bringing India into view (99), she herself "looks far away over our heads, beyond India" (100). Although it may seem natural to compare Percival to his schoolmates, the male characters in *The Waves,* his role in Woolf's novel becomes clearer if one recognizes the subtle comparisons she draws between Percival and Rhoda, who also dies but is not elegized, and Jinny, who exudes a similar charisma, but whose power fades with her beauty. After all, that great elegiac trope, the sun, is present in the interludes of *The Waves,* but only in the figure of a woman.

Unlike Neville and Bernard, who identify as writers, Rhoda never claims to be a poet, but if Shelley is the most-quoted writer in *The Waves* (Hite, Introduction xli), Rhoda is the character who is most clearly tied to him and the only female character who uses allusions with anything like the frequency of her male counterparts. Although classical references litter *The Waves,* it is the Romantics who appear most frequently, an indication that one should be looking for a poet, rather than a hero, for elegizing. Unlike the male characters, however, Rhoda's literary education appears to come largely from her own reading rather than from formal schooling, and from library books rather than her own (*TW* 39).[17]

Although Woolf reconsidered her early plans to make Rhoda a writer of fiction (*The Waves: Two Holograph Drafts*), her revision is not a retrenchment. Rhoda's writerly role in the published version of *The Waves* is more amorphous but no less significant. In an early section of the published novel, just after Bernard weaves his first story, Rhoda sits with a basin full of white petals and water, an image with which her character is allied for the remainder of the novel:

> I will drop a stone in and see bubbles rise from the depths of the sea. . . . I have a short time alone, while Miss Hudson spreads our copy-books on the schoolroom table. I have a short space of freedom. . . . And I will now rock the brown basin from side to side so that my ships may ride the waves. Some will founder. Some will dash themselves against the cliffs. One sails alone. That is my ship. It sails into icy caverns where the sea-bear barks and stalactites swing green chains. The waves rise; their crests curl; look at the lights on the mastheads. They have scattered, they have foundered, all except my ship which mounts the wave and sweeps before the gale and reaches the islands where the parrots chatters and the creepers . . . (11; final ellipses in original)

When Percival dies, she characterizes him as "like a stone fallen into a pond round which minnows swarm. Like minnows, we who had been shooting this way, that way, all shot round him when he came. Like minnows, conscious of the presence of a great stone, we undulate and eddy contently" (99). In a novel that teems with web imagery—from the lines on

Louis's trade maps to Neville's net of scholarly discernment (121, 157)—the recurring image of the waves offsets the elegiac web with which Bernard attempts to "sum up" all that came before (176). It also draws on a recurring elegiac trope: since Milton's *Lycidas,*—which Woolf, in the company of W. B. Yeats and Walter de la Mare, declared to be the work to which she could return "unsated" (*D* 3:330)[18]—a setting by the sea reappears in elegies such as Hardy's for Swinburne, "A Singer Asleep," and T. S. Eliot's "The Waste Land" (Kennedy 6). In Woolf's elegiac novel, the sea operates as a disruptive force, recasting the more rigid forms that Bernard hopes to impose in its stead.

The conclusion to Bernard's final soliloquy, in which he calls on the heroic Percival to defend him against death, is followed by "*The waves broke on the shore*" (220), a line whose italics tie it to the nine italicized interludes that preface each section of the novel. It also recalls Rhoda's basin and the ships that she rocks to and fro. This final link between the book's form and Rhoda's image suggests that the difference in the ways Percival's and Rhoda's deaths are received may be explained not by Bernard's limited imagination but instead by Rhoda's design. Percival serves, like a dropped stone, as a locus of attention for a moment, enabling Rhoda to sail off alone while the others founder in the wake of his loss. The image of her play with the basin of white petals, appearing so early in the novel, suggests that she holds the world in which the others move. In this narrative, her solitude is a sign of her victory, even if it is only for "a short time," within "a short space of freedom" (11). That victory stands in marked contrast to the rest of her experience: "Alone, I rock my basins; I am mistress of my fleet of ships. But here, twisting the tassels of this brocaded curtain in my hostess's window, I am broken into separate pieces; I am no longer one" (76). Rhoda's sense of being fragmented when she is out in society echoes the novel's other images of fracture and indicates her awareness of the risks of remaining a player in such a world. It also ties her to Jinny, that figure of the point of impact, and to Louis's game of hide-and-seek.

Despite her allusions to Shelley, Rhoda does not seem to write poetry. Instead, she looks beyond familiar poetic language to express what Woolf calls the "feelings which seem at the moment to be balked by poetry" (*E* 4:435). Rhoda is like the speaker of Shelley's *Epipsychidion,* who acknowledges that the "wingèd words" with which he elevates his subject beyond worldly concerns are also "chains of lead around its flight of fire" (ll. 588–90). In describing herself as a girl with "no face" (22, 88), Rhoda conjures up the paintings of Woolf's sister, Vanessa Bell, exploring the boundaries between one artistic medium and another.[19] When she finds herself "broken into separate pieces" at a social function, she regains composure by replacing the room full of "tongues that cut me like knives" with "faces rid of features, robed in beauty" (77). In her elegy for Percival, Rhoda does not share Bernard's and Neville's monumentalizing impulses but instead gives herself over to the clarity of sight that such moments provide. In one of the most well-known scenes in *The Waves,* Rhoda's mourning leads her to describe orchestra members as taking a "square" and placing it "upon the oblong" (118). She makes the music visual, just as she made the individual abstract by insisting on facelessness. She strives beyond the known words to do justice to the "gift" of the shock of Percival's death, even as the faded violets she carries indicate her awareness of the futility of such a gesture. When her willingness to struggle with the limitations of language is set against Bernard's desire for phrase making, her potential as a modernist poet comes into focus. Her alternative elegy looks beyond order and control, exhibiting a flexibility of imagination that is in pointed contrast to Bernard's self-conscious efforts. Unlike Bernard, Rhoda considers directly one of the ethical aspects of elegy that R. Clifton Spargo explores most movingly: "our desire to spare ourselves the perceived lack of control over what happens" to the dead (3).

Rhoda's claim to just a moment of narrative authority is political as well as aesthetic, since it challenges the educational paradigms that break along gendered lines. She emerges as a figure of education, but not of dominance, of books, but borrowed ones. Both Jinny and Rhoda exhibit characteristics that place them outside the social institutions that shape the poetic elegy. Even Louis, hypersensitive to class divisions, cannot readily classify them: "Susan's father is a clergyman. Rhoda has no father. Bernard and Neville are the sons of gentlemen. Jinny lives with her grandmother in London" (*TW* 12). He equates fathers and social position; Jinny and Rhoda are, conveniently, unmarked by the social legacy of their fathers, and thus intriguing candidates for alternative elegiac voices, particularly given the elegy's ties to issues of inheritance. Both female characters suggest an alternative to the traditions of male education that dominate *The Waves,* an alternative that emphasizes flexibility and the embrace of new forms over established ones.

Jinny's and Rhoda's emphasis on the significance of a moment, rather than on the unfolding of an epic history or poetic tradition, sets them at odds both with Bernard's elegy and the genre as a whole. As Zeiger argues, women elegists do not, "in critiquing a monumental tradition, produce a monumental countertradition. Cumulatively, instead, they make a difference to the way the tropes of the mainstream elegiac tradition are amplified, redeployed, and read" (82). Women elegists, in effect, put their trust in literary tradition as a conversation in which any given writer plays only a part; they exchange the desire for a central role for the imagination needed to envision an elegy built of a community of mourners. Ironically, Woolf's alternative elegists lean more heavily on the elegiac tradition than do the traditional ones; as Bernard seeks to replace his predecessors' work, Rhoda and others add to it. Jinny offers a shining figure for order when she enters the restaurant, but then the control dissolves, immobility giving way to ripples of movement that Jinny transfers to those around her. Rhoda too shies away from the through line: "I cannot make one moment merge in the next. To me they are all violent, all separate; and if I fall under the shock of the leap of the moment you will be on me, tearing me to pieces. I have no end in view. I do not know how to run minute to minute and hour to hour, solving them by some natural force until they make the whole and indivisible mass that you call life" (94). Rhoda's approach to each moment, receiving them as individual shocks, stands in contrast to Bernard's historian tendencies, and it upholds Ramazani's claims for the modern elegy: "The modern elegy at its best is not a timeless sanctuary, immune to historical change; rather, its rough and ravaged contours indicate the social realities it must withstand" (*Poetry* 14).

Although Bernard claims "to long for some little language such as lovers use, broken words, inarticulate words" (176), the design that he eventually weaves is much grander, part of his plan for "some final statement" (138). Unlike the discrete events that Jinny and Rhoda create and observe, Bernard's elegy relies on a major event—that of Percival's death—and a narrative of mourning that unfolds from that point onward. Traditionally, a poet used the elegiac form to announce his own literary emergence through the mourning of a lost comrade, thus binding himself to the tradition of the elegy and the community of poets it represents. But Woolf's use of multiple speakers causes one to consider the cost of such community building:

Does one need the body of a Percival to facilitate such communion? Must one deny him the ability to speak in order to make him the occasion for the gathering of friends and the writing of the novel as a whole? Such questions put a great deal of pressure on the "occasional" nature of the elegy, making what is ostensibly an act of mourning appear more like opportunism.

In her critique of Bernard's elegy, Woolf suggests a reframing of history, subtly detaching it from the event, particularly the First World War, and allowing a greater variety of voices to add to the history. At a time when many of her contemporaries were rejecting the elegy, Woolf reclaims it from its cultural baggage, shifting the aesthetic ground of elegy to keep the ideological uses of order from closing in. Although Bernard's words cast doubt on the elegy, the novel form allows Woolf to continue the conversation with tradition rather than take a solely oppositional stance to it. It folds in elegy, or swallows it up. Woolf's novel's structure keeps the voices of elegy continually at play with one another.

Although Alex Woloch intends his theory as a means of studying narrative space in the novel, it also provides the necessary grounds for comparing the differences in narrative distribution *between* genres, a comparison that brings to the foreground the ethical as well as the aesthetic resonance of Woolf's negotiations between the elegy and the novel. Perhaps most importantly, Woloch's system reminds readers that fiction offers an unusual opportunity for an author to enlarge the role of a socially marginalized figure by granting him or her greater narrative space. The hide-and-seek of the children at the beginning of *The Waves* offers a new model for characterizations of the modernist novel, an opportunity to move beyond the smashing and fracturing called to mind by events of the historical period and into a critical exploration of the dynamics at play among the survivors. Woolf's hide-and-seek games speak to the kinds of negotiations at the center of Woloch's study of character: her new novelistic elegy has no central figure, but it does challenge the traditional use of the dead to memorialize public institutions and solidify existing social roles rather than to seek the individual who was lost. Her elegy makes room for new mourners who do not shoulder the full burden of representing the dead but instead offer a fleeting contribution to the chorus of mourners whose varied stories and styles reflect the multiplicity of ways in which the dead are remembered.

Through the elegy, Bernard preserves what Jinny calls "this globe whose walls are made of Percival, of youth and beauty, and something so deep sunk within us that we shall perhaps never make this moment out of one man again" (105). Although Jinny only asks to hold that globe for "a moment," Bernard suspends what he calls "the swelling and splendid moment created by us from Percival. We have proved . . . that we can add to the treasury of moments. . . . We are creators. We too have made something that will join the innumerable congregations of past time. We too . . . stride not into chaos, but into a world that our own force can subjugate and make part of the illumined and everlasting road" (106). The artifice of the elegy, rather than the grief that it articulates, emerges as the genre's most prominent feature when placed in Bernard's hands. In Woolf's critical rendering of the traditional elegy, the losses she conveys are surprising ones: the disappearance of the individual as he is rewritten into a suitable elegiac subject, the sudden silencing of the other mourners when the elegist seizes his chance, and the neglected opportunities for recognizing marginal characters whose elegiac qualities suggest great potential. Even as Bernard gallops toward the conclusion, Woolf's careful orchestration leaves the reader wondering after the Jinnys and Rhodas whom tradition left behind.

3

The Lively Response of the Dead in *As I Lay Dying* and *Jacob's Room*

> I measure every Grief I meet
> With narrow, probing, eyes—
> I wonder if It weighs like Mine—
> Or has an Easier size—
> —Emily Dickinson, Fr 550

Although Woolf's *The Waves* revolves around Percival, only once does another character express interest in what he has to say. Neville notes that Bernard exhibits "a certain effort, an extravagance in his phrase, as if he said 'Look!' but Percival says 'No.' For he is always the first to detect insincerity; and is brutal in the extreme" (26). Neville devalues the act of speaking by linking it to insincerity, a criticism that implicitly undermines the narrative form that has propelled the novel forward. The six speakers' words are prefaced by phrases such as "Bernard said" or "Susan said," but here Neville amends that formal tic with "as if" and in so doing demotes the speakers' declarations to merely hypothetical contributions. At the same time, his abrupt shift to the present tense distances Percival's purported "No" from the "as if" earlier in the sentence. One might be forgiven for thinking that Percival had indeed spoken, and with greater authority than all the rest.

Through these slight shifts in grammar, Woolf frames the attitude of the dead toward elegists as one of resistance, with Percival's alleged "No" a protest against profligate storytelling. In *The Waves,* opposition appears only through the words of a character not yet dead, as they are imagined by another. It is a small opening. But Neville's fancy enables readers to imagine how the elegiac subject could lay claim to his or her own narrative. In literature, where the rules of reality can be bent or thrown out, authors have an opportunity to set the voices of the dead alongside those of the living and hold elegists accountable for trying to "finish their stories" (*TW* 26).

In *The Sound and the Fury* and *The Waves,* Faulkner and Woolf highlight the competition for the elegist's position, a dynamic that has always lain beneath the elegiac tradition but that is rarely acknowledged by it. When the authors' novels are considered separately, as they are in this book's first two chapters, the differences in style suggest the modern elegy's range of voices and effects. But when the authors' works are brought together, they argue for the consonance of the authors' imagination in using fictional—even fantastic—perspectives to revivify a genre so that it can better speak to the needs of the world beyond literature. Although Addie of *As I Lay Dying* (1930) and Jacob of *Jacob's Room* (1922) share with Caddy and Percival a measure of absent centrality, their voices irrupt into the text in a joint challenge to the unilateral relationship between elegist and elegiac subject.

Like the war poets whose antielegies dominate discussions of literature and the First World War, Woolf and Faulkner reject palliative phrases such as "He did not die in vain" as propaganda masquerading as consolation. Just as limiting, Woolf and Faulkner make clear, is the dictum "De mortuis nihil nisi bonum," or "Speak no ill of the dead," since it ensures that the dead will not be remembered as having been once among the (flawed) living. Before proposing alternatives to the traditional elegiac dynamic, Woolf and Faulkner challenge not only the elegist's authority but also the pervasive assumption that elegy need be eulogistic. To dispel that notion, they call up the idiosyncratic voices of the dead to contest an elegy of unrealistic perfection. Even as both authors claim the voice of the dead as their literary prerogative, they dispel the mystique of "last words" and the "second sight" that proximity to death is supposed to bring.

Woolf's and Faulkner's emphasis on flawed speakers reflects their long-standing reluctance to rely on a single voice to represent their work. At the end of her life, Woolf begins work on a new project, titled "Anon," that traces anonymous influences on readers and writers, teasing out communal qualities rather than the individual ones prized by society. Faulkner would prefer to have no public record of his life beyond his books, so that they stand without comment: "It is my ambition to be, as a private individual, abolished and voided from history, leaving it markless, no refuse save the printed books; I wish I had had enough sense to see ahead thirty years ago and, like some of the Elizabethans, not signed them. It is my aim, and every effort bent, that the sum and history of my life, which in the same sentence is my obit and epitaph too, shall be them both: He made the books and he died" (*SL* 285). Faulkner's reticence stems from a larger set of concerns that distinguishes the right to speak as an ordinary citizen from the power of speaking as a representative or figure of authority.

Such concerns come to the fore in political situations, such as when he was asked to speak at the seventh national conference of the US National Commission for UNESCO, to be held in Denver in October of 1959. In his reply to the request, Faulkner expresses unease not with appearing at the conference but with appearing as an "officially delegated mouthpiece":

> If I will have any value here (the Denver Conference) I believe it will [be] negatived, maybe destroyed if I am more than present. I mean, to be the official speaker delegate. Because I would go there having no confidence whatever in the idea of me being that officially delegated mouthpiece. For the reason that I believe that speech is mankind's curse, all evil and grief of this world stems from the fact that man talks. I mean, in the sense of one man speaking to a captive audience. Except for that, and its concomitants of communication—radio, newspapers, such organs—there would have been no Hitler and Mussolini. I believe that in the case of the speaker and his captive audience, whatever the reason for the captivity of the audience, the worst of both is inevitably brought out—the worst of the individual, compounded by the affinity for evil inherent in people compelled or persuaded to be a mass, an audience, which in my opinion is another mob. (*SL* 424)

Faulkner writes elsewhere of the audience or mob, most notably the lynching crowds of *Intruder in the Dust* and "Pantaloon in Black." His fear of a mob may account for the silence of so many of his novels' central characters: "It's that single voice that's the important thing. When you get two people, you still got two human beings; when you get three you got the beginning of a mob. And if you get a hundred all focused on one single idea, that idea is never too good. Man has got to be, if he's got to be a collection, or a gang, a party or something, he's got to be a party of individual men" (*LG* 102–3). Woolf's portrayals of silent young men in *The Waves* and *Jacob's Room* reflect social values that Woolf desires to call into question even as she suggests alternative models of narrative attention. The silence of Faulkner's characters, however, reflects his sensitivity to the problems of the central position, an element that is often overlooked in Faulkner criticism, where it is common to intuit the author's opinions from those expressed by talkative characters such as Gavin Stevens.

In drawing out the voice of the dead, Faulkner and Woolf take opposing tacks: *As I Lay Dying* is dogged by the presence of a corpse that appears early and intrudes upon the narrative until its end, while *Jacob's Room* is notable for the absence of its dead soldier's body. Through both methods, the authors acknowledge the body as the staging ground for grief, since mourners incorporate the rituals of burial into their own lived experience in order to stand in new relation to the dead. Even as Woolf and Faulkner acknowledge the traditional correspondence between laying the body in the ground and "laying the dead to rest," in their fiction they make it difficult to take such rest for granted. Their response to elegy begins with the body, as they challenge the link between stillness and the surrender of human agency that enables mourners to act on behalf of the dead without fear of accountability. Everything about the dead is to be reconceived, starting with a corpse whose stillness may mask the presence of a forceful, continuing will.

In one of the earliest scenes in *As I Lay Dying,* Faulkner trains his reader to see the animation that lies behind stillness as the character Jewel attempts to control his half-wild horse: "Then they are rigid, motionless, terrific, the horse back-thrust on stiffened, quivering legs, with lowered head; Jewel with dug heels, shutting off the horse's wind with one hand, with the other patting the horse's neck in short strokes myriad and caressing, cursing the horse with obscene ferocity" (12). Woolf, in a similar move, makes clear that the force of London traffic reverberates in the body of the policeman who directs it: "as smoothly sculptured as the impassive policeman at Ludgate Circus. But you will observe that far from being padded to rotundity his face is stiff from force of will, and lean from the effort of keeping it so. When his right arm rises, all the force in his veins flows straight from shoulder to finger-tips; not an ounce is diverted into sudden impulses, sentimental regrets, wire-drawn distinctions. The buses punctually stop" (*JR* 125). Both scenes retrain the reader to align stillness with effort. As André Bleikasten observes of Faulkner's work, "Immobility is scarcely ever absolute or final. Stillness is almost always throbbing with latent motion; it is movement beginning or ending, energy dying or gathering force, a tense interval like the lull before the storm" (*Ink* 165).

Faulkner and Woolf resist the temptation to treat the dead as objects of memory. Through recurring images of tense stillness they create an opportunity for the dead to cut through the objectification that lies at the heart of the elegiac tradition. If stillness reflects what the mourner sees, then Woolf and Faulkner take the part of the dead, imagining a much more active internal life than what is usually granted them. Both authors couch the voice of the dead in narratives that, as Claire Raymond says of other posthumous literary voices, make death "a direction rather than a graphic site of burial" (16). Like other modern writers, Woolf and Faulkner are leery of characterizing mourning as a process that is to be completed. To argue for the ongoing nature of mourning, they first lay claim to the continued existence of the dead through active corpses that prepare readers to engage corpses as characters with voices of their own. Woolf's and Faulkner's "character-system," to use Alex Woloch's term, makes room for the dead, thereby acknowledging the ongoing effects of the dead on the social interactions of the living.

Uprooting the Dead

The protagonists' initial absence in *Jacob's Room* and *As I Lay Dying* renders them vulnerable to characterization by minor figures, capricious narrators, and readers' own desires; character making is the dominant sport in these novels. But both Woolf and Faulkner challenge the elegiac conventions that entitle others to speak for the dead by making clear the costs of such portraits, even—perhaps especially—when such sketches are eulogistic. In *Jacob's Room*, Seabrook Flanders, the protagonist's father, is present only through the carefully constructed role that his widow has created in his absence: "'Merchant of this city,' the tombstone said; though why Betty Flanders had chosen so to call him when, as many still remembered, he had only sat behind an office window for three months, and before that had broken horses, ridden to hounds, farmed a few fields, and run a little wild—well, she had to call him something. An example for the boys" (9–10).[1] In making her husband an "example for the boys" Betty Flanders has made of him a fiction. Freud speaks to such urges to rewrite the lives of the dead in "Thoughts for the Times":

> Towards the actual person who has died we adopt a special attitude—something almost like admiration for someone who has accomplished a very difficult task. We suspend criticism of him, overlook his possible misdeeds, declare that '*de mortuis nil nisi bonum*,' and think it justifiable to set out all that is most favourable to his memory in the funeral oration and upon the tombstone. Consideration for the dead, who, after all, no longer need it, is more important to us than the truth, and certainly, for most of us, than consideration for the living. (290)

What Woolf captures, however, is that consideration for the dead is often performed in service of the living. It is for the future generation that Betty chooses such an inscription, intending to guide her sons toward a more stable, bourgeois life than the one her husband actually lived.

After foregrounding the ways in which mourning practices perpetuate social ideals, Woolf proceeds to uproot such practices. Seabrook's tombstone, "a solid piece of work" that lends gravitas to Betty's chosen epitaph (9), gives way to "a mason's van with newly lettered tombstones recording how some one loved some one who is buried at Putney" (89–90). Here the identities of the dead are blurred both by multiplicity and by movement: "Then the motor car in front jerks forward, and the tombstones pass too quick for you to read more" (90). It is a chilling vision of the ways in which the tools of grief have been shaken by the First World War, during which individual deaths give way to mass casualties. The bodies of the dead are not brought home, forcing mourners to abandon funeral practices that rely on putting the body of the dead to rest in English soil.[2] Since tombstones comfort the living rather than represent the dead, Woolf puts them on a truck and renders them illegible, making the names and lives of the dead something to seek rather than reify.

Not to be outdone, in *As I Lay Dying* Faulkner puts both coffin and corpse on a wagon after Addie Bundren's corpse has lain at home for three days, an echo of Christian resurrection that anticipates the unsettling animation of Addie's body after her death. Although as she dies Addie is aligned with inanimate objects, "her eyes like two candles," her body making "no more of a hump than a rail would" (8), upon her death the descriptions of both body and coffin challenge the assumption that Addie has been put to rest. As the men carry the coffin into the house they speak of it "as though, complete, it now slumbered lightly alive, waiting to come awake" (79–80). By making Addie's death the beginning rather than the end of the Bundren story, Faulkner appears to entertain a theory put forth by Addie's husband, Anse: "The Lord put roads for travelling: why He laid them down flat on the earth. When He aims for something to be always a-moving, He makes it long ways, like a road or a horse or a wagon, but when He aims for something to stay put, He makes it up-and-down ways, like a tree or a man" (35–36). Living men are to remain fixed, but upon their death they become subject to new rules. If coffins were meant to be stationary, then they would be placed in the ground vertically, as Leopold Bloom proposes in Joyce's *Ulysses* (6.764). Such theories emphasize the conventionality of the public treatment of the dead. As Faulkner uses fiction to reconsider such conventions, he opens the door to remaking them in a world in which the old signs of respect no longer fit the circumstances of grief. Just as Anse refuses to adjust to a more mobile modern culture, so too the reliance on burial for solace becomes a problematic practice in a world that is both overcrowded and missing its war dead.

Faulkner and Woolf shift from physical markers of mourning to less tangible ones when they refuse to pinpoint their characters' moment of death and burial. In Woolf's novel, we learn that Betty Flanders's sons are "fighting for their country" only one paragraph before the final chapter of the novel, when she is left to contend with the belongings Jacob leaves behind (143). Jacob's death occurs in the yawning gap between the two chapters. By depriving her readers of the battlefield and the final moments of Jacob's death, Woolf denies the elegiac identification of the lost individual with the circumstances of his death. Although she knows that much elegiac literature presents the moment of death as a confrontation and her soldier-subject is well suited to such an allegory of death, Woolf denies her reader information that the soldier's loved ones do not have, maintaining the perspective of those who mourn for him at home. Jacob's body and the circumstances of his death remain beyond reach, leaving his family to mourn him only through empty shoes and an empty room.

Whereas Woolf elides the moment of Jacob's death, Faulkner makes Addie's moment of death uncertain by offering the reader too many options. The eyes that "gutter down into the sockets" finally "go out as though someone had leaned down and blown upon them" (48). But the metaphor reverberates among several different characters, all of whom seem to speak of different moments in time. The clearest rendering of the moment of death comes from Addie's son Darl, who is not present to witness the event and who thus must be understood as clairvoyant if his words are to have any weight with the reader. Even Peabody, the doctor, begins his very unclinical ruminations on Addie with "When we enter she turns her head and looks at us. She has been dead these ten days" (43). This unusual diagnosis echoes the medical expert in Faulkner's first novel, *Soldiers' Pay,* who declares the returning soldier one who "should have been dead these three months were it not for the fact that he seems to be waiting for something" (122). Through Addie, Faulkner brings home the lessons of the First World War: "that the boundary between life and death does not hold" (Limon, "Addie" 41). For Faulkner, such conditions are not simply an explanation of the war as a unique context but rather a lingering effect of warfare that must now be grappled with on the home front. Without a clear moment of loss, Addie's family members struggle to move past a death that is always in process. Addie's youngest son, Vardaman, conceives of his mother's experience in the coffin in terms of his own nightmarish memory of being trapped in his crib (*AILD* 65). Vardaman's sense of suffocation, his identification of his mother as a living being rather than a corpse, contributes to the pervasive sense that Addie is arrested in the act of dying, as the grammar of the novel's title would suggest. The perpetuation of the act of dying undermines the elegiac emphasis on death as the moment from which poetic mourning is born, and in which consolation might be found. Instead, Addie's dying state is recorded and reimagined in an endless loop throughout the novel. Although Addie, unlike Jacob, is afforded a burial, it offers both reader and characters little resolution. Faulkner alters the regard for the body of the dead merely by keeping the corpse around for nine days: "For the Bundrens, the cadaver is not so much a source of horror and revulsion as a nuisance" (Bleikasten, *Ink* 169–70).[3] As Addie's son Cash reports, "We got it filled and covered and drove out the gate and turned into the lane" (237). Buried in a subordinate clause, Addie's burial barely registers on the level of narrative because the mourners' attentions are elsewhere.

By denying the reader and the bereaved characters a clear portrayal of the moment of death and the ritual of burial, Woolf and Faulkner withhold the moment that allows one to "sum up" a character, to begin recasting his or her life in familiar narrative arcs. Although storytelling may be consoling to the bereaved, it also exchanges life for a more limited story that suits the needs of the storytellers. Such concerns resonate with novelists, whose literary form offers the pretense of an all-inclusive story while yet allowing characters room only inasmuch as they serve a larger narrative purpose. In treating mourning as a messier, more multifaceted experience than it appears in either traditional elegy or Freud's characterization of grief work, Faulkner and Woolf challenge the assumption that mourning follows the arc of storytelling, with a clear beginning and end.

The mourning may be messy in *As I Lay Dying* and *Jacob's Room*, but neither author can be accused of careless technique. Faulkner characterized *As I Lay Dying* as a "tour de force" in which both form and goal were so clear that he considered the writing "simply a matter of fitting bricks together" (*LG* 244). When Woolf began work on *Jacob's Room*, she deliberately set out to master "looseness & lightness" in its form, her primary concern being that this formal play yet "enclose the human heart" (*D* 2:13). Woolf's first critic, her husband Leonard, echoed her doubts about the marriage of form and character upon reading the final draft of *Jacob's Room*: "He says that the people are ghosts.... Thinks I should use my 'method,' on one or two characters next time" (*D* 2:186). That the form would make "ghosts" of the characters—a sentiment echoed in the novel's earliest reviews—and that limiting the set of characters would make clearer the "one or two," should not be accepted uncritically. In making their protagonists apparitions, like the "phantom" characters of *The Waves*, Woolf and Faulkner facilitate the presence of minor characters and challenge their cultures' larger narrative of the uniqueness of grief. No one, in the wake of the losses of the First World War, could sustain such a view, and yet few proved ready to subsume their loss within a larger cultural shift.

Fittingly, for two authors so concerned with the marriage of form and culture, Woolf and Faulkner draw on literary predecessors to support their challenge to the integrity of the story arc of mourning. Sidestepping the elegiac tradition, Faulkner draws his title from book 11 of the *Odyssey*, when Odysseus's descent into Hades gives the dead the opportunity to tell their own stories, a desire that, like Addie Bundren's, persists beyond the grave. In *Jacob's Room,* Woolf draws from the same *Macbeth* soliloquy that gives Faulkner the title for *The Sound and the Fury,* a passage that speaks to the unraveling of story and significance. The "tale / Told by an idiot, full of sound and fury, / Signifying nothing" that attracted Faulkner is immediately preceded by the declaration, "Life's but a walking shadow, a poor player / That struts and frets his hour upon the stage / And then is heard no more" (5.5.24–28). Or, as Woolf rewrites the lines, "In any case life is but a procession of shadows, and God knows why it is that we embrace them so eagerly, and see them depart with such anguish, being shadows" (*JR* 56). Faulkner and Woolf use each allusion to underscore the disarray of life and mourning, fending off those who would see their characters' deaths fitting a larger narrative.

The Speaking Dead

As is clear from Bernard in *The Waves,* speaking for the dead brings with it a number of opportunities for personal gain. Becoming Percival's elegist allows Bernard to lay claim to a poetic identity, to rein in his diffusiveness through an established literary form, and to secure for himself an audience. In *As I Lay Dying,* Faulkner formulates the mourner's gains in coarser terms: although Addie's husband and children claim to honor the wishes of the dead by taking her body to Jefferson to be buried, forty miles from home, her request is the pretext for their own desire to go to town to acquire bananas, an abortion, a set of false teeth, and a new wife.[4]

Anse, Addie's husband, whose rain-wet face looks like "a monstrous burlesque of all bereavement" (78), makes the most of his new widowerhood. There is no room in Anse's mourning for what David Sherman calls "mortal obligations," the care of the dead that reflects one's role as a member of a larger cultural community (9). Instead, Anse claims, "But now I can get them teeth. That will be a comfort. It will" (111), enacting a parody of other mourners' search for consolation. Of all of Woolf's and Faulkner's characters, Anse offers the most cynical rendering of the opportunistic mourner. If psychoanalysis has figured grief as that which seeks compensatory substitution, Tammy Clewell argues that "Faulkner's novel ... demonstrates how commodity culture plays on this substitutive drive" (*Mourning, Modernism* 59). Even more disconcerting, however, is the way in which mourning convention has enabled Anse to use his wife's death to amplify both his voice and his status. He enjoys being able to "look folks in the eye now, dignified, his face tragic and composed" (86). His new status gives him leverage even within the bereaved family, as when he takes ten dollars from his daughter, Dewey Dell, quelling her protests with a rebuke: "My own daughter, the daughter of my dead wife, calls me a thief over her mother's grave" (256). Anse takes Dewey Dell's money on grounds that he should be compensated for the loss of his wife, and yet in doing so he denies Dewey Dell her own grief. In Addie's death, Anse has been made irreproachable, removing him from community—and criticism.

Thus when Addie speaks, much to the surprise of the reader, more than halfway through the novel, at issue is whether her voice is sufficiently powerful to contradict the portrait that has been painted by the characters and community members who precede and outlive her. It is an unusual confrontation in literature of mourning. If we consider the question in narrative terms, what room is there for a central figure who comes so late to the story? The words of the dead have a strange power, coming as they do from a peculiar narrative and ontological space, and the majority of Faulkner critics read Addie's monologue as authoritative.[5] But Faulkner's attention to the voices of the mourners earlier in the novel equips the reader to reject Addie's character as she represents it in her monologue.

Much of what Addie says can be read as an insistence on her continued presence in the world, through teaching, marriage, motherhood, and even death. Her use of violent language combats the objectification that the other characters enact even before she is dead. Her insistence that she be buried in Jefferson delays the moment of burial, relying on the difficulty of the journey to unravel family bonds, since their unity would enable the Bundrens to share the burden of death and mourning and thus move past the loss.[6] She hopes, in effect, for an experience like the whippings she inflicted on her students when she was a schoolteacher: "I would think with each blow of the switch: Now you are aware of me! Now I am something in your secret and selfish life, who have marked your blood with my own for ever and ever" (170). Everything from the smell of her decaying corpse to the trials of the family's slow journey to Jefferson contribute to her impressing herself on her family even as they prepare to dispose of her.

Addie's family members remind themselves and others of Addie by invoking her name throughout *As I Lay Dying*. For silent characters such as Percival in *The Waves* and Caddy in *The Sound and the Fury*, such invocations can make them seem superhuman or mythical, bigger than life. But as Addie demonstrates, if the power of narration is in one's hands, it is possible to make another person disappear by gradually draining the signifying power of their name: "Why are you Anse. I would think about his name until after a while I could see the word as a shape, a vessel, and I would watch him liquify and flow into it like cold molasses flowing out of the darkness into the vessel, until the jar stood full and motionless: a significant shape profoundly without life like an empty door frame; and then I would find that I had forgotten the name of the jar" (173). Having eliminated Anse's name and, through it, the individual that it signifies, she moves on to a discussion of Whitfield, her lover, whom she carefully does not name. In eliding his name she protects him from the erasure that she enacts on her own husband, and that she fears is being enacted upon her by her family as they invoke her name during their interactions with one another.

Addie's desire to leave her mark on others emerges in a postmortem voice that makes very little sense except as a literary trope, one that exuberantly calls attention to itself as a freak of storytelling. By giving Addie prime narrative space in *As I Lay Dying,* Faulkner reconceives the "character-space" of fiction, challenging the tendency to expunge the dead from our social and narrative relations. That Addie's fight is, at least in part, a literary one is clear from the fact that she is haunted by her father's legacy. She begins her narrative by recalling that "my father used to say that the reason for living was to get ready to stay dead a long time" (169). His is the narrative arc that Addie fights and against which she compares each of the successive events in her life. Addie's chapter, though ostensibly a monologue, carries the marks of a debate Faulkner is continuing from his first novel, *Soldiers' Pay:* Margaret Powers challenges the predatory Januarius Jones, "The next time you try to seduce anyone, dont do it with talk, with words. Women know more about words than men ever will. And they know how little they can ever possibly mean" (199). Faulkner's Addie fights to make sense of her life beyond the words of her predecessors. As she empties and reshapes her father's words, Addie makes clear her reason for rejecting words as "just a shape to fill a lack" (172), and her resistance to substitution more generally.

In speaking, Addie addresses her desire to maintain a presence after death to the novel's readers, who have likely eliminated Addie from their character lists by this point in the novel. Some critics attempt to get around the problem of a speaking corpse by declaring Addie's section a record of "Addie's dying thoughts" (O. Vickery 55), a flashback of sorts, while others, such as Paul Lilly, assert that her voice simply takes place outside the chronological sequence of narratives that makes this novel a relatively straightforward read.[7] But either of these interpretations would obscure the ways in which Addie's monologue is in conversation with those that precede and follow hers, as well as the textual similarity between her monologue and the others of the book. In other words, they would remove Addie's section from the social network out of which the novel is fashioned. Ironically, the only way to preserve Addie's place in the conversation and in the community is to accept the voice of the dead in the midst of the living.

Faulkner's teasing description throughout the novel of a coffin that is resistant, "volitional" (*AILD* 97), prevents the reader from dismissing the claim that Addie has been dead for several days at the time her monologue appears in the text and that it is from that place and time that she is speaking. In the midst of such gruesome evidence of decomposition, as neighbors shake their heads and strangers turn in shock when they get a whiff of the smell, readers are presented with Addie's voice as she takes a turn in composing the narrative. Through the visual gag of the rotting corpse being carted to town, Faulkner forces readers to realize the difficulty of determining the position from which Addie speaks and the role of her voice in the narrative, exposing characters' and critics' prior literary, metaphysical, and theological commitments. The biological process of decomposition keeps the narrative *in* time, such that her voice appears after she has been dead for five days.

Setting Addie's position in time and place aside, Faulkner complicates even the position and perspective of those who merely observe the dead. Rather than join the community in gawking at Addie's coffin, Darl gazes upward, drawing attention to the buzzards who begin to follow the corpse: "Motionless in tall and soaring circles, they diminish and disappear" (104). Darl emphasizes their stillness in an echo of his characterization of Addie on her deathbed: "[Her face] is like a casting of fading bronze upon the pillow, the hands alone still with any semblance of life: a curled, gnarled inertness; a spent yet alert quality from which weariness, exhaustion, travail has not yet departed, as though they doubted even yet the actuality of rest" (51). The "still" suspends the sentence ("the hands alone still") before it goes on to stress the persistence of animation ("the hands alone still with any semblance of life"), neatly capturing the dual focus on rest and vigor in

Faulkner's novel. The hands that at first seem "still" are not at all still, but rather "still" in readiness for further activity, and thus readers must restart their interpretations partway through this garden-path sentence.[8] Faulkner allows Addie's willful stillness to be obscured by the coffin, but the buzzards then appear, seeming still in their high arc, making stillness a trope that resonates beyond Addie and draws our eye toward Darl's narrative priorities.

In 1956 Faulkner told Jean Stein in an interview for the *Paris Review*, "You know if I were reincarnated, I'd want to come back a buzzard. Nothing hates him or envies him or wants him or needs him. He is never bothered or in danger, and he can eat anything" (*LG* 243).[9] Eric Sundquist interprets this statement as an indication of Faulkner's "detachment from his materials" (28). But any sense that the buzzard is at a remove from life arises from those who observe it from the ground: it seems still from such a distance, which preserves it from demands and interruptions. But the buzzard is not, himself, unconcerned with what goes on below. After all, he still has an appetite to satisfy.

The buzzards in *As I Lay Dying* are a constant reminder that the coffin in the wagon is not an empty box. But the buzzard, "as still as if he were nailed to [the sky]" (122), is also a visual manifestation of an aural allusion:

> I heard a fly buzz—when I died—
> The Stillness in the Room
> Was like the Stillness in the Air—
> Between the Heaves of Storm—(Dickinson, Fr 591)

That opening stanza from one of Emily Dickinson's most famous poems draws readers back to the deathbed that they had left behind as the wagon moves through Mississippi, Faulkner's "still" "buzzards" echoing Dickinson's buzzing fly and still room. Although the Bundrens' journey bears the marks of an epic (complete with flood and fire), Faulkner draws readers' attention back to the domestic space Addie has only recently vacated.

Although Faulkner admitted to being "still rather Victorian in my prejudices regarding the intelligence of women, despite Elinor Wylie and Willa Cather and all the balance of them," he was well read in English and American poetry and could not have overlooked Conrad Aiken's work on Dickinson, given Faulkner's regard for Aiken's own writing (*SL* 32). Aiken published an edition of Dickinson's poetry in 1924 that paid particular attention to her poems on death and what one might call the posthumous voice, nearly all of which are gathered into the last of four sections in the volume, thereby amplifying their theme.[10] In his introduction to the selection, Aiken quotes from two such poems and then pauses to observe:

> Both these poems, it will be noted, deal with death; and it must be observed that the number of poems by Miss Dickinson on this subject is one of the most remarkable things about her. Death, and the problem of life after death, obsessed her. She seems to have thought of it constantly—she died all her life, she probed death daily. "That bareheaded life under grass worries one like a wasp," she wrote. Ultimately the obsession became morbid, and her eagerness for details, after the death of a friend—the hungry desire to know *how* she died—*became almost vulture-like*. But the preoccupation, with its horrible uncertainties—its doubts about immortality, its hatred of the flesh, and its many reversals of both positions—gave us her sharpest work. (xv; second emphasis mine)

Faulkner's buzzard may have yet another source. By making Dickinson's detailed exploration of death the landscape on which Addie Bundren seeks relief, Faulkner extends his novel's aesthetics of restless stillness beyond the bounds of his fiction.

One in ten of Dickinson's poems feature death or the dead, though Max Cavitch does not include Dickinson in his survey of the American elegy, nor does Jeffrey Weinstock in his study of nineteenth-century women writers' stories of the supernatural. Dickinson's poems are, perhaps, somewhat outside the purview of ordinary elegy or ghost stories, and it is in this "strange and original genius" (xvi), as Aiken called it, that she aids Faulkner in considering literature of mourning anew. For both Woolf and Faulkner, elegiac success comes not in providing a container for grief, validation of the elegist, or even an aesthetic substitute for loss; instead, it requires that one negotiate space within one's story for the dead, making them part of the story without that space either being claimed and manipulated by other characters or becoming a platform from which the dead's priorities can stifle the living.

The Dickinson poems that feature a postmortem voice, such as "I heard a fly buzz," are part of a genre that Diana Fuss has called the "corpse poem," which is "poetry not about the dead but spoken by the dead, lyric utterances not from beyond the grave but from inside it" (2–3). The key difference from elegy, Fuss claims, is that the corpse poem "rarely presumes to console the living for losses so profound they transcend the compensation of mourning" (67). Dickinson fills her corpse poems with female voices that Fuss calls "spirited personalities: gruff, overbearing, peevish" (51), a description that also suits Faulkner's Addie Bundren. The similarity between Dickinson's voices and Faulkner's suggests Dickinson's influence on the later author and may explain why Faulkner chose for his speaking corpse a woman when so many of his other female characters are silent. David Minter sees in some of Faulkner's early poems a voice that is, like Dickinson's, "distinctly post-mortem" (21). But in his poetry, Faulkner's female characters appear as nymphs, "Smooth-shouldered creatures in sheer scarves" (*Green Bough* 7). They share almost nothing with Emily Dickinson's pointed, playful voice or her nimble movement between high terms and low. In *As I Lay Dying,* however, the postmortem voice emerges in full[11] and begins to show some of the spirit of Dickinson's speakers.[12]

In an essay that answers its title question, "Who Is Faulkner's Emily?" Peter Hays reads the protagonist of Faulkner's widely anthologized short story "A Rose for Emily" as modeled after Emily Dickinson herself, or at least a popular interpretation of her life: an overprotective father, a reclusive lifestyle, and a fascination with death. Conrad Aiken's biographical sketch of Dickinson in his introduction to *Selected Poems of Emily Dickinson* contributes to the view of Dickinson as a "hermit" (ix), as he both laments and marvels at "her almost inviolable solitude" (vii). But her influence on Faulkner runs deeper than popular caricature, in large part because her work was ubiquitous in the decade preceding Faulkner's writing of *As I Lay Dying.* As Hays notes, Dickinson emerged in the American consciousness after the First World War, with a wildly popular biography by Dickinson's niece, an edition of what were, at the time, thought to be her complete poems, followed by a volume of additional poems, and publication of several new-found Dickinson poems in the *Atlantic* and *Nation* (Hays 107). Although the editors of the *Faulkner Encyclopedia* cast doubt on Faulkner's having read Dickinson, noting that he did not own any Dickinson books "nor did he mention her in any published essays or interviews" (Rowley 102), Faulkner did speak of her in at least one public appearance. In the midst of a series of informal lectures at the University of Mississippi in 1947, he reminds the class that "primarily I'm not a prose writer, I'm a poet. I write that way because I can't write like Shakespeare or Shelley" (qtd. in Inge 78). He then replies to a question about women poets with the comment that he liked them "when they were good," and he names Emily Dickinson first in a short list of women poets he admires (78).

The disregard Dickinson's speakers show for the line between life and death has a theological basis that helps to explain the presence of Addie Bundren's postmortem voice beyond her formidable will. In Dickinson's era, the status of the dead hinged on the answer to a doctrinal dispute: "Was the soul judged at the moment of death, passing directly out of the body and out of the grave, or did soul and body occupy the grave together until both were resurrected on Judgment Day?" (Fuss 50). Dickinson's poems investigate the latter possibility, implicitly supporting the notion of a transitional state in which consciousness and voice endow the human cadaver with a distinct presence of its own. It is the possibility of a voice in transit that Faulkner captures in matching Addie's moving, rotting corpse to a voice that continues to churn over questions of subjectivity and language well after one would assume such questions are behind her.

In Dickinson, as in Faulkner, the journey of death is made literal as well as figural. Most famously, Dickinson offers her speaker an elegant carriage:

> Because I could not stop for Death—
> He kindly stopped for me—
> The Carriage held but just Ourselves—
> And Immortality. (Fr 479)

Just as Addie is buried in her wedding dress, Dickinson's speaker's journey to death bears the trappings of a wedding (Raymond 17), and she looks out at a schoolyard scene that calls to mind Addie's fraught days as a teacher: "We passed the School, where Children strove / At Recess—in the Ring—" (Fr 479). When placed alongside Dickinson's poems, Addie Bundren's resistance to convention becomes more than idiosyncrasy or selfishness; instead, she echoes Dickinson's speaker's dissatisfaction with pat stories of salvation, such as the one that Addie's neighbor, Cora Tull, trots out. Like Addie, Dickinson's character flirts with rejecting an unknown heaven:

> I never felt at Home—Below—
> And in the Handsome skies

> I shall not feel at Home—I know—
> I don't like Paradise—
>
> Because it's Sunday—all the time—
> And Recess—never comes—(Fr 437)[13]

Dickinson, who identified herself as one of the minority of young women "without hope" of salvation during her year at Mount Holyoke, confesses in a letter to a friend that "it is hard for me to give up the world" (qtd. in Leiter 8). Schools and Sundays mark the institutional nature of what both Dickinson's character and Faulkner's have been told are the pinnacle of one's life. Is it any wonder, then, that Dickinson's speaker threatens to "run away" (Fr 437) were it not for Judgment Day?

The matter of escape consumes both Dickinson's speakers and Faulkner's character. In "Because I could not stop for Death," Dickinson's speaker is taken to a "House" that is, of course, a grave, and yet her repeated figuring of that grave as a house insists on the grave as a place to be inhabited, rather than one in which to be merely deposited.[14] Dickinson pays equal attention, however, to the house in which the individual dies. In one of her many deathbed poems Dickinson draws attention to the activity that follows the deathbed vigil:

> The Bustle in a House
> The Morning after Death
> Is solemnest of industries
> Enacted opon Earth— (Fr 1108)

Even as the mourners care for the body in one home, Dickinson's dead speakers become mistress of another:

> The grave my little cottage is,
> Where "keeping house" for thee
> I make my parlor orderly
> And lay the marble tea. (Fr 1784)

The doubled house-keeping of these poems offers a new slant to Addie Bundren's final rejection of her father's words, as she claims a domestic role unavailable to him: "I knew at last what he meant and that he could not have known what he meant himself, because a man cannot know anything about cleaning up the house afterward. And so I have cleaned my house.

With Jewel—I lay by the lamp, holding up my own head, watching him cap and suture it before he breathed—the wild blood boiled away and the sound of it ceased. Then there was only the milk, warm and calm, and I lying calm in the slow silence, getting ready to clean my house" (175–76). Addie does not trust other women to prepare her body after death or put her house in order, and she shows little regard for Judgment Day. Her narrative seeps with satisfaction at her own forethought in preparing a house that need not be tended upon her death, and that will not leave her, like her father, empty-handed. She rejects her father's seeming indifference to Addie as the fruit of his life, and she claims one of her children as the means by which she will triumph in death.

In Dickinson's poetry, it is the thought of Judgment that holds the speaker back, and she frequently grants it the last word in her poems, even if her teasing, questioning articulation of the reality of Heaven makes one wonder what could make it alluring. Addie, however, has drawn on the difference of gender to sidestep her father's claim that the point of living is "getting ready to stay dead a long time," an expectation either of annihilation (Clewell, *Mourning, Modernism* 70) or of Christian Judgment, if Addie's father prepares to be judged for eternity on the life that he has lived. The tidy house that Dickinson's speaker prepares for Christ becomes, in Faulkner's novel, the means by which to escape the taste of eternal judgment. When Addie turns again to her father's declaration about death at the close of her monologue, she acknowledges its dialogic use to her in shaping her own conception of life's purpose, but she reworks it to suit her own emphasis on the legacy of the dead to the living. Although she acknowledges the pull of her dead father's words, Addie lays claim to the ability of the living—of women, in particular—to empty out those words and infuse them with different meaning, a capacity that comes with "cleaning up the house" of the dead and taking up his or her burdens. That burden has traditionally rested on women, though by the time of *As I Lay Dying* the bulk of such work has become the purview of funeral directors—who are predominantly male (Sherman 27, 29). It is, then, as a kind of reclamation of domestic power and suspicion of the new shifts in culture that Addie stakes her claim.

Although both Dickinson's speaker and Faulkner's Addie inhabit houses in their deaths, the composition of their houses turns on opposite responses to the biblical narrative of redemption. In poems in the vein of "A Word made Flesh," Dickinson plays on the famous opening of the Gospel of John,[15] in which Christ is both Word and man, to breathe life into her own poetry. She soundly rejects the view that the language of poetry is calcified experience. As Steven Monte argues, the poem is densely woven with puns, both linguistic and theological, sounding a delight in language and drawing strength from echoes of the Christian narrative (39). Addie, however, contests the capacity of language to embody sacrament: "I learned that words are no good; that words dont ever fit even what they are trying to say at" (171). But she, like Dickinson's speakers, draws on Christian parallels. Whereas Dickinson turns to the Word, Addie turns to the flesh, using motherhood as an alternative to poetry as a means of fashioning her own terms for life. Thus her son Jewel becomes a new salvation for Addie, the means by which she can set her future in order, even after her own flesh gives out. Although Dickinson chooses poetry over progeny, even she occasionally couches her ambitions in terms of motherhood. As Sharon Leiter observes, in "A Word made Flesh" Dickinson repeats a query she first poses in a letter to Thomas Wentworth Higginson: "Are you too deeply occupied to say if my Verse is alive? . . . Should you think it breathed . . . I should feel quick gratitude" (qtd. in Leiter 55). The quickening of gratitude engenders the form for Addie Bundren's new reclamation of meaning.

Throughout her monologue, Addie resists her father's view of life's purpose, using each of her pregnancies to reimagine his words. Through acts of creation she makes his words no longer abstract but concrete, linked to the particularities of her own life. Upon learning of her first pregnancy she concludes, "I knew that living was terrible and that this was the answer to it" (171). When she finds herself pregnant for the second time, she reports, "I asked Anse to promise to take me back to Jefferson when I died, because I knew that father had been right, even when he couldn't have known he was right anymore than I could have known I was wrong" (173). Later, upon deciding that she would take up the affair that results in her beloved son Jewel, she explains, "I believed that I had found it. I believed that the reason was the duty to the alive" (174). Although Addie's monologue can be read through a variety of lenses, none so precisely captures her conflicts with language and blood relations as her struggle to understand, and ultimately to challenge, her father's pronouncement.

Although Dickinson's relationship with her father was complex, one is struck by a handful of comments that catch at the tacit understandings that shaped their relationship: "I never knew how to tell time by the clock till I was 15. My father thought he had taught me but I did not understand & I was afraid to say I did not & afraid to ask anyone else lest he should know"; "I had promised to visit my physician for a few days in May, but father objects because he is in the habit of me"; "He buys me many books, but begs me not to read them, because he fears they joggle the mind"; "I had no portrait.... It often alarms father. He says death might occur, and he has moulds of all the rest, but has no mould of me; but I noticed the quick wore off those things, in a few days, and forestall the dishonor" (Higginson). Even after his death, Emily Dickinson's letters and poems reflect a consciousness of his role in defining her life.

In Faulkner's novel, the striking description of family that Addie Bundren gives Anse during their courtship makes clear that she shares Dickinson's unusual understanding of family's hold on an individual:

> Later he told me, "I aint got no people. So that wont be no worry to you. I dont reckon you can say the same."
> "No. I have people. In Jefferson."
> His face fell a little. "Well, I got a little property. I'm forehanded; I got a good honest name. I know how town folks are, but maybe when they talk to me......."
> "They might listen," I said. "But they'll be hard to talk to." He was watching my face. "They're in the cemetery."
> "But your living kin," he said. "They'll be different."
> "Will they?" I said. "I dont know. I never had any other kind."
> (171)

That Addie enjoys Anse's discomfort is clear, but such convolutions also serve a rhetorical function: her contradictory descriptions reveal her father's voice to be, just as impossibly as her own monologue, the voice of the dead. Thus Addie makes the corpse poem an inherited narrative position, a rather unusual literary creation. It allows her to criticize the voice of the dead even as she herself speaks from such a position. Addie's acute awareness of the voices of both the living and the dead underlies her concerns with language and pregnancy, since only through the voices of those that follow her can she still be present after she can no longer punish her students, bear her children, or engage a lover.

By framing her narrative in the terms of a succession of pregnancies,[16] Addie's voice departs sharply from Dickinson's many child speakers. She shares, however, their acute awareness of Judgment, and their canny calculations in preparing to face it. In "'Twas just this time, last year, I died," Dickinson's speaker pauses to consider the shape of the hole she will leave behind in her family's life, using metaphor to test the link between the world she inhabits and the one she leaves behind:

> I wondered which would miss me, least,
> And when Thanksgiving, came,
> If Father'd multiply the plates—
> To make an even Sum—
>
> And would it blur the Christmas glee
> My stocking hang too high
> For any Santa Claus to reach
> The altitude of me—
>
> But this sort, grieved myself,
> And so, I thought the other way,
> How just this time, some perfect year—
> Themself, should come to me— (Fr 344)[17]

The speaker finds it difficult to measure a space for herself in the old world, and her tone falters as she realizes how much depends on her father's choice about plates or the pretense of Santa Claus's arrival. Her place in the world of the living, which she left only a year ago, depends on the nostalgia and whim of others. This thought disturbs, so the speaker instead shifts the ground of evaluation: rather than consider an absence in the world of the living that can be obscured by simply outgrowing the belief in childish fairy tales, she will instead see her own family members as coming late to the place where their places are already arranged. She does not fear a gap in the old world so much as the closing of that gap, and to recover from such thoughts she must invent a calculus of death that is in her favor.

Faulkner's Addie also concocts a new arithmetic: "I gave Anse Dewey Dell to negative Jewel. Then I gave him Vardaman to replace the child I had robbed him of. And now he has three children that are his and not mine. And then I could get ready to die" (176). Like Dickinson's speaker, Addie is concerned about her presence in two realms, but for her those two realms are society and her sense of herself as set apart from such society. She can only have the latter through theft. Whereas Dickinson's speaker advises, "Ample make this Bed—/ Make this Bed with Awe—/ In it wait till Judgment break / Excellent and Fair" (Fr 804), Addie is just as energetic, but she circumvents the marriage bed, lying with the Reverend Whitfield in the weeds. She throws off Cora Tull's prayers and judgments, noting that "people to whom sin is just a matter of words, to them salvation is just words too" (176). Addie cannot control how she was brought into the world, but her rigid stillness expresses her desire to control how she will leave it and where she will go. Her violence, like that of Jewel, is not destructive or impulsive but rather a means of exacting control over the world she has left behind that is echoed in the fierce way he reins in his horse.

Critics who have focused on Addie's maternal role in *As I Lay Dying* frequently express disappointment that Faulkner stops at a maternal rather than a defiantly sexual woman (Bergman) and follows tradition in associating women with death and illness (Blaine). If we read Addie not in the tradition of ill and dying women but in the elegiac tradition, her voice rings out unexpectedly and, precisely for that unexpectedness, more fully than it would if she were alive.[18] *As I Lay Dying* is not an elegy, but in placing a "spirited" corpse poem in Dickinson's line against the other characters' manipulative use of elegiac liberties, Faulkner offers the novel as the site of new elegiac formation. If elegy is to have a future in the modern era, it must take into account the ways in which the dead demand a continued narrative presence. It is a kind of ethics predicated on the existence of continued "character-space," even though the dead cannot—Dickinson's and Faulkner's characters excepted—make their wishes known.

Faulkner fends off condescending uses of the dead by endowing Addie with a powerful sense of agency that extends into death. She has used her life to prepare a chain of reactions that will occur long after she is gone, and it is that continued activity, of which she is the original cause, that sustains her existence as a subject. For Addie, salvation is an act of creation, not a fate to be anticipated. As the buzzards remind us, there is a purposefulness that lies behind stillness, and they prompt a new reading of the Dickinson poem to which they allude. The fly that attracts the attention of Dickinson's speaker is frequently regarded as the thief of the last moment of consciousness, a distraction from eyes and thoughts turned toward heaven, but it may instead be the outward sign that she has *already* died, one of many flies that are attracted to a corpse. The speaker's jarring recognition of this further missed moment, or misrecognition, brings the poem to its swift conclusion. Diana Fuss argues that Dickinson emphasized "the radical privacy of death" (18), but Addie Bundren's characterization of her husband as one of the dead and her own parents as significant though dead suggests another motive behind both authors' failure to describe the final moments before death: the line between the two states is simply beside the point. The social and ethical bonds between the dead and the living obscure the line between the two, and the flies and buzzards serve not to underscore death but rather as a reminder of the ongoing activity—biological and otherwise—of the dead.

Addie's monologue is a resistant form that irrupts from within Faulkner's parade of living mourners and thus offers readers an opportunity to reassess the elegy as it is challenged by the corpse poem. But the textual similarity between Addie's monologue and the others of *As I Lay Dying* works against a too-easy division between the two sets of voices. By making Addie's section appear in the same form as that of the other characters, Faulkner underscores the relationship between the two worlds, encouraging comparisons between narratives that run "side by side" like the dual inflection of Reverend Whitfield's voice as he gives Addie's eulogy: "Whitfield begins. His voice is bigger than him. It's like they are not the same. It's like he is one, and his voice is one, swimming on two horses side by side across the ford and coming into the house, the mud-splashed one and the one that never even got wet, triumphant and sad" (91). Whitfield speaks from his clerical office and as an individual, but Faulkner never lets the reader lose sight of the fact that Whitfield is also a character, one whose affair with Addie colors his role as mourner and minister. Neither Addie nor Whitfield has the final say on her character, as Faulkner shows not only the familiar modernist skepticism with regard to religious authority but also a new reluctance to accept the dead as an unquestioned authority in narrating their own public narrative. Addie's monologue continues the critique of authoritative voices rather than replace them.

In arguing that the corpse poem brings back the lost art of consolation, Diana Fuss makes a stinging—and accurate—critique of the cult of resistance in modern critical discourse: "Are inherited models for writing about sudden or enduring grief ipso facto unethical, and can modernist despair truly be said to be the only real ethical response? Does it not matter what is being resisted or refused and when, how, and why? By the same token, does it not matter what is being reclaimed or restored?" (108). Fuss argues that "it is the *effort* to restore or redress, the *desire* either to acknowledge those lost to us or to address those suffering like (or even instead of) us that powerfully articulates the ethical force at the heart of modern elegy" (109; italics in original). Her sketch of the modern elegy elegantly illustrates the ethical costs of dividing the judgment of elegy along Freudian lines—swallowing up the dead in elegy or losing them in an attempt to respect their alterity in melancholic antielegy—but her ethical picture is incomplete. Is it really only the elegist's own desires and efforts that matter? She emphasizes the ethics of effort and desire, indicating that we demonstrate respect for the dead and the living by continuing to extend the affect of engagement with the dead after they are gone. But the effect of one's efforts and desires is relevant in any ethical analysis; terrible things can be done from beatific motivations. In a traditional elegy, only the speaker's motivations can be judged, but in other forms, particularly the novel, the voices of multiple parties contribute to a larger ethical picture. When Anse speaks for Addie, and then she speaks for herself, the reader can begin to see the effects of elegiac desires, proclamations, and acts on others. Woolf and Faulkner fashion from elegy a more socially responsible tool in holding the speaker accountable for their words' effects on others.

Neither Woolf nor Faulkner adopts traditions, such as Christianity, that make claims about the continued existence of individuals after death, so the rights of the dead seem moot. But both authors are clearly concerned about how our treatment of the dead shapes the way that the rest of us live. What effect will our characterization or caricature of death and those who once lived have on the ethical world of the living? What, to use David Sherman's term, are our "mortal obligations"? It matters not only that we make an effort or that we desire the dead but also that we treat both elegist and elegiac subject as subjects or, in Faulkner's and Woolf's fiction, characters. The dead remain personas as full and rich and complicated as when they were alive. Any conventions or traditions that indicate radical transformation sever the link between living and dead in a way that makes our portrait of the world both narrow and incomplete.

Flashes of Distinction

Although not as supernaturally startling as Addie's postmortem voice, a similar surprise awaits the reader of *Jacob's Room* when Jacob—who to that point had been characterized in genteel terms—grumbles, "But this service in King's College Chapel—why allow women to take part in it?... No one would think of bringing a dog into church" (23–24). Such pettiness lends credence to Alex Zwerdling's reading of *Jacob's Room* as a satirical elegy[19] and Judy Little's interpretation of the novel as a parody of the bildungsroman.[20] As with Addie Bundren, Jacob's self-representation undermines his suitability for the lead role he is to play, and yet such moments allow Jacob to be a character and not a mythical figure like Percival.[21] Jacob's portrait, as sketched by admiring female characters, is of a promising young man who follows the familiar path of privilege and power. His being described repeatedly as "distinguished" reads as a bit of Woolfian satire, since it is precisely that he is indistinguishable from other young Cambridge men that makes Mrs. Norman, for example, so satisfied with her assessment of him.[22] Her portrait, early in *Jacob's Room,* is an exercise in making the figure fit the form. Jacob is initially threatening to her because he "seemed so out of place, somehow, alone with an elderly lady" (21), but he is soon swallowed up in the "young men all day long" that Mrs. Norman sees when the train stops in Cambridge (22). It is only on the train, as he moves between settings that might allow her to place him more readily, that Jacob could be truly distinguished, since once he is given a familiar environment, he becomes indistinguishable from that setting.

But Jacob's own words fight such portraits. Just as Addie methodically dismantles the collective portrait of her as an unstinting wife and mother, Jacob's comment about women in chapel should be jarring for more than its misogyny. When he compares the women to a dog, Jacob is protesting not only their manifestations of femininity, but also their insistence on individuality: "Surely, if the mind wanders ... it is because several hat shops and cupboards upon cupboards of colored dresses are displayed upon rush-bottomed chairs. Though heads and bodies may be devout enough, one has a sense of individuals—some like blue, others brown; some feathers, others pansies and forget-me-nots. ... Though separately devout, distinguished, and vouched for by the theology, mathematics, Latin, and Greek of their husbands" (33). The women's sartorial distinction is, in Jacob's eyes, a mark of their unsuitability in an environment that is marked by the uniformity of academic gowns. Such distinction of dress is opposed to the kind of "distinction" to which he refers at the end of the passage, when he acknowledges the women's respectability. This latter kind of distinction is one that Jacob shares with the Cambridge wives; it is what enables him to carry off his shabby attire and awkwardness in other settings, the good breeding that obscures individual quirks. Jacob speaks to the reality of those who have not only embraced the pressure to conform but will also work to uphold such conformity.

The dynamics of the chapel scene are replayed late in the novel when Jacob, on a visit to Greece, again displays the kind of inattention that the unsympathetic narrator is quick to point out in the chapel scene, when "Jacob looked extraordinarily vacant, his head thrown back, his hymn-book open at the wrong place" (23). In Greece, Jacob's distraction is heightened by "all the French ladies opening and shutting their umbrellas just beneath him," and then, when he tries again to focus, by another woman with a camera (121). Thinking of his romantic entanglements as much as any woman present, he vents his frustration with "Damn these women—damn these women! ... How they spoil things" (121).

Through the reverberation of the word "distinction" throughout *Jacob's Room*, Woolf captures a particularly dangerous form of social hypocrisy: although English culture may rely on particular class and educational institutions to produce young men who are intended for "distinguished" careers, it does so only while encouraging the compliant rather than the individual aspects of those young men. It should not be surprising if, like Jacob, those young men firmly embrace the conformity in which they were nurtured and disparage new arrivals—such as women in university settings, or modern literature—that might threaten such conformity.

Just before Jacob makes his surprising comparison of women and dogs in chapel, Woolf's narrator offers two images of order whose contrast is itself something of an elegy for the possibilities that Jacob loses when throwing in his lot with conformity. The first image is that of worshippers filing into chapel: "What sculptured faces, what certainty, authority controlled by piety, although great boots march under the gowns. In what orderly procession they advance.... Inside the Chapel all was orderly" (23). The chapel is compared to the sides of a lantern, which "protect the flame so that it burns steady even in the wildest night" (23). The second system operates outside that protective lantern, in the wild night itself, a prefiguration of the order that makes Jinny so mesmerizing in *The Waves:* "If you stand a lantern under a tree every insect in the forest creeps up to it—a curious assembly, since though they scramble and swing and knock their heads against the glass, they seem to have no purpose—something senseless inspires them" (23). Although the forest scene echoes an earlier one in which Jacob sees such things while catching butterflies, his comments on the women in chapel suggest that his loyalty has shifted toward the order of the regiment. Whereas it was precisely the spots of color that he looked for in lepidopterology, as he hunted the elusive flash of the red underwing or spied the "pale clouded yellows," "blues," and "painted ladies and peacocks," in the later scene the women's distinctive colors are deemed reason for scorn (16–17).

Jacob's dismissal of the women in chapel reveals a greater institutional exclusion of women that Woolf challenges in the novel's early drafts. Jacob confidently asserts that the women in chapel are the wives of Cambridge men, but he may be mistaken. Although Woolf's narrator laments that the chapel "has shut out a great deal" (Bishop 27), it may not any longer shut out female students. A decade after Woolf's novel was published, the teaching faculty of the women's colleges of Cambridge, Girton and Newnham, were still frequently taken for faculty wives at university functions, but the female student body was growing (Tullberg 178). Woolf's manuscript for *Jacob's Room* outlines an alternative to Jacob's interpretation through a parallel story, that of Angela, a female Cambridge undergraduate. Although Cambridge was slower than Oxford to grant degrees to women, Girton College opened to female students in 1869, and the women of Girton and Newnham Colleges were attending lectures at the men's colleges within a few years. Angela's story offers an intriguing contrast with Jacob's, one that echoes the dynamic of Rhoda and Percival in *The Waves.* In both novels, the elegy of the promising young man is shadowed by the story of a promising young woman. By including references both to Angela's story and to the attitudes of those who seek to foreclose such educational opportunities for women, Woolf begins to indicate how the elegiac novel is to play a role in urging social change. For both Faulkner and Woolf, the elegy is charged with political and cultural responsibility, a theme that becomes most apparent in *Mrs. Dalloway* and *Go Down, Moses,* but that first flares in *Jacob's Room.*

Although Woolf eventually removes Angela's Cambridge experience from *Jacob's Room*, she publishes the sketch in *Atalanta's Garland* in 1926 as "A Woman's College from Outside."[23] The opening language of Angela's story invites intertextual comparisons; both Jacob's room at Trinity College and hers at Newnham are introduced with "The feathery white moon never let the sky grow dark" (Bishop 50; *CSF* 145; *JR* 28). After thus signaling the comparison, the remaining elements of Woolf's story highlight the contrast between the two university students. Although Jacob's room is empty, Angela stands in hers like a beacon: "A double light one might figure in Angela's room, seeing how bright Angela herself was, and how bright came back the reflection of herself from the square glass" (*CSF* 145). Unlike Jacob's shadowy form, which is always slipping between darkness and light, distinction and anonymity, "the whole of her was perfectly delineated—perhaps the soul" (145).

Although Woolf initially describes Angela as if the latter is returning from a ball, her subsequent elaboration not only dispels such assumptions but explains a great deal about what causes Jacob to remain undefined when Angela is so "perfectly delineated": "Angela Williams was at Newnham for the purpose of earning her living, and could not forget even in moments of impassioned adoration the cheques of her father at Swansea; her mother washing in the scullery: pink frocks out to dry on the line; tokens that even the lily no longer floats flawless upon the pool, but has a name on a card like another" (145). Like the majority of women students of the era, Angela is from the middle classes and attends out of economic necessity. Her sex and situation make her Cambridge experience very unlike that of Jacob and capture postsecondary education at a watershed moment in which the lives of women and men run parallel to one another. Parallel, of course, because, as Woolf makes clear, the women are sequestered from the male students: the narrator notes Newnham's resemblance "to a dairy or nunnery, a place of seclusion or discipline" (146).

The reminder that "none but women's faces could meet [the moon's] face" in the garden of Newnham (145), as well as the late hour in which the story takes place, suggests that Angela's Cambridge takes place on the edge of the university man's experience and the waking hours. Krystyna Colburn claims that Angela's cry at the end of the story, as she watches the sunrise over the college garden, comes forth because "the women's world is giving way to the everyday; life is returning to 'normal,' and that is to be mourned"

(78). The first Newnham students had no garden, and they could only envy the freedom of little boys playing in the open common outside their windows (Tullberg 45). The carefully circumscribed conditions of the women's presence at Cambridge are the result of their precarious status there. When the proposal to grant degrees to women at Cambridge was roundly defeated in 1897, "the result of this defeat was that for the next twenty years their college life and behaviour continued to be minutely ordered" (Tullberg 118).

For the women of Cambridge, their political and educational disenfranchisement requires that they attempt to minimize the distinctive dress of their gender so that Cambridge can remain a visibly male institution. Henry Sidgwick, one of the heads of Newnham, lamented the fact that three of the first five Newnham students were both attractive and fashionable, since "their unfortunate appearance" would make it difficult for them to go about their education without drawing attention to themselves (qtd. in Tullberg 58). Though a French tutor once complained that he could hardly be expected to teach with such bedecked female students before him (121), anticipating Woolf's character's remarks, the majority of the women of Newnham and Girton contributed to the perception of university women as "drab" (212). At the turn of the century, color or ornament might be a sign of newfound courage in claiming "distinction" in an environment in which women had been too long a neglected faction.

Not all male undergraduates scoffed at such efforts. Frank Raphael Waley arrived at King's College, Cambridge, in 1912, and spent much of his time sketching the fashions of his female classmates before he joined the war. He was certainly aware of the stereotype of drab women students, as evidenced by his unflattering sketch of "a typical Girtonite." And yet, although he lived in the same space in which Woolf's fictional character groused about a chapel filling up with "hat shops" and "cupboards of colored dresses," Waley's portraits suggest delight at the state of affairs. He devotes an entire page to "Newnham Fashion for 1913," a collection of more than two dozen women's hats. A scribbled poem in his sketchbook also attests to the women students' effect in smartening up their male classmates' attire as the male students seek to impress. But Waley does not seem to forget the women's real purpose in being there. His sketches are dotted with records of the women's names, with their colleges in parentheses, and his more elaborate classroom scenes show row upon row of women with pen in hand and phrases from history lectures on their pages. They are not wives

Sketches by Raphael Waley, 1912–13: *upper left,* "A Typical Girtonite"; *upper right,* "Newnham Fashion for 1913"; *bottom,* "Divinity Lecture Room." (Images courtesy of King's College, Cambridge, with permission from Joyce Morton)

of students but students themselves. Waley does, however, match Jacob in exuberant exaggeration; both Jacob's imagined and Waley's real classes at King's College would have been predominantly male, and yet both envision a powerful female presence. Whether the sentiment that accompanies those images is complaint or pleasure, both men offer a vision of the future of Cambridge.

Angela's presence, both in the early drafts of *Jacob's Room* and in the published short story, is a reminder of the narrowness of the world Jacob inhabits. When Woolf imagines an ideal university for women, she instructs, "It must be built not of carved stone and stained glass, but of some cheap, easily combustible material which does not hoard dust and perpetuate traditions. Do not have chapels" (*TG* 143). As with the chapel that appears in *Jacob's Room,* on which her narrator dwells at length, Woolf links the architecture of the ideal university to the views that might be generated within it. It is no accident that her character Angela is part of Newnham College, Cambridge's first secular institution, which has no chapel. When Jacob complains about the women's presence in what he assumes to be an exclusive environment, he confirms a suspicion that Woolf voices only much later, in the lectures she delivered at Newnham and Girton Colleges in 1928: "I thought how unpleasant it is to be locked out; and I thought how it is worse perhaps to be locked in" (*A Room of One's Own* 24). Although Woolf's readers may blame the institution for excluding the world, Jacob Flanders makes clear that some enclosures happen as much in the mind as in the institution itself.[24]

Woolf removes Angela's story from *Jacob's Room* to keep pressure on Jacob, but her choice also reflects her awareness that Angela's story points beyond prewar sensibilities to the fallout of the war. The 1920 bid for women to be granted degrees at Cambridge resulted in a crushing defeat that brought to the public eye the great hostility toward women at the country's two most prestigious educational institutions. Although women were granted degrees at University College London by 1880 and the war casualties created an even greater need for women to look beyond husbands to support them, the lives of women at Cambridge became only more difficult during and after the war, since they were seen to be taking the place of men, particularly servicemen, both in schools and in the workforce (Tullberg 168). It is precisely because Angela may be Jacob's replacement in the postwar world that Woolf extracts Angela's story from the novel; she is well aware of the animosity exposed by the 1920 Cambridge vote. Woolf's readership is not ready to consider a world in which a young man is replaced by a female student who will do more than he to distinguish herself with the education she receives.

Jacob is, as Judy Little characterizes him, conventional "except for the war" (118). This exception is an intriguing one, since in one sense the war is precisely what makes Jacob conventional, as his lost future is enveloped by the larger story of the war dead. Kelly Walsh reads Jacob's war death as swallowing up his particularity, though elsewhere she notes that the novel's "poignancy derives from the singularity of its synechdochical figure" (8–9). The vacillation in the critical literature between Jacob's singularity and his conventionality is already contained within the word that Woolf uses throughout the novel to characterize him: "distinguished," both set apart from his peers and manifesting a bearing that situates him within a particular class of men.

It is a critical commonplace that *Jacob's Room* is "an excursion into... the making of a set of beliefs and world views which could plausibly have led to war" (Bucknell 761). What is most striking about the novel, however, is how Woolf uses the central character's own words to make such a critique. Jacob's protest against signs of individuality may raise an eyebrow in a novel in which the description of war casualties as an undistinguished mass has such a chilling effect. Jacob eventually becomes a soldier, one of the "dozen young men in the prime of life" or part of the "blocks of tin soldiers" that fall flat on the battlefield; the only individuation comes when most have been wiped out and "one or two pieces still agitate up and down like fragments of broken match-stick" (125).[25] The novel's elegiac echoes are particularly poignant at such moments, since the elegy can only remind the reader of the difficulty—perhaps even impossibility—of mourning a particular individual in the context of such mass death. Thus when Jacob judges that a woman in chapel, like a dog, "makes the blood run cold in horror," that, though "separately devout," the women ruin a communal service, Woolf draws a clear connection between the voice of complacent conformity and the war to come (23).

In such moments of self-revelation Jacob's novel takes on some of the horror of Faulkner's more overtly macabre *As I Lay Dying*.[26] Addie's chapter is sensational in that she speaks from the coffin even as her corpse remains insistently present throughout, and in that she speaks with such fierceness against the other characters and their stories. The horror of *Jacob's Room* comes from Jacob's using his irruption into the text to register his discontent with those who do not conform. Tammy Clewell argues that in making Jacob a shadowy figure from the beginning of the novel, rather than only once he has died in the war, Woolf "refuses to allow even the novel that commemorates her protagonist's life to compensate for his death" (*Mourning, Modernism* 28). And yet it is not his absence but rather his presence—including a peevish voice—that aids Woolf in resisting elegiac substitution.

    What Jacob chooses instead of the flashing colors of the forest insects is disturbing. Changes from the manuscript version show that Woolf highlighted the martial tone of the chapel procession as she revised, underscoring the ominousness of the "great boots [that] march under the gowns" as they "advance" (23).[27] Not only will Jacob not live up to the "distinguished" future that is expected of him, he participates in a kind of seeing that, Woolf indicates, makes it easier to imagine how culture has changed such that war casualties can be compared to matchsticks. He is part of the war not only as a victim but also as one who cultivates the conformist environment that led to it. Woolf's attempts to implicate English patriarchal culture in the Great War are, of course, well known. What is striking here is her unwillingness to spare even the war victim his place in the line of culpability.[28]

    Through Jacob's voice, Woolf reshapes perhaps the most fraught poetic ground of the First World War. Jay Winter chronicles the "resurrection of the dead in poetry" produced during the war, both those who imagined the dead rising up to fight once more and also those who insisted that fallen soldiers be left to rest rather than be called in to mouth propaganda (205). The poetic use of the dead was widespread: "In Britain, France, and Germany, many writers used verse to keep the voices of the fallen alive" (204). Not only does Woolf's soldier not get an opportunity to urge his fellow soldiers to victory after his death, but he does not, as in other war poetry, have an opportunity to express guilt at his own "complicity in the monstrous crimes of war" (213). That latter sentiment, Woolf knows, too neatly wraps up the war experience, via confession and communion. Instead, nearly every word Jacob expresses unwittingly charts his culture's and his own complicity in cultivating an environment that forecloses others' viewpoints and prizes order above all else. The most damning aspect of that portrait, Woolf knows, is that Jacob articulates these values unreflectively. There is no recognition of wrongdoing, and there is no repentance.

In *As I Lay Dying*, Addie's son Darl also joins the war, but unlike Jacob, Darl survives it. Like Septimus Smith of Woolf's *Mrs. Dalloway*, Darl's postwar future is monstrously shaped by wartime. His war experience colors his reading of his mother's death and offers a new way into understanding how the larger cultural losses shape the contours of mourning after the war:

> In a strange room you must empty yourself for sleep. And before you are emptied for sleep, what are you. And when you are emptied for sleep, you are not. And when you are filled with sleep, you never were. I dont know what I am. I dont know if I am or not. Jewel knows he is, because he does not know that he does not know whether he is or not. He cannot empty himself for sleep because he is not what he is and he is what he is not. Beyond the unlamped wall I can hear the rain shaping the wagon that is ours, the load that is no longer theirs that felled and sawed it nor yet theirs that bought it and which is not ours either, lie on our wagon though it does, since only the wind and the rain shaped it only to Jewel and me, that are not asleep. And since sleep is is-not and rain and wind are was, it is not. Yet the wagon is, because when the wagon is was, Addie Bundren will not be. And Jewel is, so Addie Bundren must be. And then I must be, or I could not empty myself for sleep in a strange room. And so if I am not emptied yet, I am *is*. How often have I lain beneath rain on a strange roof, thinking of home. (80–81)

David Sherman highlights Darl's conundrums as a way of considering how modernist thought opens up new relations between living and dead: "Darl's impossible access to the death of his mother is a violation of the novel's narrative economy, a warping of narrative logic under the irrational pressure of an ethical obligation to the dead that cannot be translated into economic terms" (137). And yet where Sherman sees Darl's character unravel under these ethical and economic pressures, the phrases that frame Darl's narrative provide greater insight into the context of his innovative criticism of mourning and identity. The "strange room" creates the impetus for the emptying of the self, a setting that is recalled in the final line's "strange roof" as he lies "thinking of home" (81). Just as Addie weaves her father's words throughout her narrative, making him into a dialogic opponent, so too Darl's framing phrases indicate how the war has become that against which everything about his known life must be opposed, reconsidered, and reinvented.

Unlike Dickinson's speaker and Addie, Darl is estranged from the place in which he lies. Unsettled by the resemblance of death and sleep from the outside, he probes whether death and sleep resemble each other too, when viewed from within. In a novel replete with violently willful stillness, sleep is proffered as a kind of erasure that may be even greater than death. Darl's mock syllogisms, spiraling out of tight logical control, register Addie's continued existence because stories of identity are so often crafted through relationship with the dead. She remains a link needed for his own identity when Darl's own confidence falters; Jewel cannot discard "himself" because he carries around a false understanding of himself. Addie crows at such a feat, giving her favorite son an identity he cannot disown because he does not know it. Darl, however, is driven by the fear that he now lacks outside confirmation of his identity, and the war—which engenders the necessity of emptying oneself for sleep when in a strange room—has made maintaining his identity and his memories intolerable.

If Woolf and Faulkner, in their initial challenge to elegy, emphasize the competitive character of elegists, and then fight for recognition of—but not submission to—the character of the elegiac subject in their second phase, they have yet achieved much more. They first establish a system of elegists and subjects that foregrounds the complex, ongoing relations among them and then open the boundaries of their fiction to illustrate how characters register the weight of other texts. It is not merely that Woolf and Faulkner become allusive in the second stage. In crafting an angry Addie who seeks a reprieve in the domestic forms of Dickinson's speakers and an Angela whose narrative haunts Jacob, they reflect their elegy's larger call to develop unknown voices. And they encourage conversations about Addie that make possible the reading of Woolf's Jacob Flanders offered here, as they foreground the intertextual study of modern elegy. Addie is emboldened by Dickinson's example, and the origin of Angela's erasure is explained by Jacob's brusque dismissiveness even as Woolf embraces the vibrancy of her narrative possibilities. In the third stage, Woolf and Faulkner ensure that the elegiac voices that are often elided, both elegists and subjects, are given their due. And they open wide the character-system so as to acknowledge the specific intrusions of historical context on elegiac character.

4

"A Host of Others" in *Mrs. Dalloway*

> [The modern novelist] will have extended the scope of his interest so as to dramatise . . . the emotions bred in us by crowds, the obscure terrors and hatreds which come so irrationally in certain places or from certain people. . . . Every moment is the centre and meeting place of an extraordinary number of perceptions which have not yet been expressed.
> —Woolf, "The Narrow Bridge of Art"

The complications Woolf and Faulkner bring to the elegy, as they multiply elegiac voices and imagine dialogues between the dead and those who speak for them, may seem merely formal exercises, but in fact they nudge the elegy closer to real, lived mourning. The traditional poem of mourning accomplishes a respectful hush around the dead and bereaved, but Faulkner's and Woolf's elegiac transformations enable them to demand of the form, "Which occasion for grief? Which loss?" Although poetic elegy tells the story of a single loss sending reverberations through a mourner's life, in reality, individuals are left to play a variety of elegiac roles in a network of mourning that crosses class, culture, and country. The First World War may have brought loss to the foreground in the public consciousness, but accounting for the grief in evidence will require a mode of mourning that connects individuals to the losses that crisscross their lives before and after the war. The traditional elegist will fall short of the customary devotion to a single loss when faced with so many losses. Such mourning is selective—and isolating. But the mourning of many affords the modern elegist a new connection to others who are also experiencing loss. Both Faulkner and Woolf expand the scope of elegiac relations to acknowledge the intricacy of those relations in the modern era. Woolf's *Mrs. Dalloway* is an invitation to make mourning not the responsibility of a single elegist, who will crumble under the weight, but rather a shared social endeavor.

Whereas the titles of *As I Lay Dying* and *Jacob's Room* point to their nearly silent subjects, *Mrs. Dalloway*'s title gives no indication of the Septimus Smith who crowds Clarissa Dalloway to the edges of "her" novel. Like Percival in *The Waves*, Septimus Smith appears only belatedly in *Mrs. Dalloway*. But whereas Bernard uses Percival to unite the six speakers' narratives, Septimus is a divisive force, calling into question the novel form's focus on a single central figure.[1] A parallel structure occurs in Faulkner's more loosely organized *Go Down, Moses*, in which Lucas Beauchamp dominates the early stories but then yields to the character Rider, whose intense violence cuts a wide swath through the middle of the novel. In both of these novels, two figures share the central position. Although in each novel only one of the two main characters dies, all four exert themselves to speak to the deaths of others, and all four are haunted by the specter of their own deaths.

By the time one returns to Clarissa Dalloway at the end of *Mrs. Dalloway*, the reader can no longer see her as a traditional protagonist who carries the weight of the novel, a point underscored by Woolf's repeated references to the strain of such a position. In Clarissa, Woolf creates a new narrative position, a hostess who draws together different characters to make the party—and the novel—work. Through Septimus and Clarissa, Woolf repudiates the Freudian narrative of mourning as a brief interlude before one's identity is fully reestablished after loss. Her portrait of mourning more closely resembles that of Derrida, who argues that the mourner may not want to reclaim his or her ego from the dead but rather may in fact "welcome" the decentering that comes from inviting the lost one into oneself (188). It is precisely in the "welcome" of shared narrative space that Woolf poses her most radical challenge to both elegiac and novel form. As Faulkner and Woolf rewrite the modern elegy, they insist that both the elegy and the novel expand in "scope," as Woolf articulates in "The Narrow

Bridge of Art," to include the demands of crowds and the wide range of occasions for the grief they carry.

Septimus the Poet, Septimus the Soldier

Woolf's character Septimus has garnered critical attention as a victim of shell shock,[2] but *Mrs. Dalloway* pulls in another direction, twice describing him as an aspiring poet (84, 184). If Woolf had structured her novel like Faulkner's *As I Lay Dying,* Septimus's artistic predilections rather than his soldiering would take center stage. Faulkner presents his character Darl as a sage for much of *As I Lay Dying,* repeatedly confirming Darl's premonitions and letting his analysis of the other characters stand unchallenged.[3] Only in the final pages, once the reader has known the character through his own voice, does Faulkner make Darl's war experience explicit. Through his careful structuring, Faulkner acknowledges how easily the war overshadows the individual, even as the author fights the marginalization of the individual's voice. In Woolf's novel, however, Septimus's war experience marks him throughout his interactions with others, and only near the end does Clarissa wonder, "There were the poets and thinkers. Suppose he had had that passion" (184–85). Woolf suggests that a stranger may better intuit Septimus's character than his own wife or doctors, since they continue to regard him as if he were in uniform. However differently they make room for the war in their narratives, neither Faulkner nor Woolf is willing to subsume the fullness of the character under the historical event.

Like Christine Froula, whose reading of *Mrs. Dalloway* as a postwar elegy is now a classic in Woolf studies, I find there is much to be gained by reading Septimus as more than a victim of war trauma. Whereas Froula posits Septimus as a "prophet" of England's postwar struggles (*Virginia Woolf* 110), I read Septimus as an elegist. David Bradshaw argues that "by deploying . . . the ancient topos of falling or fallen leaves, an age-old simile for the numberless dead (see, for example, Isaiah 34:4), Woolf plainly encourages the reader to conceive of her book as an elegy" (107).[4] But in making only the *book* elegiac, critics fail to notice that Woolf also stages an elegy within the fiction so as to illustrate the challenges faced by the modern elegist, whose traditional conception of an elegist's devotion to the dead will break him when he is faced with a flood of war casualties.

As she writes "The Hours," the manuscript that becomes *Mrs. Dalloway*, Woolf wonders, "S's character. founded on R[upert Brooke?]? . . . or founded on me? . . . might be left vague—as a mad person is . . . so can be partly R.; partly me" (qtd. in Froula, *Virginia Woolf* 118). Critics have leaped at the opportunity to read Woolf's own fight with mental illness in the character of Septimus Smith, but the relation to Rupert Brooke has been sidelined. In Brooke, however, Woolf identifies a figure who, beyond being widely elegized after his death in the war, maintained multiple public identities. The day of Brooke's death, which is both St. George's Day and Shakespeare's death date, "sealed his claim to chivalric action, and . . . to poetry" (Parker 218). In his double role of soldier and poet, Brooke seems to offer the clearest exemplar for Woolf's character Septimus. One has to wonder whether Septimus's name is a reference to Brooke's cause of death, as reported in the *Times* on 26 April 1915: "septicaemia" (Levenback, *Great War* 15).[5] But in considering both herself and Rupert Brooke as a model for Septimus, Woolf was not choosing between madness and poetry or civilian and soldier but rather between one writer and another, both of whom struggled with mental illness. In a letter to Woolf during her breakdown in 1912, Brooke wrote to her with particular sympathy: "'Hypersensitive and Introspective,' the good doctor Craig said I was," acknowledging that he, like Woolf, was susceptible to nervous breakdowns (Brooke 364). By situating Septimus somewhere between herself and Brooke, Woolf draws on not simply their shared mental anguish but also the tendency of the medical community to treat hypersensitivity and introspection as problems to be solved. Doing so ignores what both writers suspect is the flip side of such tendencies: their contributions to poetic facility. Or, as Brooke puts it, "I feel drawn to you, in this robust hard world. What tormented and crucified figures we literary people are!" (364).

Clarissa Dalloway may imagine Septimus as a poet, but she also immediately thinks of the medical establishment that would deem him a madman. Madness waits to discredit the voices of both Faulkner's and Woolf's characters. When Faulkner was asked about his character Darl's clairvoyance, he replied: "Who can say how much of the good poetry in the world has come out of madness, and who can say just how much of the super-perceptivity the—a mad person might not have? It may not be so, but it's nice to think that there is some compensation for madness. That maybe the madman sees more than the sane man. That the world is more moving to him. That he is more perceptive. He has something of clairvoyance, maybe, a capacity for telepathy" (*FU* 113). Woolf's *Mrs. Dalloway,* written five years before Faulkner's novel, reflects a less wistful philosophy. She keeps Septimus's ability to see in question throughout the narrative, challenging her reader to follow Septimus's lead without proof of his insight. By balancing soldier and poet, sanity and insanity, Woolf prevents readers from diagnosing and dismissing Septimus, as the doctors Holmes and Bradshaw do within the novel.

When Sigmund Freud ruminates on the First World War losses in "Thoughts for the Times on War and Death," he initially dismisses the combatant as "a cog in the gigantic machine of war" (275), implying that the soldier does not share the noncombatant's unease at the ideological changes afoot. In his second essay, Freud reconsiders, acknowledging that it would be interesting to look into the psychology of the combatant, "but I know too little about it. We must restrict ourselves to the second group, to which we belong" (291–92). In *Mrs. Dalloway,* Woolf does not restrict herself to the second group, instead incorporating the combatant's viewpoint into her novel and resisting the separation of combatants and noncombatants in the war's aftermath. Woolf's novel points not only to the effect of the war on Septimus and his fellow Britons but also to the impulses that led him to such an experience: "He went to France to save an England which consisted almost entirely of Shakespeare's plays and Miss Isabel Pole in a green dress walking in a square" (86). Septimus was, like Rupert Brooke, "one of the first to volunteer" (86). Woolf wrote of Brooke, "No one could have doubted that as soon as war broke out he would go without hesitation to enlist" (*E* 2:281). By linking the war and the poetic impulse, Woolf acknowledges art's political significance even as she holds poetry responsible for its part in the devastation of the war.

Woolf creates two elegiac strains in *Mrs. Dalloway,* with Clarissa's drawn from Shakespeare and Shelley and Septimus's from classical literature.[6] Although Greece ties Septimus to Rupert Brooke, whom D. H. Lawrence called a "Greek god" and Winston Churchill characterized as of "classical symmetry of mind and body" (Levenback, "Rupert Brooke" 5), Woolf uses classical allusion to distinguish postwar England from classical Greece. Repeatedly in her otherwise restrained review of *The Collected Poems of Rupert Brooke: With a Memoir,* Woolf resists the Rupert Brooke of legend, aligned with classical Greece, and instead figures him as a writer poised to confront the present: "You felt that to him literature was not dead nor of the past, but a thing now in process of construction by people many of whom were his friends" (*E* 2:280); "he showed his power of being in sympathy with the present" (2:281). Woolf's sketch of Brooke succeeds in breaking from an elegiac portrait that ties Brooke to his past and literature's past. She credits him with considerable sensitivity to culture's hand in shaping literature's future.

Through Septimus Smith, Woolf is able to write less guardedly about the minefield of the hero's home reception. Longing to escape the postwar life, Septimus contests the claim that he "served with great distinction in the War," thinking instead, "Had he served with distinction? He really forgot. In the War itself he had failed" (96). Unlike the protagonist of *Jacob's Room*, Septimus endures the clash between poetic sensitivity and the brute nature of the London to which he has returned. London is no longer full of Shakespeare and Miss Isabel Pole; instead, the postwar city bears the marks of a Greek tragedy. In her essay "On Not Knowing Greek," published in the same year as *Mrs. Dalloway*, Woolf argues that in Greek literature, "we meet them before their emotions have been worn into uniformity" (28):

> In the vast catastrophe of the European war our emotions had to be broken up for us, and put at an angle from us, before we could allow ourselves to feel them in poetry or fiction. The only poets who spoke to the purpose spoke in the sidelong, satiric manner of Wilfred Owen and Siegfried Sassoon. It was not possible for them to be direct without being clumsy; or to speak simply of emotion without being sentimental. But the Greeks could . . . march straight up, with their eyes open; and thus fearlessly approached, emotions stand still and suffer themselves to be looked at. (34)

Interested in neither the melancholic, satirical elegies of the war poets nor what she would characterize as the stiflingly ritualistic mourning of her Victorian childhood, Woolf instead turns to the Greeks' direct approach to tragedy. As Anne Fernald observes, "What Penelope, Antigone, Electra, and Clytemnestra all show is the power of inconsolability, the fidelity and courage of a mourning that never ends" ("Mourning in Greek"). Notably, Woolf's interest in the classical world shows her seeking a kind of mourning that is neither maudlin nor melancholic in the Freudian sense.

It is not, then, solely madness that makes Septimus hear birds sing in Greek in Regent's Park, but rather a realignment of his aesthetic sympathies (24). Before the war he had read of Shakespeare and the Romantics, but he is now the inheritor of an older tradition. In her novels, Woolf draws from the conventions of epic and tragedy (Fowler 218) so as to emphasize, as she wrote in an early diary entry, that "any live mind today is of the very same stuff as Plato's & Euripides. It is only a continuation & development of the same thing. It is this common mind that binds the whole world together; & all the world is mind" (*Passionate Apprentice* 172–73). And yet Rupert Brooke's legacy serves as a warning: classical allusions may well bring her close to the "sentimental" writing of which she had such a lifelong abhorrence. Thus the sharp irony when the narrator of *Mrs. Dalloway* observes, "So prying and insidious were the fingers of the European War [that it] smashed a plaster cast of Ceres, ploughed a hole in the geranium beds, and utterly ruined the cook's nerves" (86). She incorporates classical conventions so as to break through the deadening effect of the war. Ironically, she draws on the dead in order to reawaken postwar England, so that "England & Greece stood side by side, each much *enlivened* by the other" (*D* 4:100; emphasis mine).

Woolf's classical world is, therefore, quite different from Milton's pastoral elegy and its legacy in the English elegiac tradition. Septimus hears "a shepherd boy's piping" (68), but the pastoral allusion quickly gives way to reality: "(That's an old man playing a penny whistle by the public-house, he muttered) which, as the boy stood still came bubbling from his pipe, and then, as he climbed higher, made its exquisite plaint while the traffic passed beneath. This boy's elegy is played among the traffic, thought Septimus. . . . The music stopped. He has his penny, he reasoned it out, and has gone on to the next public-house" (68). Although threads of poetry appear, they are quickly perverted, the young shepherd replaced by an old beggar, reflecting the realities of Septimus's situation and creating a trajectory of decrepitude in place of the flowering of civilization. The strains of elegy here are not akin to poetry that "bids us take refuge in the past" (*E* 4:434) but are, rather, brought wrenchingly into confrontation with the realities of the present.

Standing in Regent's Park, Septimus mistakes the character Peter Walsh for Septimus's dead friend and fellow soldier Evans. Woolf's reader knows Peter only as Clarissa Dalloway's former suitor, but here he serves as a stand-in for a dead soldier who is, in Septimus's eyes, just as present and in need of our attention as is Peter. When Septimus's wife, Lucrezia, notes that "it is time" to leave the park (69),

> the word "time" split its husk; poured its riches over him; and from his lips fell like shells, like shavings from a plane, without his making them, hard, white, imperishable words, and flew to attach themselves to their places in an ode to Time; an immortal ode to Time. He sang. Evans answered from behind the tree. The dead were in Thessaly, Evans sang, among the orchids. There they waited till the War was over, and now the dead, now Evans himself—
>
> "For God's sake don't come!" Septimus cried out. For he could not look upon the dead.
>
> But the branches parted. A man in grey was actually walking towards them. It was Evans! But no mud was on him; no wounds; he was not changed. I must tell the whole world, Septimus cried. (69–70)

However immortal the ode, Septimus finds himself ill-prepared to answer the returned soldier. With Evans's appearance, the division between the living and the dead, the elegist and the elegiac subject, is no longer clear. Like the Greek-singing birds that suggest to Septimus that there is life "beyond the river where the dead walk" (25), Evans appears from the shrubbery. He is evidence of the renewed life of the dead, despite Septimus's persistent description of him as a "dead man" (70).

Evans has come closer to life even as Septimus himself edges toward death. Before the former's death, the two men "had to be together, share with each other, fight with each other, quarrel with each other" (86). With Evans's death comes a death of feeling in Septimus: "[He] congratulated himself upon feeling very little and very reasonably. The War had taught him" (86). The lack of feeling continues after the war, marking a death of a different kind than Evans's, but one that puts Septimus "behind a pane of glass" before he breaches it by throwing himself out a window (87). Septimus is like Faulkner's character Donald Mahon in *Soldiers' Pay*, published the year after *Mrs. Dalloway*. Mahon is initially mistaken for a British officer (17–18), and though he suffers from no physical ailment, he is encased in an unreachable "apathy" and "detachment" from the people and things that surround him that lead him to an early death (92). Both Mahon and Septimus are caught between physical health and mental devastation.

Septimus's withdrawal from everyday life leads Lucrezia to describe him as "Septimus, who wasn't Septimus any longer . . . a dead man" (65). If "it was cowardly for a man to say he would kill himself" and yet "Septimus had fought; he was brave," then Lucrezia concludes that "he was not Septimus now" (23). In her mind, as well as Septimus's own, the Septimus who had fought in the war was dead. Severing war efforts from postwar life may help to set soldiers and the war beyond critique, but it comes at the cost of a unified identity for veterans and creates a yawning gap between veterans and civilians. Karen Levenback notes rightly that Woolf "knew that misrepresenting the lived experience of the war on the front widened the chasm between civilians and combatants" (*Great War* 25).[7]

In a war where the only body to return to England was that of the Unknown Soldier (Trumpener 1097), Evans's return home, even if only in Septimus's mistaken identification, is remarkable. No less fantastic than the narration by a dead Addie Bundren in *As I Lay Dying*, Evans's presence in postwar London shows the impossibility of, as the doctors have recommended, Septimus's living in the present. He struggles not only between past and present but also between literature and reality. If, as Jay Winter argues, "many writers used verse to keep the voices of the fallen alive" (204), Septimus shows readers the terror of such a possibility, of the dead being revivified through poetry for a symbolic return home from the battlefield (210). Fictional accounts of the unrelenting patriotism of the dead contribute to a terrifying present for Septimus and other veterans like him. Although it is no secret that Woolf's novel contests the professions of patriotism that indicate Britain is unwilling to wrestle with the complex war that Septimus has witnessed, a different historical disagreement is at play here. Septimus is fighting not only his own memories of the war but also the ghostly creations of those who speak for the war, as the Shakespeare for whom he went to war is transformed into patriotic specters created by war poets. In his terror, Septimus critiques the literary world for its willingness to prioritize the idealized voices of the dead over the complex reality expressed by the living. If elegiac speakers jockey for position in the character-system of *The Waves*, Woloch's formulation once again proves fruitful for indicating that a return of the voice of the living is likely to cost others who remain in that world.

The figures of the past reappear in what Septimus reads as a request that he, the "giant mourner" (70), speak for their loss. But, as the close pairing of Evans and Septimus makes clear, the modern elegist is not far removed from the dead. The elegist and elegiac subject are bound together in a way that contemporary London does not seem to recognize. Dr. Bradshaw counsels Septimus to focus on the "brilliant career" before him, but for Septimus there is only the "crime" of the past (98). The desire to label Septimus as either damaged or a hero renders him without a place in postwar London and undermines the elegiac role that might otherwise provide him with a place and purpose that extends well beyond those who have seen battle.

Septimus is, throughout, the character who has "that look of apprehension ... which makes complete strangers apprehensive too" (14), but because strangers do not like to admit to such feelings in public, he bears the burden of his apprehension almost entirely alone. Like the motor-car grazing something "very profound" in the social fabric of its spectators (18), Septimus's feeling that "some horror had come almost to the surface" (15) grazes something that many of the other characters express throughout the story. Peter Walsh is haunted in his midday dozing by the sense that spectators were about to be swept into "complete annihilation" (58). Clarissa's memories of Bourton on the first page of the novel are marred by the sense that "something awful was about to happen" (3), immediately followed by her sense of "a particular hush, or solemnity; an indescribable pause; a suspense" (4). Anxiety is not simply a product of Septimus's delusion but rather a widespread phenomenon that cannot be easily categorized as shell shock or any other medical ailment. It takes an outsider, Peter Walsh returning from a long absence, to note that "a change of some sort had undoubtedly taken place.... Those five years—1918 to 1923—had been, he suspected, somehow very important" (71). For those who draw the line directly from Greek civilization to that of Britain, who see civilization progressing, the Great War unravels all that had been and undermines any clear sense of narrative. Through Septimus and a new elegiac narrative, Woolf refashions narrative and historical expectation, making room for mourning earlier losses—and, implicitly and explicitly, one's own damage from such horrors—and, through this new role, a place for oneself in the world of the survivors.

Septimus the Messenger

Septimus is left to bear the burden of being an elegiac subject, a victim of war trauma who eventually commits suicide, and also the elegist for Evans and other war casualties. Continually pressed by his visions to carry secrets to the prime minister (67), Septimus is compelled to tell a story, but it is, perversely, only upon seeing Evans "returned," whole and unharmed, that Septimus feels the need to speak. As both Faulkner and Woolf recognize, when the dead are recharacterized and given space within the story, their loss prompts action. Karen DeMeester, one of many critics to read Septimus through trauma theory, sees in Septimus the need to tell a story so that he might work through the trauma of his war past. And yet his storytelling pains him in large part because he hopes to speak of others' experiences as well as his own as he reshapes trauma into elegy. Septimus's hopes for the prime minister show him to be less well equipped to find satisfactory solutions than Clarissa—whose social standing provides her with a clearer sense of the limits of governmental power. Society has let him down in enabling him to hope that the prime minister who sent him to war could address the brokenness he brings home.

When Evans / Peter Walsh appears to Septimus in Regent's Park, Septimus regards him as Tennyson might Arthur Hallam; his one true friend, destroyed and with such promise, must be elegized appropriately. But Evans is there merely to announce the return of the dead en masse. The elegizing of such a body overwhelms Septimus:

> I must tell the whole world, Septimus cried, raising his hand . . . like some colossal figure who has lamented the fate of man for ages in the desert alone with his hands pressed to his forehead, furrows of despair on his cheeks, and now sees light on the desert's edge . . . and with legions of men prostrate behind him, he, the giant mourner, receives for one moment on his face the whole—
>
> . . .
>
> The millions lamented; for ages they had sorrowed. He would turn round, he would tell them in a few moments, only a few moments more, of this relief, of this joy, of this astonishing revelation— (70)

Septimus attempts to be the mourner large enough for that crowd of men, a burden of mourning larger than that of any prior elegist. But, as both subject and elegist, he is caught between his experience with Evans during the war, in which his role was clear, and the present to which Lucrezia asks him to return, in which society gives him no elegiac purpose. As Susan Bennett Smith argues, by the beginning of the twentieth century, "physicians considered it their duty to aid the grief-stricken, but without acknowledging the source of the pain" (315). In such a world, Septimus's scribbled elegiac messages have no place.

Although Dr. Bradshaw is wrong in his attempts to turn Septimus into a "case" for his own medical and political aims, he may be right in assessing Septimus's trouble as a matter of "proportion": "When a man comes into your room and says he is Christ (a common delusion), and has a message, as they mostly have, and threatens, as they often do, to kill himself, you invoke proportion" (99). Dr. Bradshaw then goes on to defy proportion in the terms of his treatment: "Order rest in bed; rest in solitude; silent and rest; rest without friends, without books, without messages; six months' rest; until a man who went in weighing seven stone six comes out weighing twelve" (99). Bradshaw's methods mock Septimus's attempts to swell to the size needed to address the loss of so many; the modern elegist is faced with a task that is simply insurmountable. He could not speak to the loss of Evans without setting aside the other men on the field, and yet as an elegist he cannot stand in "proportion" to the wave of loss to be mourned. Woolf draws out the sorrow of the modern elegist and the impossibility of his task when it is attempted alone. Through his agonizing, Woolf implies that what is called for is a chorus of elegists and elegiac roles if literature is not to crack under the pressure of the war dead.

In their final stage of elegiac reinvention, Woolf and Faulkner play a double game. They draw attention to the casualties of thwarted elegiac longing even as they suggest that many others could be enlisted to elegize those who have died. Clarissa is not, in this reading, the central character but rather simply one who could join Septimus in his seemingly impossible task. Although both Faulkner and Woolf incorporate public rituals such as bear hunts and dinner parties into their novels, they also foreground the ways in which interruption, spectacle, and arrested daily life create openings for shared grief. Through the reverberations of loss throughout the public, Septimus might find an elegiac chorus that would not shortchange

Evans and the other dead. But he can only do so if the rest of London sees the dead as clearly as does he.

Since Septimus is unable to be the elegist that England needs, what is left is for him to embody the loss himself; since such losses have not been fully mourned as they occur overseas, his death brings the loss home to England. By such means he takes part in the "melodrama" of the present, offering himself up as the center of spectacle, the desire of which lies just beneath the bustle of the modern life. As David Kennedy argues, scholars such as Philippe Ariès may have lamented the "denial of death" throughout much of the twentieth century, but in recent decades "death and mourning have become participatory; public spectacles" (7). Woolf's and Faulkner's novels predict such a shift in linking the dead and the mourner to the many who watch, particularly in *Mrs. Dalloway* and *Go Down, Moses.* Septimus's is a failed elegy, as it means simply another bodily substitution rather than the story that the public needed proclaimed. But in the repetition of loss there is also an insistence on bringing the loss home, where it cannot be ignored.

At the novel's beginning, the "pistol shot" Clarissa Dalloway hears in the London street draws the attention of the reader away from her (13), and attention does not return to her for another dozen pages. Although "the throb of the motor engines sounded like a pulse irregularly drumming through an entire body" (15), it is only when the crowd is gathered around a particular car—which, they suspect, carries royalty—that there is a sense of order, a sense of "sobriety" (14). The car and the crowd are spoken of as a single, collective body, of which the car is the heart (15). By denying the reader and the spectators an individual at the center of the event, however, the scene demands more from the crowd. Instead of allowing an exchange of glances between passenger and observer, the window simply acts as a mirror for the patriotism of the bystanders. Each of the bystanders seems to feel the burden of the car's passing: "Tall men, men of robust physique . . . stood even straighter . . . and seemed ready to attend their Sovereign, if need be, to the cannon's mouth, as their ancestors had done before them" (18). This central incident, marked by an impersonality that differentiates it from Percival's role in *The Waves,* places demands on the bystanders; it seems a call to service. And yet it is a mockery of the vulnerability and shared sorrow that would help Septimus. Although those in the crowd gathered at the gates of Buckingham Palace get a thrill "at the thought of Royalty looking at them" (19), such mutual recognition seems unlikely. The blind had been pulled, mutual recognition denied. The sense that little relies on the individuality of the figure at the center is confirmed much later in the novel: the prime minister's appearance at Clarissa's party causes a flurry of excitement, but only when one did not look directly at the man, since "he looked so ordinary" (172).

In a 1926 journal entry, just one year after *Mrs. Dalloway* was published, Woolf bemoans the lack of community at such junctures:

> Two resolute, sunburnt, dusty girls, in jerseys & short skirts, with packs on their backs, city clerks, or secretaries, tramping along the road in the hot sunshine at Ripe. My instinct at once throws up a screen, which condemns them: I think them in every way angular, awkward & self assertive. But all this is a great mistake. These screens shut me out. Have no screens, for screens are made out of our own integument; & get at the thing itself, which has nothing whatever in common with a screen. The screen making habit, though, is so universal, that probably it preserves our sanity. If we had not this device for shutting people off from our sympathies, we might, perhaps, dissolve utterly. Separateness would be impossible. But the screens are in the excess; not the sympathy. (*D* 3:104)

It is, George Eliot concurs, entirely possible that "our frames could hardly bear" such frequent demands of our sympathy (182). And yet Woolf is even less inclined than Eliot to refrain from holding her reader to the attempt. Just as, in her diary entry, Woolf's throwing up of a screen prompts rumination about herself, the window screen in *Mrs. Dalloway* prompts a kind of reflection on the part of the observers. They become self-conscious in ways that seem to challenge Woolf's assertion that "the screen making habit . . . preserves our sanity." A pub fight breaks out as a result of the heightened nationalism the spectacle of the car produces (*MD* 18).

Septimus's terror reflects his awareness of the fickleness of such spectacle. For it may well be that a body, a particular body, is needed to sustain the roving attention of the crowd. Septimus's war-deadened senses prevent him from taking part in the "unity of identity in the form of shared affective response" that, as William Egginton argues, marks crowds from the nineteenth century onward (106). Without shared emotion, Septimus has only his person to offer up to the crowd if it should attempt to claim him.

Feeling abandoned by his wife, who has attempted to secure him a doctor, Septimus believes the "whole world was clamouring: Kill yourself, kill yourself, for our sakes. . . . It was at that moment . . . that the great revelation took place. A voice spoke from behind the screen. Evans was speaking. The dead were with him" (93). Through his own death Septimus will provide an occasion for elegy, a substitutive spectacle for the losses that happened abroad. His melodramatic re-creation of loss for the London public feeds an unnamed hunger for spectacle on the home front. But he will also defer the work of elegy making, offering instead only an additional body to add to the lists of those to be mourned.

Elegy could keep Septimus from participating in what he perceives as the public's desire to rid themselves of him, and for much of the novel he appears invested in his elegiac undertaking. If his death is a foregone conclusion, a careful calculus for the formal purposes of the novel, the character seems unaware of such a decision. He is, instead, enjoying life only a few minutes before his death. His elegiac role enables him to resist those who, like Dr. Holmes, have their own conceptions of Septimus's role. Alex Zwerdling has written extensively of the tendency by Septimus's doctors to see Septimus as simply a "case" of a broader medical category. According to Septimus's wife, Lucrezia, he had been exhibiting symptoms of shell shock for nine months, which places the onset during the same year that the British government produced the *Report of the War Office Committee of Enquiry into "Shell-Shock."* Septimus's plight coincides with formal acknowledgment of such things; his life is prescribed by what the British government does or does not acknowledge to be the case. Sir William Bradshaw, the expert to whom Lucrezia takes Septimus on the afternoon of Clarissa Dalloway's party, later speaks of Septimus's suicide in the context of current legislative issues: "They were talking about this Bill. Some case Sir William was mentioning, lowering his voice. It had its bearing upon what he was saying about the deferred effects of shell shock. There must be some provision in the Bill" (183). Septimus is that case, buried in the repeated reference to "the Bill," and once again serving as the center of a spectacle, this time in a drawing room rather than the street. In seeing himself speaking to the prime minister, then, Septimus was not far off; at the Dalloway party, legislators, the prime minister, and Sir William Bradshaw are all on hand to turn Septimus into a case that promotes their own interests and the interests of the British establishment. The difference between Septimus's understanding and Bradshaw's understanding, of course, is that Septimus has a message of his own to deliver. Bradshaw sacrificed the individual for concerns of his own, turning the "Christs and Christesses, who prophesied the end of the world, or the advent of God" (99) into "cases" for the furthering of medical knowledge.[8]

It is clear why, when he is pursued by the doctors, Septimus's internal thoughts have the rhythm of a conversation that he has had before. He alternately resigns himself to the role and resists it: "At last, with a melodramatic gesture which he assumed mechanically and with complete consciousness of its insincerity, he dropped his head on his hands" (90); "But why should he kill himself for their sakes? Food was pleasant; the sun hot" (92). Having previously rejected the role of the sacrificial lamb, Septimus is aware of his current situation as a role to play. Settling on the window as the means of suicide, he thinks that there is only the "rather melodramatic business of opening the widow and throwing himself out. It was their idea of tragedy.... Holmes and Bradshaw like that sort of thing" (149).[9] Awareness of "melodrama," the social expectations that underlie Bradshaw's and Holmes's attention, sets Septimus apart from the other figures in the novel. He is aware that there are only two places for the individual: away, as in the "homes" that will keep disconcerting figures out of the public consciousness, or playing a role that will make them suitable for a "case" study by specialists.

Although Septimus best expresses the elegiac tensions introduced by the war, Woolf's narrative efforts prevent him from playing a particular "role" within the novel even as he seeks escape from social or elegiac responsibilities. Instead of pinning her novel's entire framework on him, Woolf allows Septimus to emerge only gradually in *Mrs. Dalloway*. When the reader moves away from Clarissa Dalloway's mind, the shift is to a collective response to the backfiring car: "Nobody knew whose face had been seen. Was it the Prince of Wales's, the Queen's, the Prime Minister's? Nobody knew. Edgar J. Watkiss, with his roll of lead piping round his arm, said audibly, humorously of course: 'The Proime Minister's kyar.' Septimus Warren Smith, who found himself unable to pass, heard him" (14). He is, here, one of many, and much of Woolf's writing in the novel works to reincorporate him into the fabric of Clarissa's world, indicating he is not alone in his anxieties or in his elegiac impulses. Even his fixation on the prime minister emerges from the rumors of the crowd around him on the street. Jane de Gay argues that

Septimus's turn to the prime minister aligns him with Jacob Flanders of *Jacob's Room* (87). Unlike Jacob, however, Septimus does not enjoy the class privileges that would engender such aspirations, and that class difference is precisely what separates the lounging Jacob Flanders from the floundering Septimus Smith.

An extended description of Septimus comes late in the novel, only well after the reader has become acquainted with his mental states. The description of him wavers, blurring his social situation and showing its fragility: "To look at, he might have been a clerk, but of the better sort; for he wore brown boots; his hands were educated; so, too, his profile—his angular, big-nosed, intelligent, sensitive profile; but not his lips altogether, for they were loose; and his eyes (as eyes tend to be), eyes merely . . . so that he was, on the whole, a border case, neither one thing nor the other" (84). This description revisits the briefer description that appears with Septimus's introduction in the novel, where he was "beak-nosed, wearing brown shoes and a shabby overcoat" (14), prompting a reconsideration of his character. Rather than describe Septimus in order to explain him, as a Victorian predecessor might do, Woolf does so in order to emphasize the mutability of his position. Molly Hite observes the deliberate awkwardness of the description, as Woolf employs "the conceit of the educated profile and hands" not to delineate Septimus but rather to make the reader aware of one's reliance on such literary conventions for access to a character ("Tonal Cues" 258).

Continually deferred and deflected, Septimus's entrance as a major figure and Clarissa Dalloway's "double" takes place only when he himself begins to express a preoccupation with centrality. First there is Clarissa Dalloway's walk, then the pistol shot of the car's backfiring, after which Septimus is only one of many onlookers in the street. Appearing just after Edgar J. Watkiss, a character who gets only a line in the novel, Septimus is not yet a figure of interest for the reader when one sees the car through his eyes: "This gradual drawing together of everything to one centre before his eyes, as if some horror had come almost to the surface and was about to burst into flames, terrified him. The world wavered and quivered and threatened to burst into flames. It is I who am blocking the way, he thought. Was he not being looked at and pointed at; was he not weighted there, rooted to the pavement, for a purpose? But for what purpose?" (15). Only in thinking of a center and the weight of that role does Septimus in fact become the center of the narrative scene. By placing himself at the center—"It is I who am blocking the way"—he assumes responsibility for the narrative; the progress of the novel seems to stop when Septimus, previously unknown to the reader, is rendered "unable to pass" by the backfiring motor car (14). Through moves like this one Woolf takes part in what Rebecca Walkowitz has called "critical cosmopolitanism," marked by "an aversion to heroic tones of appropriation and progress, and a suspicion of epistemological privilege, views from above or from the center that assume a consistent distinction between who is seeing and what is seen" (*Cosmopolitan* 2). As she did with the narrator in *Jacob's Room* and the hide-and-seek play of *The Waves*, Woolf uses a character to call into question the limits and benefits of his own position.

If Septimus assumes responsibility for the narrative, he does not retain it for long. When his wife catches his attention and encourages him to resume walking, he "jumped, started, and said, 'All right!' angrily, as if she had interrupted him" (15). And indeed she had, calling for not only his attention but also that of the reader. For after the remark from Septimus the narrative attention shifts to Lucrezia's concerns:

> People must notice; people must see. People, she thought, looking at the crowd staring at the motor car; the English people, with their children and their horses and their clothes, which she admired in a way; but they were "people" now, because Septimus had said, "I will kill myself"; an awful thing to say. Suppose they had heard him? She looked at the crowd. Help, help! she wanted to cry out to butchers' boys and women. Help! Only last autumn she and Septimus had stood on the Embankment wrapped in the same cloak and, Septimus reading a paper instead of talking, she had snatched it from him and laughed in the old man's face who saw them! But failure one conceals. (16)

The lengthy quotation merits attention because in this introduction to Lucrezia, she enumerates the aspects of public spectacle that shape both her actions and those of the other characters of the novel. Lucrezia feels her vulnerability to the crowd in ways that she did not when she was happy. Her thoughts establish that the shell-shocked character is not the only one who is fearful of becoming the object of attention. Like the backfiring car that intrudes on the scene, Lucrezia contributes to the disintegration of a neat contrast between Septimus and Clarissa.

Clarissa's Selective Elegiac Inheritance

The question Woolf puts to readers is how one should assess Clarissa's relation to the dead. Alex Zwerdling and others contend that Clarissa is the only member of the governing class who connects to Septimus as an individual and feels empathy rather than clinical interest (*Virginia Woolf* 128). But I join Deborah Guth in thinking that Clarissa makes her own use of Septimus when she retreats from her party to consider the implications of his death. Guth argues that Clarissa uses Romantic, pagan, and Christian imagery to fashion out of Septimus's suicide a renewed connection to life.[10] Clarissa may have sympathy, but not for the Septimus who resisted becoming "the eternal sufferer" (*MD* 25), and who, even in his final moments, desires to continue living. Instead, her sympathy is for a figure of glorious sacrifice who acts so that others might be driven closer to the meaning of life. It may, however, be Clarissa's sympathy for Septimus as one of "the poets and thinkers" that makes it difficult for her to see him clearly (184). Rupert Brooke and other war poets fused the identity of the poet with that of the soldier, and the "soldier-poet" played a significant role in national identity. Even as Clarissa attempts to imagine Septimus's prewar ambitions, she can only do so through a postwar lens, in which poets are also soldiers, and both have been removed to a patriotic distance. She cannot access him even through imagination in order to elegize him.

Despite his explicit rejection of sacrificial typology, Septimus is forced to embody that very role, through Clarissa's eyes. Earlier in the novel, Peter Walsh flirts with the same conclusion when he sees Septimus's ambulance pass, before naming its dangers: "But thinking became morbid, sentimental, directly one began conjuring up doctors, dead bodies; a little glow of pleasure, a sort of lust too over the visual impression warned one not to go on with that sort of thing any more—fatal to art, fatal to friendship" (151). Reducing the dead to the self-satisfaction of the living is fatal to both art and life, Woolf suggests, since art relies on the preserving of socialization—friendship—and a recognition of the full-bodied character of the dead.

Although Clarissa is reinvigorated through contemplation of Septimus's death, there are also, as with any elegy, significant literary gains. One might think of Woolf's own response to the many deaths in her family. She admits that her development as a writer relies on her learning to welcome shocks.

They are, as she writes in "A Sketch of the Past," inevitably followed by a desire to make sense of it, "a revelation of some order," which was the desire to write (*MOB* 72). Although Clarissa is no writer, her weathering of such shocks—not grimly bearing them like Lady Bexborough, but regarding them as opportunities—marks the development in her character from the cruder version Woolf offers in the short story "Mrs. Dalloway in Bond Street." Mark Spilka expresses dismay at the changes Woolf makes in the turn to the novel, since what he sees as "Woolf's original impulse to burden Clarissa with the problem of mourning" (60) is almost entirely given over to Septimus. And yet in Clarissa the social responsibility for mourning and mourners is given body and voice. Her decision to link his loss to her own and her sympathetic withdrawal from her party reflect the final place on which Woolf places responsibility for mourning in modern society. Septimus's fear, while striking, does not help us to determine what, precisely, he is afraid of losing. Clarissa, in her delicate balance of private and social selves, begins to address such a concern.

Although Septimus is the only one described as a poet in *Mrs. Dalloway,* Clarissa shows herself fluent in elegiac poetry in all three of her major appearances in Woolf's fiction. In *The Voyage Out* she claims to love Shelley's "Adonais," though she qualifies that with "I always think it's *living,* not dying, that counts" (58). As she walks through London in "Mrs. Dalloway in Bond Street," Clarissa Dalloway thinks of the lines from that poem:

> From the contagion of the world's slow stain
> He is secure, and now can never mourn
> A heart grown cold, a head grown grey in vain.
> (Shelley ll. 356–58, qtd. in *CSF* 154)[11]

Clarissa's walk continues to the refrain of Shelley's line "And now can never mourn, can never mourn," turning the attention from the dead to the difficulty of mourning in the current age; one "can never mourn" again because the traditional modes of mourning are disintegrating. "For all the great things one must go to the past," Clarissa thinks; "the moderns had never written anything one wanted to read about death" (*CSF* 155). Through Clarissa's dissatisfaction, Woolf registers a failure on the part of modern poetry to address the needs of mourners who seek consolation and find only cynicism in the poems of Sassoon and Wilfred Owen. Clarissa's thoughts outline a rift in the elegiac tradition, from when "it used . . .

to be so simple," to now, when, she thinks, "simply one doesn't believe ... any more in God" (158). The burgeoning secularism of the twentieth century presents a problem for the modern elegist. In this postwar, posttranscendental time, Woolf forces her readers to see the unraveling of poetic tradition that comes with a loss of belief.

As Peter Sacks and Jahan Ramazani trace the elegiac tradition over centuries, it becomes clear that whereas older elegies generally concluded by offering the dead to God or gods for immortality, modern poets are far less certain that there is some means of offering the dead immortality other than through their own poetry. Although, as Ramazani points out, Lord Tennyson wrestles with his position throughout the entirety of "In Memoriam," by the end the poet does trust that his friend will "live in God" (qtd. in Ramazani, *Poetry* 68). Thomas Hardy, on the other hand, struggles with "the burden of the personal elegist in a secular time" (47). Ramazani suggests that that the hundred-plus elegies Hardy wrote for his wife are the poet's attempt to take on the burden of securing immortality for the dead when he thinks God no longer can.

Through her disappointment with contemporary elegists' use of satire and cynicism and her impatience with religious transcendence in elegies such as Milton's *Lycidas,* Woolf makes her own path between the two positions. But in Clarissa's turn to Shelley, Woolf forges a strong connection to the elegiac tradition. Shelley, whose pamphlet *The Necessity of Atheism* got him sent down from Oxford without his degree (Shelley xii), resists the influence of religious belief on the English elegy.[12] But he too ends his elegy for Keats by trusting in transcendence, concluding that Keats's soul "Beacons from the abode where the Eternal are" (l. 495). It is this search for transcendence unconnected to Christianity that Woolf echoes in her portrait of Clarissa Dalloway. In drawing on Shelley rather than Tennyson or Milton, Woolf connects her search for alternative modes of mourning with a particular atheist strain of the English elegy. T. S. Eliot puts the link between death and poetry most succinctly in "Tradition and the Individual Talent": "No poet, no artist of any art, has his complete meaning alone. His significance, his appreciation is the appreciation of his relation to the dead poets and artists. You cannot value him alone; you must set him, for contrast and comparison, among the dead" (37).

In facing her lack of belief and her need for an alternative reason for continuing to breast the "slow stain" of her world, Clarissa forms a "transcendental theory" that, as Peter elaborates in the novel, "allowed her to believe, or say that she believed (for all her scepticism), that since our apparitions, the part of us which appears, are so momentary compared with the other, the unseen part of us, which spreads wide, the unseen might survive, be recovered somehow attached to this person or that, or even haunting certain places after death . . . perhaps—perhaps" (153). Although this emerges as the major theory guiding Clarissa's life and it strongly echoes Shelley's vision of Keats as being "made one with Nature" (l. 370), Peter does note that "in those days—they had heaps of theories, always theories, as young people have" (152), indicating that this may not be the best theory Woolf could offer. In her search for a modus operandi, Clarissa makes little of the living apparitions (the part of us which appears) in order to invest herself in the dispersal of the unseen other, a choice that may contribute to what Woolf called the "tinselly" quality in Clarissa (*D* 3:32). Just as Shelley introduces a number of mourners in "Adonais" whose mourning he finds insincere, so too Woolf offers through Clarissa the picture of a mourner caught between modes and motivations. Septimus may have been a poet, but now he is a soldier-poet, which alters considerably Clarissa's willingness and her ability to set herself in elegiac relation to him. But Woolf pushes further, working to see modern mourning speak to the fullness of an individual's character, reclaiming both poet and soldier from the mass mourning into which they have been absorbed.

The mass nature of modern war losses deprives the public of its ability to mourn loudly and at length for any lost individual. Woolf's awareness of such a problem reveals itself through the young men of *Jacob's Room*, as we have seen, and also in *To the Lighthouse:* "A shell exploded. Twenty or thirty young men were blown up in France, among them Andrew Ramsay" (133). As the narrator moves from "twenty or thirty" to the full name of one who is of concern to the reader, Woolf joins contemporary poets and prose writers in using literature to reclaim the right to mourn the individual, building up a story around the character to combat the mass nature of his or her death. Woolf's movement through many characters' minds in *Mrs. Dalloway* is an extension of this individualization, enabling her to attend to the range of frustrations, grief, and beliefs that govern not only the mourning of individuals but the mourning that is done by individuals who attempt to find their way without the baroque machinations of Victorian mourning. As Woolf's poetic allusions remind her reader, much has changed from the time of earlier elegists, leaving the war survivors with the burden not only of mourning the dead but also of creating a form in which that mourning can take place.

Woolf uses Shelley to ground her own inquiry into secular elegy, but she also, in the process, implicitly criticizes Shelley's transformation of the dead for his own purposes. He, like Clarissa, refashions Keats's fate to suit his own system of beliefs,[13] illustrating the uneasy relationship that develops between elegiac subject and elegist when devotion to the dead and self-promotion conflict. Clarissa echoes Shelley by turning outward in her grief; as Peter puts it, "To know her, or any one, one must seek out the people who completed them; even the places" (152–53). Both Woolf's fiction and Clarissa's philosophy turn from a search for transcendence to an attempt to reenliven the secular world with a deep sense of sympathy. In Clarissa, Woolf practices a selective elegiac inheritance, circumventing the English elegy and its traditional call for the dead to be lifted up by the God in whom neither Woolf nor many of her contemporaries believed. And in Clarissa Dalloway's survival and near-continuous elegiac work, Woolf works around the demands of a central position and the weight of the elegiac burden.

Part of the reason *Mrs. Dalloway* does not easily fit the existing novel form is that it was not originally intended as a novel. In her earliest notes, Woolf conceives of *Mrs. Dalloway* as "a short book consisting of six or seven chapters each complete separately, yet there must be some sort of fusion" (Dick 3). "Mrs. Dalloway in Bond Street" was to be the first of those stories. But as the writing continues, Woolf notes, "Now I break off . . . to write Mrs. D. (who ushers in a host of others, I begin to perceive)" (*D* 2:189). It is not simply that Clarissa is to be joined by other characters in the book; Woolf had envisioned that all along, with her notion of separate chapters strung together. Instead, Woolf's wording here reveals something useful about her conceptualization of Clarissa as both a character and a formal force in her project. Clarissa's "ushering in" already positions her as a hostess, both on a thematic and on a formal level, and that dual hostessing is preserved through the writing and revising that Woolf does from there on out.[14] Clarissa moves from the center of the novel to a peripheral perspective and a peripheral role. She feels that she lacks "something central which permeated" (31) and conceives of Septimus's death as an attempt to fill the void created when people felt "the impossibility of reaching the centre which, mystically, evaded them" (184). Clarissa, however, remains unaware of her author's attempts to make use of such discomfiting decentering.

In her moments of self-doubt, Clarissa struggles with feelings of being "just anybody, standing there; anybody could do it" before appreciating the flexibility of that position (170): "Yet this anybody she did a little admire, couldn't help feeling that it marked a stage, this post that she felt herself to have become, for oddly enough she had quite forgotten what she looked like, but felt herself a stake driven in at the top of her stairs. Every time she gave a party she had this feeling of being something not herself, and that every one was unreal in one way; much more real in another" (170–71). Unreality is here posed as a powerful position rather than one that is necessarily self-alienating. Clarissa does not perform this role solely at her party—indeed, she ties individual to individual, past to present, throughout her day—but the party helps her to become aware that she plays such a role. Her position on the periphery offers a kind of freedom for Clarissa and for the protagonist of the modernist novel. By orchestrating a social space in which she holds a position on the periphery, Clarissa preserves, formally, a division between the individual and the event, leaving her free to explore the various facets of this anyone that she has become. If Clarissa frequently fails, in her own mind, to fix her personality, she has instead the ability "to be; to exist; to sum it all up in the moment as she passed" (174). Unlike Bernard's "Now to sum up," in which he attempts to hold the momentary "illusion . . . that something adheres for a moment, has roundness, weight, depth, is completed" (*TW* 176), Clarissa's centering is explicitly momentary, much like Jinny's fleeting coherence.

In "Character in Fiction," a later form of "Mr. Bennett and Mrs. Brown," Woolf compares the role of the novelist to that of a hostess in reaching for conventions to engage a reader:

> Both in life and in literature it is necessary to have some means of bridging the gulf between the hostess and her unknown guest on the one hand, the writer and his unknown reader on the other. . . . The writer must get into touch with his reader by putting before him something which he recognises, which therefore stimulates his imagination, and makes him willing to co-operate in the far more difficult business of intimacy. And it is of the highest importance that this common meeting-place should be reached easily, almost instinctively, in the dark, with

one's eyes shut. . . . House property was the common ground from which the Edwardians found it easy to proceed to intimacy. (*E* 3:431)

But in her own case, Woolf says, the conventions of the past are no longer useful, and "how keenly I felt the lack of a convention" (3:431). Woolf does not, of course, say what the new conventions are to be in the "Georgian" era of literature, just that there must be crashing and destruction as the old ones are pulled down. What seems essential, however, as seen in both her essay and her novel, is that the reader must see the characters themselves striving with the old and with the new.

Through her hostessing as a novelist and that of her character Clarissa, Woolf ushers the city, other characters, and other times into the limelight, consequently relieving Clarissa of the burden of the protagonist position. If the modern subject is to move beyond the "horror" of the central position, it is not, perhaps, surprising that Woolf turns to the peripheral position from which she advocates for "outsiders" in *Three Guineas*. I join Christine Froula in reading the novel as a "communal postwar elegy" (*Virginia Woolf* 88). But whereas for Froula, Clarissa is the "central elegiac consciousness" (87), here Clarissa is a peripheral elegist, one who turns away from the traditional relationship between elegiac subject and elegist to a network of relations drawn together through the figure of the hostess. Clarissa is hindered in her direct attempts to elegize Septimus, since she is unable to pierce the veil of his role as soldier. He is a soldier-poet, in her mind, and so it is not surprising that her elegiac moment is defined by her inability to do more than return to her own needs. What she does preserve, however, in that moment, is the imaginative desire for connection that denies the poet or the fellow soldier the sole duty or privilege of elegizing. Septimus is not to carry the burden alone. Modern elegy is a communal art, one that follows the network of connection Woolf traces with such painstaking detail in her London street scenes. Clarissa exemplifies Derrida's claim that the mourning subject "welcomes" the decentering that comes with bereavement, as it is the foundation for "hospitality, love or friendship" (188).

The party hostess as a model of social function speaks powerfully to the changing theater of London life in postwar Britain. Rebecca Walkowitz declares *Mrs. Dalloway* a cosmopolitan novel not despite the apparent frivolity of Clarissa's party but rather in large part because of it (*Cosmopolitan* 10). Within the novel Clarissa herself seems uncertain whether to make of her party a big thing or a small one: "Here was So-and-so in South Kensington; some one up in Bayswater; and somebody else, say, in Mayfair. And she felt quite continuously a sense of their existence; and she felt what a waste; and she felt what a pity; and she felt if only they could be brought together; so she did it. And it was an offering; to combine, to create; but to whom? An offering for the sake of offering, perhaps. Anyhow, it was her gift. Nothing else had she of the slightest importance" (122). Although tempted to make of her parties a grand achievement, one that will match the affairs of the men in her life, Clarissa stops short of fully articulating her parties' significance. Although there is the suggestion that something very grand might come of the meeting of those three people, she is unwilling to determine precisely what should occur. And in doing so she acknowledges her role in providing the opportunity for something dynamic.

Breaking the Center

In his 1908 analysis of the "social gathering" or "party," sociologist Georg Simmel draws a distinction between a small gathering of friends and a party. In a party, he observes: "a complete harmony of mood, which is so characteristic of the small group, is neither sought, nor could it be attained if it were. On the contrary—and this is a further difference—there easily occurs the formation of subgroups. The nature of a friendly gathering among few persons strenuously militates against its splitting up into two moods, even only into two conversations. In fact, the moment there is a dualism instead of an undisputed single center, we have a 'party'" (113). In a small group of friends, the attention of all is focused on a single speaker and conversation. Their shared histories and interests enable them to sustain this single focus. But in a party, as Simmel wryly notes, the group is large enough and the interests disparate enough that what they can be said to have in common likely goes no further than their interest in food and amusement (113). There is a lowering of "the level of the personality" (112) that must be compensated for by "an intensification of external and sensuous attractions" (113). Such analysis speaks to the pressure on spectacle that Septimus expresses when the backfiring car passes early in the novel. But Simmel notes two effects that mark a party: there is an emphasis on entertainment, and there is a splitting of focus.

Much sociological research has focused on the "cocktail-party effect," or the individual's ability to single out a particular sensory thread amidst a profusion of others. But, as Franco Moretti asks, "Do you go there to 'concentrate' on a single interlocutor, or rather . . . to 'follow simultaneously' more than one, even at the cost of superficiality and confusion? And the same wish, on a vastly larger scale, holds also for the metropolis—whose fascination does not lie in any specific promise, however seductive, but in the *many* choices that appear equally possible there" (138–39; italics in original). At Clarissa's party in *Mrs. Dalloway,* the split focus of the group relieves her from the pressure of entertainment, which allows her to slip away to contemplate the disturbing news of Septimus's death.[15]

Though I do not want to press too hard on the party metaphor, Simmel's analysis sheds light on Clarissa Dalloway's role as hostess of both an evening party and Woolf's novel. Woolf did, after all, begin the writing of *Mrs. Dalloway* by noting that she wanted to explore "party consciousness" (*D* 3:12). By hosting, rather than assuming the role of the protagonist, Clarissa Dalloway engages in a more fluid relationship with those around her than would be possible otherwise. As Simmel puts it, establishing party relations allows one to alternate "between involvement and release which, according to the nature of the individual, affects him as the most unbearable superficiality, or as a playful rhythm of aesthetic charm" (113–14). In *Mrs. Dalloway,* Peter Walsh gives voice to the former opinion; his sudden appearance makes Clarissa self-conscious about her party, as she remembers that, many years earlier, Peter had called her "the perfect hostess," "whereupon she winced all over" (62). Her fear of superficiality recurs throughout the novel.

And yet, of course, numerous critics have argued for a reading of Clarissa's role that claims far more than Simmel's delight in the "playful rhythm of aesthetic charm." Clarissa is the one who unites souls, sensitive to the delicate threads that bind humanity together. And then there is Clarissa as political statement.[16] Woolf suggestively compares Clarissa's activities with those of her husband and the other officious persons who appear in the novel. What, the reader is given to ask, is the difference between Clarissa's dinner party and the political one of her MP husband, Richard? Although Woolf plays with the analogy between Clarissa's occupation and that of her husband, one should be careful not to transform Clarissa's party into something more overtly didactic than Woolf intended. It was Clive Bell, rather than Woolf, who used a party metaphor to criticize those who push the effects of the war under the rug and return to class-appropriate activities. In his 1928 *Civilization,* Bell writes: "And after the handsome sample of savagery offered us between August 1914 and November 1918, we, nostalgic intellectuals, know that we have returned to the artificial pleasure of a fashionable dinner-party, where we can sit and rail in security against the unheroic quietude of civilized life, with a secret but profound sense of relief" (141). Woolf famously dismisses Bell's book with a reference to that depiction: "In the end it turns out that Civilization is a lunch party at no. 50 Gordon Square" (qtd. in Q. Bell, 2:137).[17] Although Woolf becomes more vocal about her disagreement with Bell once his book is published, the seeds of their dispute are apparent even in 1923, when his work *On British Freedom* was published. In her own 1925 novel, Clarissa's party enables Woolf to connect larger political issues to everyday decisions and settings: the suicide of a war veteran to dinner parties with the prime minister.

Hostessing enables Clarissa to remove herself from the central position that bears down on Septimus Smith for much of the center of the novel. Septimus articulates what one might see as the individual's terror at being made the object of attention. He is always, whether observing the backfiring car with the rest of the crowd or at home in his apartment, surrounded by observers, "faces laughing at him" (67). Through Clarissa, Woolf turns the protagonist-driven novel on its head, offering instead the hostessing model of involvement and withdrawal as a new form of novel. It is a rhythm Clarissa performs throughout the novel, from the busy city street to the refuge of her attic and from the hubbub of her evening party to a room where she can be alone to consider the death of the unnamed Septimus Smith. It is the same movement performed by Woolf's narrator, alternately deep within a character's thoughts and winging away to another figure on the street. Although Clarissa's party offers a climax for the action of the novel, the event anticipated from the opening lines in which Clarissa sets out to buy flowers for the event, there is also a sense in which Woolf has dispersed the party throughout the novel, so that the party becomes as much a literary attitude as an event. If the modernist novel is to draw attention away from the moment of death that propels the elegy, it will do so not by replacing the climactic moment of death with a party but rather by filling the novel with the attitude of the party.

Upon reentering her house after the walk through London, Clarissa goes upstairs "as if she had left a party" (30), drawing upon the mood of that moment in order to reflect on her life and her connections to others. The streets of London have offered a parallel for her party, an occasion on which to open oneself up to observation, and an occasion to observe others. Although critics frequently focus on the significance of the party in the novel, Clarissa's true hostessing—and the narrative benefits of it—are derived from her having never truly taken off that role in her daily life, even if she feels the difference between her party self and that of her solitary time.[18] In this shift in attention, Woolf tacitly undermines the narrative suspense of the novel, redirecting one's attention to the events of the day. Not only did Clarissa not "need" to die, Septimus did not "need" to, in a narrative sense, at all. Neither's significance is derived from mortality, and neither is the sole elegist required to "sum up" the significance of another. Redistributing the weight of the narrative away from the protagonist and toward a streetscape of networked characters is Woolf's ultimate renewal of both the novel and the elegy.

In a move that only underscores the role of the hostess in redistributing attention, Woolf offers the most sustained theory of hostessing through the character Peter rather than through Clarissa herself. As he moves throughout London on the day of Clarissa's party, he reacts to the tolling of St. Margaret's bells:

> Ah, said St. Margaret's, like a hostess who comes into her drawing-room on the very stroke of the hour and finds her guests there already. I am not late. Not, it is precisely half-past eleven, she says. Yet, though she is perfectly right, her voice, being the voice of the hostess, is reluctant to inflict its individuality. Some grief for the past holds it back; some concern for the present. It is half-past eleven, she says, and the sound of St. Margaret's glides into the recesses of the heart and buries itself in ring after ring of sound, like something alive which wants to confide itself, to disperse itself, to be, with a tremor of delight, at rest—like Clarissa herself. (49–50)

By linking the sound of the bells to Clarissa's hostessing, Peter draws attention away from the single event of the party and offers an implicit rationale for the bells' moderated tone. The "grief for the past" and "concern for the present" are occasions not for wailing or satire but rather for reserve and measure. Clarissa illustrates the discipline of repeatedly throwing oneself into the midst of others, as she does in party after party.[19]

One of the most frequently cited lines in Leonard Woolf's biography is that in which he judges Virginia to be "the least political animal that has lived since Aristotle invented the definition" (*Downhill* 27). Although Virginia herself expresses similar sentiments in her diary, recent critics who are interested in trumpeting Virginia Woolf's social and political engagement have taken issue with this characterization.[20] But what is of interest is not simply that both husband and wife classify her as a nonpolitical animal but rather how both qualify the statement. Virginia writes in her diary, "I am not a politician: obviously," but she completes her thought with "[I] can only rethink politics very slowly into my own tongue" (*D* 5:114). Even as she says she "obviously" is not a politician, she does not cede the subject but rather takes the role of an interpreter. Similarly, even as Leonard says that she is not a "political animal," he is quick to acknowledge her sensitivity to the world: "She was not a bit like the Virginia Woolf who appears in many books written by literary critics or autobiographers who did not know her, a frail invalidish lady living in an ivory tower in Bloomsbury and worshipped by a little clique of aesthetes. She was intensely interested in things, people, and events, and, as her new books show, highly sensitive to the atmosphere which surrounded her, whether it was personal, social, or historical. She was therefore the last person who could ignore the political menaces under which we all lived" (*Downhill* 27). If she is not a "political animal," it may be because she must be implicitly compared to Leonard, who labels himself "very much a political animal" after his seven years in Ceylon (*Beginning* 99). His involvement with the League of Nations, among other projects, may well have made Virginia look apolitical by comparison.

Leonard begins his discussion of Virginia's politics by acknowledging that the First World War had changed the very nature of political involvement, saturating the lives of everyone: "I have reached the period in my autobiography in which our lives and the lives of everyone have become penetrated, dominated by politics. Happy the country and era—if there can ever have been one—which has no politics. Ever since 1914 in the background of our lives and thoughts has loomed the menace of politics, the canker of public events. (One has ceased to believe that a public event can be anything other than a horror or disaster)" (*Downhill* 27). When he later reflects on the periods that mark his life, he notes that they have been "ruthlessly" divided by the two World Wars, which invaded his individual life, as well as the global scene: "If I am to continue with the story of my life, I shall have to deal with the events of each of these four periods, the effect of each upon me and my life, and my reaction to each of them. But even in our cruel, mechanized, barbarous age, we have not yet become completely robots, puppets jerked through life by history, governments, and computers. We still have, at any rate in Britain, some shreds of private life, which we can preserve unaffected by public events" (48). Virginia Woolf's talent lies in not searching for any remaining bits of privacy, those pieces untouched by war, but rather in speaking, as she does in *Mrs. Dalloway,* to the invasion of that "public event" in even the most domestic of affairs. Although "event" implies a temporal dimension, Woolf's novel argues strongly for seeing the war as a frame of mind or a culture under which society will continue to live without the promise of telos.

If the language of politics is that of "case making," as in the case of William Bradshaw and the bill that is mentioned at Clarissa's party, then Woolf's rethinking of politics fights such abstraction by recharacterizing the "case," emphasizing the effects of the war on a world that can no longer be divided into political and nonpolitical animals. Even if Clarissa cannot hope to elegize Septimus in detail, she joins him in recognizing that death is no longer synonymous with the war or confined to such an event. Woolf, like Faulkner, sidesteps the debate over elegy as consolatory or anticonsolatory by making clear that mourning is ongoing, woven into various aspects of one's life. It is fueled and shaped by social factors, but it is also itself a source of motivation for political and social action. The first two phases of this project make clear that mourning conventions are the product of many motivations in addition to grief, but in the final stage of elegiac reinvention both authors help one see how mourning itself helps to reshape social concerns. Clarissa's depressive mood is not something to overcome. Like the memories of the war itself, it can be used to extend sympathy and understanding to those who act on their emotions, serving as a means of bridging the gap between combatant and noncombatant rather than cleaving the two.

5

"Unproductive" Grief in *Go Down, Moses*

> We showed an unmistakable tendency to put death on one side, to eliminate it from life. We tried to hush it up.
> —Sigmund Freud, "Thoughts for the Times on War and Death"

It is tempting to read this book as having summed up all that Woolf and Faulkner have to say about the meeting of grief, elegy, and modernist narrative. But just as each stage of their elegiac innovation multiplies rather than simplifies elegiac relations, so too this final chapter balks at summation, insisting instead on a messy landscape of modern mourning into which this project offers only inroads. In Faulkner's *Go Down, Moses* (1942), mourning is not a task to be completed but rather a facet of human experience that lingers, connecting disparate individuals across family and community lines. Recognizing ongoing mourning makes visible political and ethical shifts that are otherwise inexplicable. By drawing on the short-story form at which both excelled, Faulkner and Woolf use their final stage of elegiac reinvention to call attention to the way that sustained mourning, shared by many, prepares the ground for revolution in the larger culture. It propels individuals to be not merely mourners and martyrs but also social critics and political agitators. This new role for mourning is only visible, however, once society abandons the idea that mourning is merely a passing phase in the life of an individual.

The genre debates that swell around Faulkner's "splendid failure" and Woolf's "playpoem" reach their peak with *Go Down, Moses,* which exists at the boundary between short-story collections and novels.[1] With *Mrs. Dalloway,* Woolf suggests an extension of novelistic boundaries, the short stories that surround the novel echoing the theme of the hostess surrounded by party guests. Faulkner's *Go Down, Moses,* however, uses the different expectations for the two genres to challenge the tendency to see the novel as an inviolate form. If seven stories can make a novel, why not eight or nine? Are there further stories buried in the existing text that are left unexplored? The "hostess" or elegist of *Go Down, Moses* is less obvious than in Woolf's novel. It must be discovered by making interpretive claims about the relations between multiple stories of mourning, a strategy that leaves room for different elegists to emerge. The literary representations of grief here are interdependent; rather than impose the conventions of another era, Faulkner's text offers a means of listening in as new mourning conventions are created, stitch by stitch.

It is not surprising that readers and critics view *Go Down, Moses* as a set of stories loosely held together by the narrative of the McCaslin family. As the successor to Faulkner novels such as *Absalom, Absalom!* and *The Sound and the Fury, Go Down, Moses* inherits expectations that the stories will outline the legacy of a white plantation family in Mississippi. But alongside the narrative of the McCaslins, Faulkner places that of the Beauchamp family, which is the black counterpart to the McCaslins and, given the shared blood between the families, its unacknowledged other half. The doubling of the family narrative and the movement between McCaslin and Beauchamp stories unsettles the primacy of the plantation family's story. Through the Beauchamp characters, the reader sees blood ties superseded by shared wounds that are inflicted by the larger culture. The stories of the black sharecroppers and tenants provide powerful challenges to Freud's conception of mourning as "grief work" (*Trauerarbeit*) that is motivated by individual, temporary interest. The black characters spend their grief in acts of social justice and challenges to racial prejudice. In this novel, family takes a back seat to a community built through grief, one that finds its role in social action and rewriting mourning for new cultures.

The novel's foremost challenge to traditional mourning is its reassessment of the assumption that mourners give voice to grief. The character Mollie Beauchamp wraps her grief in the words of African American spirituals, using biblical narrative to give shape to her modern grievances. Her words meet with a sharp "Hush" from the white woman who earlier described herself and Mollie as having grown up "as sisters" (*GDM* 357, 362). As Faulkner makes clear, giving voice to grief is not an option for all who mourn. Another black character, Rider, refuses to join in the singing of his fellow mill workers; when he is overcome with grief for his dead wife, he feels "the muscles of his jaw beginning to drag his mouth open, tugging upward the top half of his head. But he stopped that too before it became sound" (137). He forces his grief into action, not sound, as he murders the white gambler who had been fleecing the black mill workers for fifteen years. Rider insists that individual mourning make itself relevant to culture, a link that is too easily overlooked when we consider only Freudian terms for mourning. Rider's fight to reclaim economic independence when he is in the grip of grief helps to recast another character, Lucas Beauchamp, in a more sympathetic light. Lucas responds to ancient grievances with what might be characterized as fiscal aggression, making him a figure who, like Woolf's Clarissa Dalloway, draws on the novel's other stories of grief to make legible his own.

This book concludes with a study of *Go Down, Moses* (1942) not because it was published later than the other novels under consideration but because it takes further than any other texts by Faulkner or Woolf the work of decentered, genre-blurring mourning, and it confronts directly the issues of cultural difference that are present only in the margins of those other texts. If in *The Sound and the Fury* Caddy Compson claims that the people in her house are gathered for a party rather than her grandmother's funeral, she does so not only in denial of death but also because of Frony's description of funerals as "Where they moans" (22). Caddy's distaste for the display of mourning prompts her ludicrous response, "That's niggers. White people don't have funerals" (22). The insistence on not hearing moaning, and characterization of moaning as the definitive marker of black mourning, forestalls inquiry into the kinds of mourning that persist past the funeral. In *Go Down, Moses,* however, Faulkner confronts racial difference in mourning head-on, no longer limiting himself to the keening that white people hear from a distance.

"All of Hit": Beyond Voice

In the final, titular story of *Go Down, Moses,* Samuel, the lost son of the Beauchamp line, returns home by train in a casket after being executed for the murder of a Chicago policeman. In Mississippi his body is greeted by "more than a dozen cars" and "Negroes and whites both . . . idle white men and youths and small boys and probably half a hundred Negroes, men and women too" (363). The solemnity of the occasion, as Samuel's body returns to the plantation on which his great-grandfather was a slave, offers ample reason for critics to read "Go Down, Moses" as a resolution to the generations of conflict between the white and black lines of the McCaslin-Beauchamp family.[2] The grandeur of Samuel's homecoming—an expensive coffin, flowers, and a vehicle procession—seems fitting, not for the dead man himself, since he appeared in the text only briefly before his execution, but for the heir of a racial and familial identity of such complexity.

But reading the final story in such a way requires that one disregard the signs that the family narrative gives way to the professional production of mourning. The undertaker's men exhibit an abrupt, businesslike manner as they "snatched the wreaths and floral symbols of man's ultimate and inevitable end briskly out and slid the casket in and flung the flowers back and clapped-to the door" (363). A white lawyer, Gavin Stevens, works to ensure the return and proper burial of Samuel's body in hopes that the family of the dead man will receive consolation from these acts. Just as he attempts to shield the dead man's grandmother from news of Samuel's crime, so too he lies about the cost of the funeral arrangements. But the reader is not so shielded. Stevens outdoes the "twenty-five dollars in frayed bills and coins ranging down to nickels and dimes and pennies" (359) that the family produces: "Stevens passed from store to store and office to office about the square—merchant and clerk, proprietor and employee, doctor dentist lawyer and barber—with his set and rapid speech: 'It's to bring a dead nigger home. It's for Miss Worsham. Never mind about a paper to sign: just give me a dollar. Or half a dollar then. Or a quarter then'" (360). This is not really about the dead man. Stevens obscures the object of his solicitation, knowing that "Miss Worsham" will get more contributions than "a dead nigger," and as a result it is money, not mourning, that comes to the foreground in his story. As Stevens tells the town newspaper editor: "It will cost about two hundred. . . . I'll get something out of Carothers Edmonds the first time I catch him; I dont know how much, but something. And maybe fifty around the square. But the rest of it is you and me, because she insisted on leaving twenty-five with me, which is just twice what I tried to persuade her it would cost and just exactly four times what she can afford to pay—" (359). Stevens performs the solicitation of funds with all the pageantry that a traditional elegist would assume in cataloging funeral flowers.

Samuel's death provides Faulkner with an opportunity to extend his study of mourning to a time contemporaneous with the publication of his novel, when professionalized mourning has become part of mainstream culture.[3] In "Go Down, Moses," however, commercial intervention is not simply an effect of capitalist enterprise but rather a means of avoiding a direct look at the family relations and social systems that identify Samuel as a member of Stevens's own community. In supporting a lavish funeral, the white business owners buy into the elaborate preparations common in African American culture, derived from West African worship of the ancestor, but they do so for fear not of an ancestor-ghost's resentment but of the dead's surviving community.[4] In "Go Down, Moses," Faulkner considers rather pointedly the way in which the preoccupation with funeral arrangements obscures the larger social implications of a death. Readers and businessmen want closure, but the grieving family may not. What matters is not the presence of flowers and the crowds who gather to witness the burial but rather the motivations of those who engineer such moments of homecoming, grief, and publicity.

Both Faulkner and his critics express interest in the white characters' incomprehension; the narrative lingers on Stevens's attempts to figure out what he misunderstood about Beauchamp's situation. At the story's end, as he reflects on his hand in arranging the funeral for Samuel Beauchamp, he "realizes" that he misread Mollie Beauchamp's desires for her grandson's burial. After learning from the newspaper editor that Mollie insisted she wanted her grandson's story in the paper, "All of hit" (365), Stevens reassesses his initial instincts to protect her from news that her grandson was hanged for murder. He need not have attempted to shield her from news of her grandson's crime and execution because "*she doesn't care how he died. She just wanted him home*" (365; italics in original). As a send-up of Stevens's elaborate chivalry, it is a satisfying end to the story, since it acknowledges the white lawyer's inability to read the ancient black woman and yet it lays claim to a final moment of understanding between them. But Stevens's realization, even if correct,[5] calls into question the accuracy of other assumptions he makes about the desires of the bereaved. Despite his first mistaken assumption, Stevens goes on to assert, "*She wanted him to come home right. She wanted that casket and those flowers and the hearse and she wanted to ride through town behind it in a car*" (365; italics in original). If Mollie discarded eulogy for the truth in print, one might wonder whether she did indeed desire the funeral trappings, since other characters stepped in to define the terms of her grandson's burial.

When Miss Worsham, the white woman who employs Mollie's brother, intervenes, her conversation with Stevens illustrates the transformation of antebellum slave-owner relations to contemporary nostalgic "family" concerns, which ultimately find expression in financial terms. Miss Worsham sat "on the hard chair where the old Negress had sat," claiming a kinship with Mollie that transcends race: "Mollie and I were born in the same month. We grew up together as sisters would" (357). And yet Miss Worsham substitutes her own concerns for Mollie's, claiming a family bond that is mixed with unmistakable racial paternalism as she attempts to preserve the dignity of a black family that had once belonged to her own. From Miss Worsham come the requests for the return of the body and for a nice coffin, as she presses Stevens with the weight of family obligations, both Mollie's and her own: "He is the only child of her oldest daughter, her own dead first child. He must come home.... He is her grandson, Mr Stevens. When she took him to raise, she gave him my father's name—Samuel Worsham. Not just a box, Mr Stevens" (358). Samuel Beauchamp cannot be buried in "just a box" because he bears the name of Miss Worsham's father. The Worsham and Beauchamp ties extend beyond shared childhood to the long-ago ownership that produced such a childhood.

In emphasizing Samuel's homecoming one must overlook both the terms of the financial transactions that drive the return of his body to Mississippi and the rather striking protests throughout the story by both Samuel and Mollie Beauchamp. When asked how, if his family did not know of his whereabouts, Samuel expected to "get home," he replied, "What will that matter to me?" (352). In her recent study of African American burial practices, Karla F. C. Holloway observes that "those who died in the North were very often buried and funeralized in the South—reflecting the facts of generation and origin of black communities in the United States" (142). But Samuel Beauchamp's ready dismissal of the consolation of returning "home" introduces a note of skepticism about funeral protocol, one of the many ways in which Faulkner uses his final story to encourage readers to reconsider assumptions about death and burial practices, particularly among African Americans.

Mollie Beauchamp did not approach Stevens in order to arrange for a funeral: "I dont know whar he is. I just knows Pharaoh got him. And you the Law. I wants to find my boy" (354). Mollie's rather cryptic announcement points to a problem among family members: she blames the current McCaslin plantation owner, Roth Edmonds, for exiling her grandson—Edmonds's cousin—from the plantation after a series of misdeeds. Finding Samuel, reclaiming him, and identifying Roth's responsibility in the matter appear to be at the forefront of her concerns. Whether or not Stevens is right to assume that Mollie would like an elaborate funeral for her grandson,[6] he fails to recognize the ways in which funerals offer opportunity not only to lay the dead to rest but also to use grief to challenge the living conditions of those left behind. Thus he attempts to comfort Mollie Beauchamp with "He'll be home the day after tomorrow" (361). Unconsciously echoing her grandson's resistance to the conflation of body and personhood, Mollie spurns Stevens's comfort, replying, "He dead.... Pharaoh got him" (361). Her rebuttal becomes the central theme of a call and response that passes between Mollie and her brother:

> "Sold my Benjamin," she said. "Sold him in Egypt."
> "Sold him in Egypt," Worsham said.
> "Roth Edmonds sold my Benjamin."
> "Sold him to Pharaoh."
> "Sold him to Pharaoh and now he dead." (362)[7]

Mollie's sister-in-law joins them, "a true constant soprano which ran without words beneath the strophe and antistrophe of the brother and sister" (363). The two white observers, excluded from this family cry, respond by fleeing or attempting to silence the mourning hymn that mingles accusation with grief and interprets Samuel's fate through the legacy of slavery.[8]

Mollie's biblical language conjures the McCaslin family history that plays out over *Go Down, Moses* and yet looks beyond it, fitting it within a larger narrative that swallows up the grandiose claims of the McCaslin family. To the lawyer, Samuel is simply "a bad son of a bad father" (357), but to Mollie, who nursed Roth Edmonds along with her own children, the trouble is fraternal rather than paternal. Stevens's ignorance of such relations is made explicit when he considers Mollie and her brother, Hamp: "They were like that. You could know two of them for years; they might even have worked for you for years, bearing different names. Then suddenly you learn by pure chance that they are brothers or sisters" (354). In drawing a racial boundary between his own sense of family relations and "they" who were simply "like that," Stevens fails to remember that the "different names" are derived from the masters of generations past, when slave ownership, as much as blood ties, defined "family." Mollie's mourning cry, however, reflects an awareness of this more complex system of familial relations, as well as the many reasons for grieving that go beyond her grandson's death. The "all" that Mollie wanted in the newspaper would include not just Samuel's conviction for murder but also his cousin's wrongdoing in banishing him from the plantation in the first place. By rejecting Gavin Stevens's consolation that her grandson's body will be coming home, Mollie resists the lawyer's attempts to limit mourning to the preparation of the dead body. In her grief, shared by her brother and sister-in-law, she puts Samuel's actions in context, making public the other betrayals that preceded the crime for which he was executed. Although Stevens acts as though burying Samuel Beauchamp will answer Mollie's accusations, in this story of Mollie's mourning Faulkner presages the role that funerals would soon play during the civil rights movement in shifting the emphasis from laying the dead to rest to inciting a commitment to change in the living.

When, in 1955, Emmett Till's mother chose not only to leave her son's casket open for fifty-five thousand people to pay their respects but also to invite black magazines to photograph his mutilated corpse, she did so "so that the world could see what they had done to my child" (Holloway 25). As Holloway explains, the tradition of an open casket was common in nineteenth-century America, and it was, in turn, in accord with West African funeral traditions that involved paying visits out of respect to the dead and his or her family. But as the twentieth century unfolded, "the tradition also represented a different kind of memorializing, as it recognized specific evidence of the racialized violence done to black bodies" (25). Mamie Till Bradley, like Faulkner's Mollie Beauchamp, met her boy's body at the train station, a homecoming (this time from Mississippi to Chicago rather than Chicago to Mississippi) that attracted almost as much attention as did the funeral.[9] As Till Bradley later recalled of that reunion at the station, "I looked up, saw that box, and I just screamed, 'Oh, God. Oh, God. My only boy.' And I kept screaming, as the cameras kept flashing, in one long explosive moment that would be captured for the morning edition" (qtd. in Suzanne Smith 127). As she responded to a horrific personal loss, Till Bradley simultaneously attended to the resonance of her grief on a national stage: "I knew that if they walked by the casket, if people opened the pages of *Jet* magazine and the *Chicago Defender*, if other people could see it with their *own* eyes, then together we might find a way to express what we had seen. It was important to do that, I thought, to help people recognize the horrible problems we were facing in the South" (qtd. in Suzanne Smith 127). As Mamie Till Bradley appreciated the way that such media attention might be used for the benefit of African Americans all over the country, she began to reshape her mourning around a new goal: not consolation through burial and a return home but a turn outward in the face of such private loss in order to advance a greater social cause. Like Emmett Till's mother, Faulkner's Mollie Beauchamp insists on having "hit all in de paper. All of hit" (365). The publication of the details of her grandson's death will likely contribute less to the consolation that Stevens has in mind than the social movement of which Mamie Till Bradley was so aware that she and her son were a part.

Less than two weeks after Emmett Till's murder, the *New York Herald Tribune* published a statement that Faulkner dispatched from Rome, where he was traveling for the State Department. He challenged Mississippians to condemn such crimes, but he did so with the underlying prod that the refusal "to present to the world one homogeneous and unbroken front" would result in the rise of "other Aryan peoples who are already the Western world's enemies because of political ideologies" (*ESPL* 222–23). Faulkner's emphatic condemnation of Till's murder provided good material for advancing the Cold War efforts of the United States.[10] Perhaps because of his own use of Till's death to advance national causes, Faulkner was sensitive to the strident criticism that Till Bradley and others in her position would come under for taking their grief public. In "Letter to a Northern Editor," published in *Life* in 1956, Faulkner describes a letter written to him by a black woman: "It went on to say that the Till boy got exactly what he asked for, coming down there with his Chicago ideas, and that all his mother wanted was to make money out of the role of her bereavement. Which sounds exactly like the white people in the South who justified and even defended the crime by declining to find that it was one" (*ESPL* 90). His defense of Till Bradley recognizes the role of the mourner as fraught cultural ground.[11]

Although the concluding story in *Go Down, Moses* prefigures Mamie Till Bradley's demand that the public acknowledge her son's lynching, it stands in marked contrast to the novel's opening dedication to Faulkner's own black "mammy," Caroline Barr, in which he offers a more traditional portrait of black motherhood. Judith Sensibar has chronicled Faulkner's lordly behavior when Barr died. Like his character Gavin Stevens, Faulkner assumed a proprietary air in making the funeral arrangements, and he ignored the claims of her biological family and her community, fixating solely on her role as his childhood nurse and that of his daughter, Jill. He offered the eulogy in a service held in his home and had the words "Her white children bless her" inscribed on her gravestone (Sensibar 100). In other words, he followed antebellum plantation traditions. Although many if not most slave graves were unmarked, favored "mammies" were routinely buried near their masters, with a headstone of their own (Henderson 74). Eugene Genovese records one antebellum funeral of a mammy for which the plantation owner led her funeral procession and ordered everyone on his plantation to walk out and witness. The performance of public mourning in these situations makes clear that, although the individuals mourned on the plantations were black, "These funerals, moving as they were, were for the whites" (Genovese 196).

Faulkner's eulogy for Barr echoes the historical accounts of antebellum culture, but it also mirrors a genre of fiction, "plantation literature," in which southern chivalry and plantation culture were romanticized and defended. A standard trope in this genre is a scene at the grave of a beloved "mammy" figure in which the narrative affirms strong emotional ties between masters and slaves and humanizes the figure of the plantation owner. In a recent study of this strain of sentimental literature, Desiree Henderson analyzes the proslavery use of the slave funeral in Caroline Lee Hentz's novel *The*

Planter's Northern Bride (1854). In Hentz's novel, her narrator notes of the dying slave woman, Dilsy, that "it was on the face of her master she gazed, with such an expression of affection, gratitude, and humility combined that his answering glance was dimmed with tears" (qtd. in Henderson 81). This literature might be usefully contrasted with the abolitionists' use of the slave burial in fiction as a site of renewed dedication to the fight for freedom.

Faulkner's treatment of mourning breaks over different modes of fictional characterizations of African American grief—modes that reflect and reinforce a larger political and cultural battle as they prioritize either the white southerner's humanity or the black southerner's autonomy. "Go Down, Moses" carries the marks of both literary strains. Faulkner includes a mammy figure, Molly Beauchamp, in his stories, and yet he shifts the object of mourning from the mammy to a young man who died a violent death, indicating that the beloved mammy figure of nineteenth-century fiction has always had sons and grandsons who bore the brunt of the violence even as she stayed near the white plantation home as a witness to both worlds. Thadious Davis evaluates Faulkner's role in Barr's funeral as "performative; it was an enactment of his relationship to her and a performance of his ability to naturalize her place as a race-marked mammy who attended to the white Faulkner family. Beyond her raced bodily functions and symbolizations, Faulkner cannot go" (193). But in this last assessment Davis is mistaken. Stevens's awkwardness in "Go Down, Moses" and his incomprehension in the face of black mourning suggest that Faulkner reconsidered his role at the head of Barr's funeral entourage. His management of this final story as he focuses the narrative through white eyes, this time to see black mourners and not white ones, signals a new attentiveness to alternative claims to grief.

What Faulkner recognizes in "Go Down, Moses," in ways that he did not at "Mammie" Callie's funeral, is that even in grief, the racial structures of the South prioritize the voice of the white mourner over the black one. For readers and critics who adopt a substitutionary model of elegy, in which language takes the place of the dead, Samuel Beauchamp is to be returned home so that the narrative descriptions of expense and effort can attest to Samuel's loss. The voice of the elegist will, however, be that of the white Gavin Stevens rather than Beauchamp's grandmother, a fact that should give readers pause. The insistence on language as the medium of mourning leads critics, most notably John Matthews, to conclude that by the end of Faulkner's novel, the modes of mourning have been "hollowed out" (Matthews 272). Stevens's elegiac overtures are, indeed, hollow, emphasizing resolution at the cost of truth and fellow feeling. But in his attention to Mollie Beauchamp's cryptic requests, biblical allusions, and silencing, Faulkner abandons elegiac consolation so that he can lament the cultural forces that keep black expressions of grief at bay.

In "Go Down, Moses," much as in Woolf's *The Waves,* the voice of the dominant elegist is preserved as evidence of the obstacles of social convention. But Faulkner traces the attempts of other mourners to find modes of expression that skirt the dominant voice. Mollie Beauchamp's call-and-response drowns out Stevens's consolation and drives him from the room. Her actions suggest that a more radical elegiac imagination can be found by acknowledging the presence of modes of mourning that are of social as well as literary significance. What if, Faulkner suggests, elegy is not literature that uses language to obviate loss but rather literature that records the mourning of others in both words and deeds? His turn toward the social and public ramifications of loss, away from the insistence on linguistic art, takes the pressure off literature to replace or offer solace for the dead and to enact resolution. Instead, it lays claim to literature's role in tracing the influence of grief on social space, articulating what too often remains undocumented and unimagined, and fighting to acknowledge duration and complexity in mourning. There is room in Faulkner's narrative for insistent, difficult, frustrated grief, not only mourning that will most quickly resolve racial and familial tension.

"But Dese Hyar Yuther Boys": Beyond Endurance

Long before Mamie Till Bradley's bereavement, funerals served as a dramatic stage for African Americans to articulate concerns about the larger culture. Despite fears of insurrection, the majority of plantation owners allowed their slaves to gather for funerals (Genovese 195). Eugene Genovese explains, however, that such actions reflected "considerations of interest and policy quite as much as considerations of humanity" (196). The planters intended to give the "wounded feelings" of the mourners time to subside, but many black mourners used funerals to link those feelings to a new sense of communal purpose (196). A 1709 letter from a merchant in Jamaica to a member of Parliament in London includes "a speech made by a black of Gardaloupe, at the funeral of a fellow-negro" (Letter from a Merchant 16). The slave's speech, in which he challenges the institution of slavery, takes place at the grave of a slave who had been murdered by his master for stealing a loaf of bread (3–4). Though the surviving slave offered no conventional poetic elegy, it is not difficult to see how one man's death fueled the survivor's speech, earning the latter a wider and more attentive audience than he could expect otherwise.

Slave owners were less concerned with angry words than with the violent revolts that developed out of such expressions of criticism and ambition. In 1687 a plot for the extermination of white Virginians was discovered in Westmoreland County, sending waves of unease through slaveholding regions in the South. The plans for this extermination were formed during mass funerals held for slaves (Aptheker 166). Gabriel's Rebellion, organized in 1800 by a Richmond blacksmith named Gabriel Prosser and his brother Martin, a slave preacher, was also organized at slave funerals and secret religious meetings. These events were followed by Nat Turner's famous rebellion in 1831, with funerals again cited as the means of hatching the plot (Henderson 73; Genovese 194). Funerals were used for planning because they offered a rare opportunity for slaves from different plantations to congregate. But at funerals African Americans also marshaled resources that many have overlooked in their quest for consolation and what Freud calls the "productive" work of mourning. Grief over the dead enables mourners to see the world anew, and it is this new sight that many African American mourners seized. Though such new sight is no replacement for loss, it is a legacy of bereavement as well as a catalyst: it enables one to get distance from things as they are in order to see, articulate, and fight for a world that is as it should be.

It is this last possibility, the action that follows new vision, that troubled the white planters. Although slaves were frequently forced to witness slave executions, such "lessons" about the cost of rebellion could backfire. When six black men were executed for involvement in Gabriel's Rebellion, mounted militia were called in to prevent the crowds from rushing the gallows. As Douglas Egerton notes, "There was always danger in bringing together large numbers of grieving bondpeople" (151). Fear of the potent mix of oppression and grief led Virginia authorities to ban public funerals for slaves in 1687; their counterparts in New York, a century later, limited the number of attendant mourners to twelve (Genovese 194). As is clear in Faulkner's *Go Down, Moses* story "Pantaloon in Black," however, it only takes one bereaved individual to bring about the violence that those in power fear.

"Pantaloon in Black" remains something of an outlier in Faulkner's novel, as it sets aside plantation concerns to speak to the burgeoning commercial opportunities for African Americans in the early 1940s. Like Woolf, who cleaved the story of Clarissa Dalloway's party with Septimus Smith's suicide, Faulkner divides the McCaslin narrative of *Go Down, Moses* with the story of Rider.[12] Just as Septimus's character drew the effects of the First World War into focus in *Mrs. Dalloway*, Rider makes racial injustice visible outside the plantation "family" dynamics that frequently temper social interactions in Faulkner's fictional Yoknapatawpha County. He does so despite significant narrative limitations. Rider's "character-space," to return to Alex Woloch's terms, is curbed by his place outside the McCaslin-Beauchamp chronicle, and unlike other elegists, whose voices are amplified by illustrious subjects, he mourns only his wife.[13] Recent critics of elegy have argued over the significance of the Orpheus myth in the elegiac tradition, with Melissa Zeiger arguing that Orpheus's attempts to reclaim his wife from death make him a powerful elegiac predecessor, since his "ambiguously successful war against mortality depends upon a poetic power to which death itself seemingly gives him further access" (11). Peter Sacks, however, would consider Rider, like Orpheus, an "unsuccessful mourner" because he "insists on rescuing his *actual* wife rather than a figure or substitute for her" (72). Rider's object of mourning would appear to limit his potential for resonant and successful mourning, as would his tendency to maintain an almost unbroken silence throughout his narrative. Though Jacob Flanders's discordant words in *Jacob's Room* and Addie Bundren's narrative eruption in *As I Lay Dying* help them lay claim to narrative significance, in Rider Faulkner makes a bid for narrative space through action rather than voice.

It is ironic that Rider finds little room for domestic loss within a novel that many read as a family saga. Richard Godden and Noel Polk consider "Go Down, Moses" and "Pantaloon in Black" "two exemplary and parallel white misunderstandings of black grief in response to violent death" (331), and yet Rider's actions elicit incomprehension on both sides of the color line. "Pantaloon in Black" opens with Rider standing at his wife's grave, newly a widower. Although he is initially joined by his family and friends in his grief, each verbal or physical exchange that follows divides him from those who surround him: he strikes a fellow mill worker who offers to relieve him of his shovel, he shrugs off his aunt's attempts to bring him to her house for a meal, and he disregards his friend's urging to drink away his sorrows in the company of his mill crew.

Although "expressive emotionalism was the most distinctive feature of the African American funeral" (Suzanne Smith 85), Rider expresses little at the gravesite. His actions, however, prompt revelations from the other mourners present. Rider's determination to return home after the funeral causes a fellow black mill worker to say "what he had not intended to say, what he had never conceived of himself saying in circumstances like these, even though everybody knew it": "You dont wants ter go back dar. She be wawkin yit" (132). Rider's seeming obliviousness to beliefs about spirits prompts the other man to make explicit assumptions about the dead who "either will not or cannot quit the earth yet although the flesh they once lived in has been returned to it, let the preachers tell and reiterate and affirm how they left it not only without regret but with joy, mounting toward glory" (132). It is an unusual revelation about the practices of grief in African American culture in the first half of the twentieth century, since it makes explicit the distance between what is believed and what is said.[14]

The mill worker's exclamation, bursting from him with great reluctance after Rider seems oblivious to the rules of mourning, makes clear the significance of exploring not only the forms of mourning that are spoken—and, in Mollie Beauchamp's and Till Bradley's cases, politicized—but also those that remain largely unspoken. If, as Faulkner's story indicates, many different cultures of mourning are at play at one time—West African beliefs running alongside the practices of Christianity—then Rider may not need to utter the emotions of grief so much as force others to articulate the social conventions that bind him. Faulkner makes clear that Rider's silence is the result of others' attempts to keep mourning within particular religious and cultural bounds. When his uncle offers him the traditional words "De Lawd guv, and He tuck away," Rider responds with a challenge: "What Mannie ever done ter Him?" (140). The uncle's subsequent "Hush" prefigures Miss Worsham's "Hush" in "Go Down, Moses" when Mollie, in an ironic parallel, calls on biblical language for her own grief. Both responses, of course, echo the "hush" that passes from adults to children in *The Sound and the Fury* as respect for the mourners at Damuddy's funeral becomes infused with competition for control.

Whereas early elegists sought consolation by concluding with an affirmation of religious transcendence, Rider punctuates his narrative with challenges to God. He turns from the Christian mourning practices of his community to half-buried West African traditions and beliefs. Faulkner's narrator records that the cemetery where Mannie is buried is littered with "shards of pottery and broken bottles and old brick and other objects insignificant to sight but actually of a profound meaning and fatal to touch, which no white man could have read" (132). It is in funeral practices that the cultural transmission from Africa appears most strongly in America (Henderson 74), which Faulkner intuited in marking Mannie's grave and Rider's grief with traces of a culture that has been erased or covered over with Christian convention in most literary treatments of African American burial and mourning. Robert Farris Thompson links the broken pottery covering African American graves in Mississippi, Georgia, and South Carolina to the burial practices of the Bakongo culture of northern Angola, in which the pottery stands as a marker of the body broken by death; Thompson notes that the practice is not found among white Americans of the same regions (Genovese 200).

Marilyn Yalom marks the frequent use of objects associated with water—conch shells, cups, vases—on graves as markers of the Bakongo belief that the dead pass through "a watery expanse" on their way to the afterlife. She also records the presence of objects believed to be the last that the dead person touched in his or her life: "In our trip through the South we found teacups, mugs, and even a bikini placed on African American graves" (35). Although Faulkner's narrator indicates that he either will not or cannot understand the significance of the items left at the gravesites, the narrative implicitly acknowledges these African beliefs. "Pantaloon in Black" is filled with reminders of the things Mannie has touched shortly before her death. The story opens with Rider standing in "the worn, faded clean overalls which Mannie herself had washed only a week ago" (131), and as Rider walks home from the funeral the narrator notes that, beneath the marks of horses and wagons going to and from church, "vanished but not gone, fixed and held in the annealing dust, [were] the narrow, splay-toed prints of his wife's bare feet" (133). Rider does not place items on Mannie's grave, but through Faulkner's narrator the reader sees them in the world she left behind.

In poring over transcribed interviews of rural African Americans who retained African folk beliefs, Yalom found one woman's explanation of grave decoration particularly compelling: "'Dey use tuh put duh tings a pussen use las on duh grabe. Dis wuz suppose tuh satisfy duh spirit an keep it from followin yuh back tuh duh house.' The conviction that 'the spirit don't stay in the grave,' as one man put it, and is capable of working evil was one of the most persistent beliefs found among coastal blacks" (125).[15] It is, in fact, precisely in hopes that his dead wife will be "wawkin" that Rider returns home. His desire to be reunited with her in death echoes African cosmologies in which "the dead and the living are never separated from one another but are, in fact, always intimately connected" (Suzanne Smith 19). At the time of Caroline Barr's death, her relatives were dismayed that Faulkner ignored "local black rituals" (Sensibar 107), but in his novel he retains vestiges of his early education under her. Faulkner's daughter reported that Barr was "a bit of a witch. It had something to do with her ancestry—something that ran on the female side of the family. I think it was voodoo, not a witch" (qtd. in Sensibar 47). As one white writer notes in a 1932 issue of the *Georgia Historical Quarterly*, "So firm a hold upon the youthful mind have the things we learned in childhood, few of those brought up with Negro nurses are really free of every vestige of superstition" (qtd. in Genovese 217). The indifference and ignorance of Faulkner's white characters and narrators in *Go Down, Moses* fail to erase substantial evidence of African American beliefs and practices in "Pantaloon." The early indications in "Pantaloon" that multiple systems of belief are at play prepare the ground for new interpretations of Rider's actions after Mannie's burial. Like Molly Beauchamp's spirituals, the grave ornaments and beliefs about wandering spirits mark ways out of the social relations that have so hobbled Rider and others in his community.

Because Rider manifests his grief in ways that depart from his community's traditions, his actions are particularly susceptible to misreading, a vulnerability that becomes apparent in the second half of the story. There Faulkner swaps the sympathetic narrator of the first half for a deputy sheriff who is eager to turn Rider's violent death into a comedy to tell his wife as she prepares dinner. Like Clarissa Dalloway's musings on Septimus Smith's suicide in *Mrs. Dalloway,* the deputy's story manifests the elegy's uneasy balance between narrating the loss of the dead and showcasing the linguistic gifts of the elegist. In Faulkner's rendering, the deputy's storytelling ostentatiously suffocates the story of Rider's death; the reader learns of Rider's fate in an aside within the sentence "After it was over . . . the sheriff's deputy . . . was telling his wife about it" (149). Faulkner's framing techniques ensure that the reader appreciates the contrast between Rider's silent action and the deputy's eagerness to be noticed through storytelling. As the deputy's wife moves from one room to another, carrying dishes from the kitchen to the dining room, "The deputy raised his voice a little to carry the increased distance" (150). Since his wife spends much of the story's duration in the dining room, most of the tale is told at high volume, underscoring the effort of narration. The deputy's wife repeatedly interrupts her husband to express her irritation with him, and she uses his rhetorical flourishes to undercut his authority: his "Now you take this one today" is met with "I wish you would. . . . Take him out of my kitchen, anyway. You sheriffs! Sitting around that courthouse all day long, talking" (150–51). Whereas Rider expresses his grief through relentless action, the deputy's wife characterizes her husband as a man whose own inaction makes him ill-suited to interpret Rider's story. In the famous *Go Down, Moses* story "The Bear," the men who mourn the dead dog Lion pay their respects by "squatting and standing in the warm and drowsing sunlight, talking quietly of hunting, of the game and the dogs which ran it, of hounds and bear and deer and men of yesterday vanished from the earth" (238). Rider's story, however, suggests a grief that is not assuaged by storytelling.

Susan Donaldson registers disappointment with the conclusion to "Pantaloon," as Rider's grief is "brought under control and confined through the storytelling efforts of the sheriff's deputy" (145), but it is precisely in undermining the significance of storytelling—through a focus on action, emotion, and calculation—that Rider's story of resistance is so successful. The deputy may tell the story, but it is clear that Rider contrived the events in the story that the deputy tells. Rider contributes to a larger body of working-class black resistance that Robin Kelley traces in the 1930s and 1940s: women singing hymns of protest in factories where they are not allowed to talk, housekeepers who quit just before an employer's social event, and bus riders who ring the bell on the bus to protest the driver's racist behavior (76). Kelley's work extends Herbert Aptheker's much earlier study of black protest, *American Negro Slave Revolts,* which, as Kelley notes, makes a point of not merely identifying acts of rebellion "but also showing how their opposition shaped all of antebellum southern society, politics, and daily life" (Kelley 77). Kelley's work highlights the struggles for freedom that took place between—not merely during—the Civil War and the civil rights movement. He also sets working-class action against the historical record that privileges "the public utterances of black elites" (76). Faulkner's story contributes to this discussion in distinguishing Rider's silent action from the insistence on storytelling and verbal memorial that dominates the discussion of public mourning, both in literature and in reality.

"Pantaloon" opens with Rider "flinging the dirt with that effortless fury so that the mound seemed to be rising of its own volition, not built up from above but thrusting visibly upward out of the earth itself" (131). Rider's feats of strength and desperation continue throughout the book, fueled by what readers are led to presume is an overpowering grief for his wife. But when the deputy sheriff rehearses the scene later in the story, he criticizes Rider's energy: "His wife dies on him. All right. But does he grieve? He's the biggest and busiest man at the funeral. Grabs a shovel before they even got the box into the grave they tell me, and starts throwing dirt onto her faster than a slip scraper could have done it" (150). Although Rider followed African American tradition by contributing to the work of burying his wife,[16] the deputy uses Rider's situation to lecture on "them damn niggers," concluding that "they aint human.... When it comes to the normal human feelings and sentiments of human beings, they might just as well be a damn herd of wild buffaloes" (149–50). For the deputy, labor and emotion are mutually exclusive. Numerous critics have folded "Pantaloon in Black" into discussions of economic policies and race relations in the South,[17] particularly as evincing a migration of black labor from agriculture to new industrial employment. But though Rider's situation reflects many larger social and economic movements in the first half of the twentieth century, the relationship between his grief and his labor gets lost in the emphasis on economic policy.

Rider's grief enables him to create a new purpose for the physical strength that is the preoccupation of both the story's narrators. At the same time, by using the deputy sheriff to revisit the story's opening scene, Faulkner draws attention to the ways that testaments to the humanity of African Americans are frequently built on their performance of mourning at the gravesite of a loved one. Desiree Henderson argues: "If . . . slave cemeteries are largely forgotten or lost in the geographic contours of the American nation, they are remarkably present in the textual spaces of American literature. This is particularly true of the abolitionist writing of the mid-nineteenth century. . . . The slave cemetery is used to stage a moment in time and space in which there may be a restructuring of relations between masters and slaves, an opportunity for whites to recognize the humanity of slaves and for slaves to demonstrate their humanity through their capacity for mourning" (70). The tropes of abolitionist literature resonate long after slavery is abolished, and the African American gravesite becomes marked not only with the shards of glass that reveal the traces of African funeral rites but also the expectation that a black mourner perform his humanity on that occasion. Faulkner's first narrator characterizes Rider's behavior in terms that never stray from the widower's physical strength, particularly the power with which Rider labors at grief as he works at the sawmill. The first narrator therefore sketches the black performance of grief that lies at the heart of the abolitionist propaganda of the preceding century. Faulkner's second narrator, however, uses the same behavior to call Rider's humanity into question, inserting a very different voice into the literary readings of African American grief.

Eric Sundquist has argued that in *Go Down, Moses* "Faulkner is moving further away from his own early 'modernism' and placing himself, deliberately or not, more clearly in the tradition of classic nineteenth-century American fiction" (113). Sundquist has in mind the ritualized hunt and frontier humor that many see as the main arc of *Go Down Moses*, as well as Faulkner's report that he was reading *Moby-Dick* while writing his novel, but we also see the effects of other genres of nineteenth-century literature: the plantation romance that serves as an apologia for that system and the abolitionist literature that so earnestly seeks to "humanize" the black man, even at the cost of putting his most painful emotions on public display. In navigating the slippery terrain of the African American grave in literature, the presence of those broken shells and bottles in Faulkner's story once again prove useful. By acknowledging the African American cemetery, which Henderson describes as the "forgotten and unrecorded spaces, a profound absence in the historical record" (75), Faulkner indicates that Rider will not play the role required for a sentimental abolitionist narrative, which has at its heart a scene at a cemetery that looks very much like a

Euro-American one. Instead, the grave markers in Faulkner's story lay claim to different traditions, both funereal and literary, and they make space for Rider's seemingly unconventional expressions of grief. Faulkner's fiction exposes the abolitionist literature's "slave cemetery" as a political and rhetorical prop, and his attention to the particular cultural markers of the cemetery in which Mannie is buried indicate that Faulkner is inclined to hew more closely to life both in the details of the cemetery and in the emotional responses of the mourner.

Faulkner's Rider does not embrace the abolitionist-literature precedent, even as the accusations of Faulkner's deputy sheriff make clear the stakes of not performing as expected. As the deputy tells his wife the story of Rider's murder of a white man, escape from prison, and eventual lynching, he reinterprets the first part of the story, reading Rider's actions as inhumane: "So he comes to work . . . when McAndrews and everybody else expected him to take the day off since even a nigger couldn't want no better excuse for a holiday than he had just buried his wife, when a white man would have took the day off out of pure respect no matter how he felt about his wife, when even a little child would have had sense enough to take a day off when he would still get paid for it too. But not him" (151). The storyteller's excesses tempt the deputy into making explicit links among economy, emotion, and social status. Just as Rider's earlier unconventionality prompted revelations about belief in walking spirits, here it forces those around him to make explicit the expectations about labor that haunt the black individual, even in postslavery times. The deputy's crude outline relies on a clear link between the suspension of work and respect for the dead, but Rider's actions indicate that he rejects any attempts to tie his physical labor to his grief.

Rider surprises his fellow mill workers by returning to work the morning after his wife's funeral but leaves abruptly before his shift is over, despite being called back by his white foreman. He shows the same disregard to the bootlegger who attempts to limit his purchase of alcohol on grounds that "This is Monday. Aint you all running this week?" (142).[18] Finally, he confounds the deputy, who thinks only in terms of excuses for laying off work under the pretext of grieving. Rider's actions appear erratic, but when considered together they bring into relief the Scylla and Charybdis of social convention; Rider will not use absence from work as a means of signaling to others the depth of his grief, nor will he allow a workhorse mentality to define him. He exhibits a seemingly inexhaustible vigor, and yet he balks at others' attempts to make that vigor productive.

Mourning, in the deputy's calculation, carries the value of a day off work, a value that is of interest to the larger community, since "he would still get paid for it too" (151). Like the "frayed bills and coins ranging down to nickels and dimes and pennies" that fill the narrative frame of "Go Down, Moses" and push grief into the ground, the economic value of Rider's labor looms large, particularly since he refuses to be paid off (359). Here Faulkner gets into new territory, exploring not only how sharecropping and other economic systems carry traces of slavery—a subject cogently argued by Richard Godden—but also how the contemporary social system assumes control over not only the physical labor of the black population but also what we might call their affective labor as well. Although Godden argues that "it would be a mistake to cast Rider as the master of his own infringements. He is a body out of control" (91), it is precisely the body—here, the black body—that Faulkner nudges the reader to see as a means of resisting control.

By not participating in the exchange of paid leave for conventional mourning, Rider registers his rejection not only of the value placed on his grief but also of a system that marks out the shape—and limit—of his mourning. He is granted time to mourn, but only within the bounds laid out for him by the white overseer and the representative of the law, much as slaves were once granted time to attend the funerals of loved ones, but only in the dark of night, once the field work was done for the day.[19] In his unwillingness to exchange physical labor for affective labor, Rider reminds the reader that (1) the latter is no more the right of white men to demand than the former, (2) the latter *is* work, and (3) the affective labor would be done for someone else, and not for Rider's own benefit. Faulkner makes clear that the next battle in race relations will be for the black man's ability not only to get a job but also to lay claim to his emotions, his attitudes, and his public presentation.

Grief and economics have long had an uneasy relationship. In the classic text for issues of grief and mourning, Freud's 1917 "Mourning and Melancholia," his clinical definitions are nearly obscured by his frustration with mourning's inefficiency: "Normally, respect for reality gains the day. Nevertheless its orders cannot be obeyed at once. They are carried out bit by bit, at great expense of time and cathectic energy. . . . Why this compromise by which the command of reality is carried out piecemeal should be so extraordinarily painful is not at all easy to explain in terms of economics" (244–45). Repeatedly in his analysis of grief, Freud speaks of the "economics" of mourning, terms that grate against the deliberate unproductivity of Rider's energy. Studies of elegy inevitably fall along Freudian lines: traditional poetic elegy consoled the bereaved until, the story goes, twentieth-century literature rejected consolation, the start of a flirtation between literature and melancholia.[20] In his criticism of Freud's "grief work," Jacques Derrida puts pressure on the implied "success" of such processes: "In the era of psychoanalysis, we all of course speak, and we can always go on speaking, about the 'successful' work of mourning—or, inversely; as if it were precisely the contrary, about a 'melancholia' that would signal the failure of such work" (174).

If reality does not gain the day, as Freud sees it, the alternative is a melancholic state that carries all the expense of mourning but with no end in sight. It is the lack of guaranteed closure—a day away from work that becomes two and three and four—that compels Freud to label such a state pathological and that Rider claims as his prerogative in "Pantaloon in Black." Faulkner's narrative seems designed to get out from underneath the burden of grief work that Freud lays on mourners. But labeling Rider's actions "melancholic" fails to capture the social ramifications of his grief. Faulkner's character refuses to uphold the link between black bodies and labor that would exchange a man's right to grieve in a manner of his choosing for the price of his day off from work. Although recent studies of elegiac literature have struggled to move beyond Freud's classification, Faulkner offers a clear, compelling challenge to that theorist whose shadow reaches not only late into Faulkner's life but also into twenty-first century criticism of Faulkner's work. This despite Faulkner's well-known claim, "What little of psychology I know the characters I have invented and playing poker have taught me. Freud I'm not familiar with" (*FU* 268).

Gambling also furnished Faulkner with the thematic device he needed to set Freud's analysis on its head. Rider's violence appears entirely self-destructive as he runs until exhausted, tests his strength against the logs at the mill, and then turns to whiskey. But in the final stage of his grief, Rider turns social, joining the Saturday-night gambling at the mill before slitting the throat of Birdsong, the nighttime security guard who runs the crooked dice game, for which Rider is lynched by Birdsong's family members. Rider brushes off the inquiries, sympathies, and invitations that are extended to him by his aunt and members of his mill gang, and he ignores his white supervisor's attempts to get him to return to work. But in killing Birdsong, making him account for years in which Birdsong cheated black men of their wages, Rider challenges Freud's characterization of melancholia as entailing a "loss of interest in the outside world" and shows Faulkner to have learned something about human emotion during those poker games (Freud, "Mourning and Melancholia" 244).

Rider's final words to Birdsong mark the difference between his attentions to his own life and those of the other players—all black men: "Ah'm snakebit. Ah kin pass wid anything.... Ah kin pass even wid miss-outs. But dese hyar yuther boys—" (148). Despite being in a state of what appears to be all-absorptive grief, Rider registers an acute understanding of the social significance of his own actions and of the insidious effect Birdsong will have on the other mill workers' economic futures if his crooked game is allowed to continue. With the reference to a "snakebit" man, Faulkner returns to the dynamics of his early story "Red Leaves," in which a slave condemned to die alongside his master takes matters into his own hands (*Collected Stories* 334–35). He will still die, but he will die by a snakebite he invites, rather than by the ritual immolation of his master's property. In "Pantaloon," however, Faulkner propels Rider beyond a desperate grab for autonomy into a larger theater of social resistance. Paul Gilroy has characterized black men's and women's frequenting of blues clubs and dance halls as a defiance of "waged work as ... a form of servitude.... The nighttime becomes the right time, and the space allocated for recovery and recuperation is assertively and provocatively occupied in the pursuit of leisure and pleasure" (274). Faulkner's character Birdsong is part of a system that attempts to profit from black labor both day and night. Rider's actions reclaim the nighttime as a time of deliberate unproductivity. As much as Faulkner's Yoknapatawpha County relies on economic transaction for both its humor and its drama, the author shows just as much interest—if not more—in the ways that people attempt to step outside the daily grind. In Kelley's study of working-class black resistance, he notes that "some of the most intense skirmishes between such blacks and authority erupted during and after weekend gatherings" (86).

Rider is emboldened as much by grief as by alcohol, but his actions reflect those of many others who found weekend nights to be a time in which the work identity is cast off and injustice appears in a new light.

The incomprehension of those who observe Rider's actions attests to the absence of a clear, socially sanctioned form of mourning for the widower. Lynching, however, that form of violence that haunts black men in America with terrible specificity, fits Rider's profile all too well.[21] Although the mass deaths of the First World War serve as the catalyst for Woolf's and Faulkner's elegiac reinvention, *Go Down, Moses* makes clear that the war is not the only occasion for rising casualties; Rider's actions are predicated on the knowledge that his body will join many more during America's peak lynching era. Although he remains isolated in life, Rider insists that his death be read in company with the many other lynching victims who precede him. Amy Louise Wood contests the claim that lynchings tended to take place in rural areas and cultural backwaters: "The most spectacular lynchings took place not in the countryside but in these newly urbanizing places, where mobs hanged their victims from telegraph and telephone poles.... Even the smallest towns were undergoing an urbanization process of sorts.... The expansion of commercial markets for rural crops, as well as the rise of new industries, such as logging and turpentine, brought new kinds of traffic and occupation to towns and cities" (*Lynching* 5–6). Ryder's lynching is, then, both a sign of the changing culture and an example of the attempts to keep African Americans within clearly defined roles despite such changes. Woolf's Septimus Smith and Faulkner's Rider recognize the power of socially recognized roles; although Septimus capitulates to them, Rider attempts to reclaim them for his own uses. Doing so requires that Rider fight his own physical vitality, perhaps Faulkner's bluntest image for the ways in which black labor has defined black individuals.

In creating a character who shuns traditional elegiac and other literary modes of mourning and instead employs a form of violence that inspires particular fear in the African American community, Faulkner posits grief as the force behind not solely literary art but also social reform. That reform may require that one return to earlier models of culture. Suzanne Smith notes that "one of the most striking similarities between the West African death practices and African American slave funerals was the importance of the 'second funeral,' which happened weeks to months—and sometimes as long as a year—after the actual burial. This second funeral, usually celebratory in tone, was considered essential because it allowed all family members to gather to honor the deceased" (29). If Rider's burial of his wife is ostensibly Christian, the shards and shells that mark the grave open up the possibility that, in seeking his own death, Rider is insisting on a second burial—even if it is his own. Early slave owners and transporters had a high stake in grasping precisely which punishments would deter mutiny. They learned that many West African societies did not regard suicide as a profane act, and thus they could not rely on their rebellious slaves' sense of self-preservation to keep them manageable (Egerton 153). Rider's act recognizes the prohibition of suicide as a belief that is not endemic to his culture. His resistance to his aunt's Christian consolation may be prompted by a recognition that the religion's prohibition of suicide goes hand in hand with slave culture's attempts at social control.

Rider's killing of Birdsong is effectively both murder and suicide, and its success relies on the lynching inclinations of the victim's family. It also, significantly, rewrites the terms of Faulkner's "Dry September," a lynching story that was published ten years earlier. In "Dry September," the lynching mob found its victim, a black man, while he was on duty as a nighttime security guard at an ice plant. One could say Faulkner was simply short on material and drew from his own stint as a night watchman, during which he wrote *As I Lay Dying*. Faulkner's possible identification with any of these fictional watchmen is a tantalizing line of inquiry. But Faulkner returns to the watchman in "Pantaloon in Black" after "Dry September" to rework the role, finally enabling the black man to step out of the role of victim, from the one who waits and "endures" to one who acts. As Edward Clough observes, Faulkner's earlier narratives of lynching read the act as a "white phenomenon, a communal and exclusionary act" (392). But in *Go Down, Moses,* Clough sees Faulkner shift into a new perspective, reading lynching as "fundamentally a traumatic black experience, a threat to domesticity and individual subjecthood" (394). Faulkner is indeed making a shift in perspective, but he does so only through black characters who have seized on lynching as a tool in their own plans, rather than allow it to keep them cowed.

Go Down, Moses marks a radical departure from Faulkner's earlier aesthetic of black endurance, which is perhaps most memorably embodied in his characterization of Dilsey in *The Sound and the Fury*. Despite Ike McCaslin's assertion in *Go Down, Moses* that "they will endure" (286), the novel is filled with black suicides and homicides. The description of Samuel Beauchamp that opens "Go Down, Moses" may note that his head resembles "a bronze head, imperishable and enduring," but within a page the reader sees his head shaved in preparation for his execution (351). Unlike Rider, who dies at the hands of a lynching mob, Samuel Beauchamp is lawfully sentenced to death for his alleged murder of a policeman in Chicago. And, unlike Rider's body, Samuel's body returns home shrouded in the trappings of public decency. Samuel's family ties ensure a decent burial, but they cannot prevent the violence of his own actions or of his end. Other stories too offer disquieting parallels. Lucas threatens a suicidal homicide in his fight with Zack Edmonds in "The Fire and the Hearth," and the threat is fulfilled by Rider in "Pantaloon." Though much in society changes between the earliest stories and the last ones, the stories underscore how much has remained the same. The deputy's incomprehension at Rider's actions matches that of Buck McCaslin when faced with the drowning of the slave Eunice, the mother of the black half of the McCaslin family: "*Who in hell ever heard of a niger drownding him self*" (256; italics in original).[22] Particularly when the line between people and property is blurred, such deliberate "unproductivity" seems inconceivable, but it is that expectation of productivity that Faulkner forces his reader to reconsider. Mules and cattle do not commit suicide, but black laborers do. At the same time, Faulkner obliquely balks at the Freudian reading of melancholic "waste," as if grief has no role to play other than to restore one's own identity after loss. In Rider, and, by extension, in Eunice and Lucas and Samuel Beauchamp, Faulkner offers a resounding rebuttal to both parties. Like Mollie's mourning cry in the final story of *Go Down, Moses*, Rider's grief finds expression in an act that arises out of his individual loss even as it underscores the deep well of grief that remains in the community despite all attempts to purchase an end to it.

In Peter Sacks's characterization of the Orpheus myth, he concludes that Orpheus's death is brought about by his "failure to reattach his affections elsewhere" once Orpheus's wife has died (72). In making that claim, Sacks precludes a reading of Orpheus as a moving elegist whose elegy is crafted not only of words but also of actions and whose "success" must be read through both forms—with a different end than the elegy of exchange and consolation Sacks has in mind. Since Rider's actions are outside convention, he must educate both his fictional community and Faulkner's readership in new modes of mourning, largely by resisting the kinds of education that are forced on them. Rider's body, "hanging from the bellrope in a negro schoolhouse" (149), is meant to serve as a perverse kind of education to the black community.[23] In *Native Son,* Richard Wright's protagonist, Bigger Thomas, recognizes a similar educational use for his corpse when he is caught: "They were going to use his death as a bloody symbol of fear to wave before the eyes of the black world" (745). Wright wrote again about the effects of such an education in *Black Boy* in 1945:

> The things that influenced my conduct as a Negro did not have to happen to me directly; I needed but to hear of them to feel their full effects in the deepest layers of my consciousness. Indeed, the white brutality that I had not seen was a more effective control of my behavior than that which I knew. The actual experience would have let me see the realistic outlines of what was really happening, but as long as it remained something terrible and yet remote, something whose horror and blood might descend upon me at any moment, I was compelled to give my entire imagination over to it, an act which blocked the springs of thought and feeling in me, creating a sense of distance between me and the world in which I lived. (84)[24]

In "Pantaloon in Black," Rider's body is put to use as a lesson that the black community receives at the hands of Birdsong's vengeful relatives. But Rider also attempts his own reeducation of the white community. As the deputy relates, Rider went to "the same crap game where Birdsong has been running crooked dice on them mill niggers for fifteen years, goes straight to the same game where he has been peacefully losing a probably steady average ninety-nine percent of his pay ever since he got big enough to read the spots on them miss-out dice" (151). Although it is precisely what the deputy finds so puzzling, Rider's history with Birdsong makes clear to Faulkner's reader that Rider's action is the result of premeditation. Much like the early photographs of lynchings, which were initially distributed with pride by lynchers but that later fueled antilynching movements, Rider proves that the very act of lynching can be used for very different purposes.[25]

In extinguishing both his own great physical strength and Birdsong's lucrative gambling nights, Rider appears to be living out Ida B. Wells's threat from her 1892 *Southern Horrors:* "The appeal to the white man's pocket has ever been more effectual than all the appeals ever made to his conscience.... By the right exercises of his power as the industrial factor of the South, the Afro-American can demand and secure his rights, the punishment of lynchers, and a fair trial for accused rapists" (158). His murder of Birdsong provides Rider with the means of rejoining his wife, of course, but it also enables him to address not only his individual trauma but also a public one as he attempts to right a long-standing injustice.[26] His ability to move from personal grief to communal wrong draws on a long history of African American mourning that navigates loss on several levels simultaneously. W. E. B. Du Bois writes movingly of his grief at the death of his son in *The Souls of Black Folk*. The power of his grief only deepens when one realizes that he mourns not only the lost boy but also the father's inability to look at his son without seeing in him the traits by which the boy would be evaluated in a white world. As Holloway argues, this story, "almost an embarrassment in its personal and elegiac excess," may make Du Bois "the first to characterize an 'African American mourning story'" (5). If so, Du Bois's lament sets the tone for mourning that moves fluidly between the personal and the public, the present and the historical. It is with a similar grasp of the relationship between these worlds that Faulkner drives Rider's grief into a kind of awakening—and action.

Rider's murder of Birdsong offers an education in the transformation of the personal to the social cause. At the late-night game in which Rider kills Birdsong, the narrator repeatedly refers to the latter as "the white man," reinforcing the difference between him and the others present, a racial difference that is matched by a difference in power: "They were the same faces—three members of his timber gang, three or four others of the mill crew, the white night-watchman with the heavy pistol in his hip pocket" (147). Although "the same" here refers to the fact that Rider is revisiting a game that he had taken part in every Saturday night before he was married, it also reminds the reader that these are the same people he sees in his work each day. The black timber gang is led by Rider, but there is also a "white foreman" (139), and the night watchman's pistol reminds all present of his authority.

Hans Skei reads Rider's "Look out, white folks" as a warning to white people "as a group" (130), a caution that should send readers looking to larger historical events to explain Rider's actions. Walter Taylor has linked Rider's warning to several texts written by black authors that exhibit a black man's grievance directed not simply against a white man but against "white folks." *Native Son,* published the same year "Pantaloon" appeared in *Harper's,* put it best: "To Bigger and his kind white people were not really people; they were a sort of great natural force, like a stormy sky looming overhead" (qtd. in Taylor 436). James Baldwin's "Going to Meet the Man," however, speaks most strikingly to the complex racial and sexual dynamics at play in Faulkner's attempts to portray black mourning. There too, the black victim of white violence calls out, "White man" when addressing his aggressor (Baldwin, "Going" 233). As in Faulkner's story, Baldwin's speaker is a white deputy sheriff who attempts to parlay his day's interactions with an inscrutable young black man into a story to tell his wife. And like Faulkner's character, in Baldwin's story the deputy's wife only discourages the storytelling: "'You awake?' he asked. She mumbled something, impatiently, she was probably telling him to go to sleep. It was all right. He knew that he was not alone" (231). Earlier that day, Baldwin's character acts out his belief that black men and women are "animals, they were no better than animals" by tormenting them with a cattle prod (231); one hears echoes of Faulkner's character's claim that black men and women are like "wild buffaloes" (*GDM* 150).

Baldwin was publicly critical of Faulkner, particularly regarding Faulkner's gradualist approach to desegregation. As Baldwin contends in his essay "Faulkner and Desegregation," "There is never time in the future in which we will work out our salvation. The challenge is in the moment, the time is always now" (214). It is not surprising, then, that though Faulkner elides the lynching in "Pantaloon in Black," Baldwin confronts it head-on in the title story of his 1965 collection. He explores the ways in which lynchings lie behind not only black fear and resistant acts such as Rider's but also the tendencies of white persecutors to regard black individuals as objects. In Baldwin's story, even as the deputy tells his wife the story of his beating a young black man senseless in a jail cell earlier that day, he thinks back to an event from his childhood, when he witnessed the burning and mutilation of a black man. Whereas Faulkner omits Rider's pursuit, capture, and lynching, Baldwin not only includes such scenes, he does so through the eyes of an eight-year-old boy who witnesses the scene from atop his father's shoulders. His story echoes the dynamics of Reginald Marsh's well-known 1934 drawing, *This Is Her First Lynching,* which was published in the *Crisis* and as a full page in the *New Yorker* before appearing in the NAACP's New York City exhibition "Art Commentary on Lynching."[27] Faulkner,

This Is Her First Lynching, Reginald Marsh, 1934, as published in the September 1934 issue of the *New Yorker*. (© 2017 Estate of Reginald Marsh/Art Students League, New York/Artists Rights Society (ARS), New York, with image courtesy of the *New Yorker*)

like Marsh, takes the black body off display in the "educational" moment, refusing to replicate the violent spectacle of lynching. All three works, however, speak to the "educational" moment that is central to the spectacle of lynching, serving as both a warning to African Americans and a reassurance to white children that people of a certain color are fully under the sway of the white public. As the deputy thinks back to the lynching he witnessed as a child, Baldwin describes him as watching "the hanging, gleaming body, the most beautiful and terrible object he had ever seen till then" (247). The educational component of lynching is one reason why Rider's act of reclamation, however partial and problematic, is so powerful: it challenges the portrayal of the black body as the abject instrument of a violence created by a white man for a white man's entertainment and to assuage a white man's grief.

Baldwin's story carries more of an air of paranoia than does that of Faulkner, even though Faulkner describes his deputy sheriff as "a little hysterical" after his encounter with Rider (149). When Baldwin's deputy begins to tell the story to his wife, he draws up, realizing that "his voice sounded peculiar" (231). When he confronted the young black man in the jail earlier that day, he felt the singing of the black men and women outside the courthouse, songs of mourning and of protest, get under his skin: "The singing filled him as though it were a weird, uncontrollable, monstrous howling rumbling up from the depths of his own belly" (235). He beat the young black man because "they were still singing and I was supposed to make them stop" (232). As his victim says, however, "Those kids ain't going to stop singing. We going to keep on singing until every one of you miserable white mothers go stark raving out of your minds" (233). The singing of the black men and women in town links the events of the day to the deputy's earlier memory, when he heard the mournful singing of black men and women on his way home from the lynching. His father surmised at the time: "Even when they're sad, they sound like they just about to go and tear off a piece" (239). In his present-day musings, Baldwin's deputy considers the singing that has formed the backdrop to his life:

> He could not remember the first time he had heard it; he had been hearing it all his life. It was the sound with which he was most familiar—though it was also the sound of which he had been least conscious—and it had always contained an obscure comfort. They

were singing to God. They were singing for mercy and they hoped to go to heaven, and he had even sometimes felt, when looking into the eyes of some of the old women, a few of the very old men, that they were singing for mercy for his soul, too. . . . He knew that the young people had changed some of the words to the songs. He had scarcely listened to the words before and he did not listen to them now; but he knew that the words were different; he could hear that much. . . . Perhaps this was what the singing had meant all along. They had not been singing black folks into heaven, they had been singing white folks into hell. (235–36)

One wonders whether the words to the songs have changed or the changing times have encouraged the deputy to listen a bit more closely to the words that were already there. Traditional spirituals frequently emphasize the "freedom" of death and the hope for a better life beyond this one. In effect, they offer the same consolations that antebellum planters encouraged in allowing their laborers to attend slave funerals at night. In times of racial tension, however, those same songs suggest a threat to white listeners. Just as with the burial of Samuel Beauchamp in "Go Down, Moses," these rituals of mourning contain the seeds of both consolation and of reawakening. There is a volatile element in the ability to embrace death openly, and that is one of the things that Baldwin's lawman finds so disturbing: the black singers articulate a system of value that lies beyond the grasp of white listeners who stand to benefit from conditions remaining as they are.

Mollie Beauchamp's song, which contains both mourning and accusation, is hushed by her white listeners, whose incomprehension limits the extent to which the text can engage the misunderstood mourning. But in recording Mollie's song, and in giving the title of his novel over to the words of the old spiritual, Faulkner distinguishes his work from Baldwin's deputy, who reads the songs as a threat. In a letter to Malcolm Cowley, Faulkner speculates about the origins of what Cowley sees as the dearth of good music from antebellum southerners as compared to their northern counterparts: "They talked too much, I think. Oratory was the first art; Confederate generals would hold up attacks while they made speeches to their troops. . . . The Negroes invented the songs" (*Faulkner-Cowley File* 78–79). Faulkner's deputy, "sitting around that courthouse all day long, talking" (151), and Mollie Beauchamp, who says little but who sings and chants her way through "Go Down, Moses," enable him to call attention to this narrative of southern history, which marks the gap between talk that holds up the action and singing that calls one to it.

In Baldwin's "Going to Meet the Man," the young people sing while standing in line at the courthouse to register to vote, and the mourners sing after the lynching is over; Baldwin pairs lament and politics through a song of mourning, one very like Mollie Beauchamp's cry in "Go Down, Moses." If the "sorrow songs" of which Du Bois wrote "tell of death and suffering and unvoiced longing toward a truer world" (538), then it is perhaps not surprising that Faulkner's black characters either remain largely silent, as does Rider, or shroud their concerns in biblical language and spirituals. Critical readings of African American mourning draw up suddenly, following the well-worn explanation of elegiac substitution: language replaces loss.[28] The story of the rise of literature out of deep grief fails to take into account instances in which cultural and social pressure to remain silent prevent such substitutions. John Matthews argues that Faulkner chooses to "figure the imprisonment of the inarticulate" in "Pantaloon" (241), in which Rider embodies a "wordless agony" that "demands the rites of speech that the subsequent stories perform" (244). But "Pantaloon" proclaims a response to grief that is no less powerful for jumping the tracks of traditional poetic elegy—and for registering a violent edge to race relations, particularly in the civil rights movement to come, that many would like to deny or ignore.

"But Them Two Nights Is Mine": Beyond Inheritance

When Rider approaches Birdsong at the lumber mill, intent on challenging him over the crooked dice game, the squaring off of Rider and Birdsong, black man and white, echoes the positions of Lucas Beauchamp and Zack Edmonds as they fight in "The Fire and the Hearth," the *Go Down, Moses* story that appears immediately before "Pantaloon in Black."[29] The black character Lucas threatens to kill Zack, who is both his cousin and his white landlord, an act for which he knows he will be lynched, a threat that echoes through both "Pantaloon" and "Go Down, Moses." Lucas's bold "*I would have paid*" shows his awareness of the fact that it would be lynching, rather than the law, which won out (57; italics in original).[30] Lucas's pistol misfires, saving both him and the white man from death as he speaks of "two lives" to be ended by a single bullet (57). Lucas goes to kill Zack because he fears he has lost his wife to Zack. This story, with the men's physical positions, the loss of the black man's wife, and the shadow of lynching, makes Rider's actions no longer anomalous or erratic. With Lucas to speak before him, Rider does not need to articulate his motivations. But an elegiac reading naturally casts a look backward; just as "Go Down, Moses" makes legible the voiceless grief in "Pantaloon in Black," so too Rider's challenge to the economic constraints of mourning prompts readers to reconsider the relation of labor and mourning in "The Fire and the Hearth."

To turn from "Pantaloon in Black" to "The Fire and the Hearth" is to reconsider the significance of the changes that Faulkner made when transforming the short stories into a novel. Rider's story echoes early magazine versions of "The Fire and the Hearth." In the stories then known as "A Point of Law" and "Gold Is Not Always"—which appeared in *Collier's* (22 June 1940) and the *Atlantic* (November 1940), respectively—Lucas's story is also told primarily through a deputy, and Lucas is cast as a buffoon. The crime under question is not murder of a white man but bootlegging. And yet Lucas's illegal activity, when it is acknowledged as a significant source of income for twenty years, is as significant of a challenge to the economics of grief as Rider's more violent one.

Lynching was regularly used to justify retribution for alleged violations of what Faulkner once called the "sacredness of womanhood" (McMillen and Polk 5).[31] But a look at the social and economic changes sweeping the South in his time makes clear that the violence is more strongly motivated by the desire to maintain racial hierarchy so as to continue exploiting black labor.[32] The lynching of black men and women did not appear until the end of the Civil War because, as McMillen and Polk put it, "the self-interest of Southern slaveholders was the best deterrent to lawless depredations against valuable human chattel" (11). And yet the appeal to sacredness gave a fire to economic concerns that prompted individuals to break the bounds of ordinary behavior. "It requires a certain amount of sentimentality, an escaping from the monotonous facts of day by day, to make a lynching," Faulkner wrote in one of his most controversial public letters, from 1931 (qtd. in McMillen and Polk 5). In the same letter, Faulkner claims that, though it is the "misfortune" of African Americans to be victims of the "sentimentality" that leads to lynching, they benefited from that same sentimentality at other times: black men taking advantage of unofficial routes to food, land, or loans (5). Setting aside the fact that one must take unofficial routes if the official ones are closed, one wonders about the dark connection Faulkner suggests between lynching and the everyday under-the-table economic relations between black and white workers. Although his opinions in that letter to the editor of the *Memphis Commercial Appeal* do not match the views he offers in the majority of other publications, they do speak to the self-justifications that many in Mississippi may have felt when confronted with the brutality of lynching.

If Woolf's Clarissa Dalloway balanced sympathy with a kind of affective exploitation of the dead, Lucas Beauchamp's role in *Go Down, Moses* is that of one who could easily have been a Rider or a Samuel Beauchamp but whose departure from such a narrative indicates the ways in which economics, rather than violence, could break through the structures of grief that govern the black man's life and the lives of his family and community. Whereas Samuel Beauchamp heads north for economic and cultural opportunities that were denied him in his Mississippi birthplace, and Rider leverages his economic value to liberate his coworkers from penury, Lucas Beauchamp lays claim both to the cash value of plantation connections and also to the opportunities for money that need never cross white hands, such as bootlegging and searching for buried treasure. It may seem an odd final turn in a book about modes of grief to shift to a character whose sympathy is frequently called into question but whose avarice is not, but it is in part to see where grief goes, what fruit it bears, that Woolf and Faulkner open up the elegiac form of *Mrs. Dalloway* and *Go Down, Moses,* respectively. If Richard Godden's reading of Lucas Beauchamp leads him to deem the character "a revenant: one who is dead and alive and tied to a place" (62), in this project Lucas's efforts are recast as a sustained endeavor to throw off the links between man and the forty years of sharecropping that are too often used to define him.

Rider's "unproductive" mourning offers a new way of considering larger social sources and ramifications of the unproductivity of other characters in the novel. If the frayed bills and clinking coins obscure rather than reflect the mourning in "Go Down, Moses," in Lucas's narrative, economy is itself the fruit of a long life of mourning. Faulkner introduces his reader to Lucas at the age of sixty-seven (114). Unlike Samuel and Rider, Lucas survived his violent youth and crafted a response to the early griefs that still haunt him. Like Clarissa Dalloway, Lucas comes out on the other side of youth with his life intact but with a brittleness that causes those around him to question his humanity.

Of the roster of characters in *Go Down, Moses*, Lucas most clearly engages his familial and racial history without being consumed by it and uses the past for present-day life in rural Mississippi. Although he does not, as Clarissa does, think in terms of lines from Shelley, Lucas's careful navigation of his social situation manifests his awareness of the many layers of cultural grief that shape that position. Ike McCaslin is the favored central character of the novel for most critics,[33] but Lucas Beauchamp proves an important contrast to Ike's withdrawal from the culture of inheritance into which he was born.[34] Ike's life is threaded through the stories of *Go Down, Moses:* "Was" is the story of his parents' courtship, "The Old People" and "The Bear" tell of his coming of age, and "Delta Autumn" finds him in his twilight years. As the McCaslin descendant who has the strongest claim to an inheritance from the original Lucius McCaslin, Ike makes for an obvious protagonist. But other cases might be made. In *Games of Property: Law, Race, Gender, and Faulkner's "Go Down, Moses,"* Thadious Davis reads Faulkner's novel through the character Tomey's Turl, the runaway slave of "Was," and develops a persuasive argument for his centrality to the novel. A reassessment of his role as a minor character seems warranted, given that Tomey's Turl colludes with Ike's mother in the opening story to bring about two marriages. He also deals the poker hand that brings about a resolution to the many hunts in the story. With a nod to Davis's reading, I argue for the significance of Lucas Beauchamp, Tomey's Turl's son, who matches Ike's role as a narrator and focalizer in ways that Tomey's Turl does not. As with Ike, *Go Down, Moses* traces Lucas's genesis and, unlike Ike, his descendants. "Was" is the story not only of Ike's parents' courtship but that of Lucas's as well. "Delta Autumn" is the story of Ike's old age, but "Go Down, Moses," the final story, describes the death of Lucas's grandson. Just as it is the second poker game of "Was" that decides the weddings that hang in the balance, so too it is the second protagonist introduced—Lucas, rather than Ike—who carries the weight of inheritance most illuminatingly in this novel. Given the tragedies of his family line, Lucas's inheritance is both elegiac and economic. But whereas Peter Sacks figures elegiac inheritance as a means of mastering mourning (37), Faulkner's Lucas Beauchamp is notable for his wariness of that inheritance, recognizing it as a snare that can tie one too closely to the dead.

Lucas's father was bequeathed a thousand dollars by his presumed father, the plantation owner Lucius McCaslin, but Tomey's Turl never claimed that legacy. Lucas's elder brother, James, "quitted the cabin he had been born in, the plantation, Mississippi itself, by night and with nothing save the clothes he walked in" (103), as did his sister, Fonsiba, but Lucas seizes the inheritance that comes to him, appearing promptly on his twenty-first birthday to claim the thousand dollars that was the only means by which Lucius McCaslin acknowledged relation to him.[35] The money remained in the bank, useful as a note in "not only... the Edmonds family annals, but in the minor annals of the town too" (105). The money, deposited in the bank under Lucas's name, becomes a symbol of his freedom to leave. Since he does need a white man's presence to speak to his respectability, he takes the opportunity to make his cousin cognizant of his financial independence.

Lucas's inheritance is not, however, his only means of extracting financial recognition from his white family members. Although he escapes the older generations' ledgers of slave ownership, he does appear in the new ledgers that the Edmonds descendants keep. Those ledgers record the goods owed by the sharecroppers, debts that bind the sharecroppers to the land and to the landowners nearly as strongly as the slaves' ownership did. But as Roth Edmonds notes: "[Lucas continued] drawing supplies from the commissary... having on the commissary books an account dating thirty years back which Edmonds knew he would never pay for the good and simple reason that Lucas would not only outlive the present Edmonds as he had outlived the two preceding him, but would probably outlast the very ledgers which held the account" (113). The accumulated debt to Edmonds makes a mockery of the owner's careful records of harvest and purchase; both parties know that generations of forced black labor were spent caring for the plantation. Lucas approaches the commissary records in defiance of their binding quality, taking exception to the "cable-strong" threads that preserved the race relations of the plantation well after the Civil War (245).

Although Lucas is a sharecropper, it becomes clear throughout "The Fire and the Hearth" that much of his time is invested in making money off the books, bootlegging and treasure hunting with a metal detector. Both pursuits provide Lucas with money that need not be recorded in either the commissary ledgers or the bank's records. It also marks the most significant shift in Faulkner's novel from the early stories he published in magazines.

In those early stories Lucas plays the part of a wily old man who outwits his white employer, a role that draws on the crude lines of stereotype: the black man who is cunning rather than intelligent, greedy, and always looking to make money without earning it. Those familiar outlines persist in the novel version, but only in the white characters' estimations of Lucas. Roth Edmonds notes wryly that Lucas was always interested in money "on which there was no sweat, at least none of his own" (119).

In the novel, Lucas's actions remain the same as in the early stories, but the shift from the stories' "Luke" to the novel's "Lucas Beauchamp" carries with it the weight of those earlier Beauchamp and McCaslin generations and the economy of black labor that marked those times. As Thadious Davis observes of the novel's additional material, "The rhetoric of law and business elevates Lucas Beauchamp's [actions] above comic buffoonery to parody" (129). Critical consensus has it that Faulkner's revision of the short stories for the publication of *Go Down, Moses* simply strengthens the McCaslin family narrative. But in those revisions Faulkner explores the antebellum racial and financial relations that give rise to Lucas's contemporary financial eccentricities, redefining those stereotyped qualities as Lucas's deliberate rejection of the economics of slavery-turned-sharecropping.

The fool's errand in which Lucas is engaged for much of "The Fire and the Hearth," hunting gold, may well provide Faulkner with comic material, but it also epitomizes Lucas's attempt to replace the work of his body with an income that is outside the purview of his white employer. In terms reminiscent of Robin Kelley's study of resistant weekend gatherings for African Americans, Edouard Glissant observed of Faulkner:

> We might say he surprises people on their holidays, almost free of their daily routines, in the exasperated moments when they literally step out of their lives in order to crazily devote themselves to their survival. Lucas Beauchamp serves as a serene example when, in "The Fire and the Hearth," he haggles with Roth Edmonds over the nights he will spend seeking buried treasure: "You aint got any complaints about the way I farm my land and make my crop, have you? ... Long as I do that, I'm the one to say about my private business. ... Besides, I will have to quit hunting every night soon now, to get my cotton picked. Then I'll just hunt Saturday and Sunday night." Up to now he had been speaking to the ceiling apparently. Now he looked at Edmonds. "But them two

nights is mine. On them two nights I dont farm nobody's land, I dont care who he is that claims to own it." (157–58)

As the economist Joseph D. Reid Jr., observes, the farming practices of early twentieth-century sharecropping preserved the balance of crop production and labor control that was developed under the slavery system: "slaves' work habits and tools aided watching as much as crop raising" (32). When alternated with corn, crops such as rice, cotton, sugar, and tobacco helped overseers maintain a compliant labor force because those crops required work stably over the year. But this balance had its costs: "Corn, for example, was cultivated too early and too late with too few tools because the labor was cheaply available and (for managers' safety) wanted employment. The slaves' legacy, therefore, was training at efficient cultivation of the staple and at too labor-intensive cultivation at inappropriate times of the complementary food crops" (38). By creating for himself a labor-intensive "hobby," Lucas creates a means of pushing back against the farming system that maintained the grooves of coercion and compliance—compliance won through physical exhaustion—that it created under slavery. Lucas's hunt through the woods with a metal detector is profitable not in the chance to discover buried treasure but in reclaiming the right to work the land however he likes and preserve his remaining labor for his own uses. Equally, his opposition to the constant use of his labor is resistance to the docility that such relentless work imposes on field hands. Coercion and compliance are yokes that Lucas throws off through his search for other kinds of labor and lucrative endeavors.

Although Lucas at the time of "The Fire and the Hearth" is an elderly man, the extended narrative turn to his childhood memories indicates the sources of the grief that motivate his yearning for economic independence. Faulkner revisits the boyhood pairing of black boys and white over and over again in his fiction. There are two sets in *Go Down, Moses,* first Lucas Beauchamp and Zack Edmonds and—one generation later—Henry Beauchamp and Roth Edmonds: "They had fished and hunted together, they had learned to swim in the same water, they had eaten at the same table in the white boy's kitchen and in the cabin of the negro's mother; they had slept under the same blanket before a fire in the woods" (54). This passage from *Go Down, Moses* concerns Lucas Beauchamp and Zack Edmonds, who, in age, "could have been brothers, almost twins too" (46), but the same childhood experiences reappear in the subsequent generation, with Henry Beauchamp and Roth Edmonds: "[They] rode the plantation horses and mules, they had a pack of small hounds to hunt with and promise of a gun in another year or so; they were sufficient, complete, wanting, as all children do, not to be understood, leaping in mutual embattlement before any threat to privacy, but only to love, to question and examine unchallenged, and to be let alone" (107). Here Faulkner emphasizes the impenetrability, the invincibility, of childhood. And yet in the next breath he moves on to explore the moments of rift and of emergent adulthood—in the case of Henry and Roth, at age seven, when Roth distances himself from his playmate because of his emerging racial consciousness. Roth's assertion of lordliness results in Henry leaving childhood play to join his father in the field, a far more significant change in status than Roth's suffusion of proprietary shame, even though Roth's feelings preoccupy Faulkner's narrator.

The sketch of Lucas's and Zack's childhood is buried in the middle of a great fight between them not as children but as men: "He was kneeling, their hands gripped, facing across the bed and the pistol the man whom he had known from infancy, with whom he had lived until they were both grown almost as brothers lived" (54). When young Roth observes Lucas and his father many years later, he notes that Lucas "refus[es] to call him mister" (110). When they were first published in magazines, Faulkner's stories about Lucas contained no flashbacks, no mention of the McCaslins, and no mention of the episode between the seven-year-old Roth and his African American playmate, Henry.[36] Faulkner's inclusion of these stories in his final text show a new attention to the effects of childhood grief on adulthood.

Pairings of black and white children appear in Harriet Beecher Stowe's *Uncle Tom's Cabin,* Mark Twain's *Pudd'nhead Wilson,* and Faulkner's *Unvanquished.* The motif surfaces again in Faulkner's quasi-autobiographical, semimythical essay "Mississippi." It also occurs in Baldwin's "Going to Meet the Man"; Baldwin's deputy had "a black friend, his age, eight, who lived nearby. His name was Otis. They wrestled together in the dirt. Now the thought of Otis made him sick" (240). And it plays a prominent role in W. E. B. Du Bois's story "Of the Coming of John," the penultimate essay in his 1903 collection, *The Souls of Black Folk.* Although Faulkner publicly refused to debate desegregation with Du Bois in 1956, there is in his work a conversation with Du Boisian themes and narrative tactics in the recurring twinned characters of Faulkner's fiction. "Of the Coming of John" is a story of two men named John, one white and one black, who were playmates as children and who went off to experience the big city life and university educations as young men. After their separate northern educations, both return home. The white John attempts to molest the black John's sister, after which the black John kills the white John. Like Faulkner's Lucas Beauchamp, who said he would take lynching if he succeeded in killing Zack Edmonds during their fight over a woman, Du Bois's story concludes with John Jones waiting for the lynching party.

At the center of Du Bois's story is a scene set in a concert hall, as the black John, John Jones, sits transfixed by Wagner while the white John argues with his female companion about race relations, claiming in his defense, "'You *will* not understand us at the South. . . . With all your professions, one never sees in the North so cordial and intimate relations between white and black as are everyday occurrences with us. Why, I remember my closest playfellow in boyhood was a little Negro named after me, and surely no two,—*well!*' The man stopped short and flushed to the roots of his hair, for there directly beside his reserved orchestra chairs sat the Negro he had stumbled over in the hallway" (526). Du Bois calls into question the effects of such intimacy when the protesting man fails to recognize his childhood playmate in the black man who stands in front of him. Then there's the white man's inability to extrapolate from that childhood friendship a warm or neutral relationship to African Americans generally speaking. This is the double consciousness of Du Bois with which everyone is familiar, but here told through story and not theory, through the bodies of these two men.

What gets lost in the discussion of Du Bois and schooling is a very different kind of education, that of relationships and intimacy fostered in childhood, that has been carefully scripted in nineteenth- and early twentieth-century literature, and that does not encourage a relationship between black and white children that survives childhood. It is, then, the priming of adult behavior through the literary representations of childhood that both Faulkner and Du Bois attempt to rewrite in their fiction. They elegize childhood friendship even as they set their sights on the adult consequences of such a loss.

When John kills John over a black woman's body, Du Bois rewrites the lynching mystique that had so long and so often put the white woman's body at the center of the discussion. When Lucas attempts to kill his former childhood playmate over what he thinks is an appropriation of his new wife in Faulkner's novel, he acts in conversation with both Rider and the black John of Du Bois's story. Faulkner builds such grief in as he reworks the stories of Lucas Beauchamp, and it is the economic resistance that develops out of that grief that forms the core of Faulkner's novel. His rewriting of grief makes clear how the centuries of "Hush" have silenced the black elegist. In seeking out the paths of alternatives, Faulkner's novel moves discussions of grief into larger discussions of violence and economic ingenuity, revealing grief and the ever-evolving cultures of mourning as increasingly significant players in larger social change.

Conclusion

> People who have recently lost someone have a certain look, recognizable maybe only to those who have seen that look on their own faces. I have noticed it on my face and I notice it now on others. The look is one of extreme vulnerability, nakedness, openness. It is the look of someone who walks from the ophthalmologist's office into the bright daylight with dilated eyes, or of someone who wears glasses and is suddenly made to take them off. These people who have lost someone look naked because they think themselves invisible. I myself felt invisible for a period of time, incorporeal. I seemed to have crossed one of those legendary rivers that divide the living from the dead, entered a place in which I could be seen only by those who were themselves recently bereaved.
>
> –Joan Didion, *The Year of Magical Thinking*

The result of Faulkner's and Woolf's efforts is a crowded landscape of mourning. Elegists look not only to the dead but also to one another, negotiating a shared narrative that may be unflinching or circumspect as a result of the presence of multiple speakers. When incorporating the voices of the dead too, Woolf and Faulkner strip such literary technique of its romantic veneer; the dead remain characters rather than ideals and are entitled to the truthfulness and agency that one would grant the living.

But it is in their final turn that Woolf and Faulkner most fully draw the elegy into the modern world, recognizing mourning as an act that is not only shaped by culture but is also a shaper of it. Grief should yield more than a respectful tip of the hat, as is granted to Betty Flanders in *Jacob's Room*. It should concentrate attention on those who connect death to injustice, such as when Mamie Till Bradley or Faulkner's Mollie Beauchamp insist that *all* the story be told in the paper and all the pictures published. Although Faulkner and Woolf have criticized and rewritten the elegiac conventions that tie the mourner to the dead, their most significant rewriting has come in reshaping the relationship between mourners and the society that observes them.

The ethical obligations of those who are merely "spectators"—not of death, as Freud presumes in "Thoughts for the Times," but of mourning—emerge as Woolf's and Faulkner's most unsettling challenge to the modern era. They would alter scenes such as the one Roland Barthes records, as his grief for his deceased mother is met with comments by friends who "prescribe some calm" or identify what they see as "bereavement, depression" in his behavior. Barthes's response is sharp: "Irritation. No, bereavement (depression) is different from sickness. What should I be cured of? To find what condition, what life? If someone is to be born, that person will not be *blank*, but a *moral* being, a subject of *value*—not of integration" (8; italics in original). He flatly rejects Freud's vision of mourning as an opportunity to restore one's ego. Although Woolf and Faulkner cannot prevent observers from attempting to medicalize or categorize Barthes's grief, they warrant his irritation by insisting on the reality of their fictional character systems, in which the dead maintain their value, their moral being, and the "infinite possibilities of a succession of days which are furled in him, & have already been spent" (*D* 1:186).

Notes

Introduction

1. As the editors explain, "In DSM-IV, there was an exclusion criterion for a major depressive episode that was applied to depressive symptoms lasting less than 2 months following the death of a loved one (i.e., the bereavement exclusion). . . . It was critical to remove the implication that bereavement typically lasts only 2 months, when both physicians and grief counselors recognize that the duration is more commonly 1–2 years" (811). The *International Classification of Diseases,* published by the World Health Organization and used in most countries outside the United States, is currently under revision, but the *ICD-10* addresses "normal bereavement reactions, appropriate to the culture of the individual concerned and not usually exceeding 6 months in duration" in a chapter titled "Factors Influencing Health Status and Contacts with Health Services" (150).

2. Other recent critics of elegiac literature include Zeiger, Clewell, Gilbert, Spargo, and Watkin.

3. Morton Bloomfield nicely summarizes the distinction that is widely assumed by scholars working on elegy in a variety of periods: "Elegy is a subdivision of the elegiac mode" (147). Bloomfield's subsequent discussion, however, shows how easily such a taxonomy breaks down. Just as early English elegy broke from the classical emphasis on a particular metrical form, so too the Romantics refuse to maintain the distinction between elegies that "praise, lament, and console," as Bloomfield summarizes, and poems that capture vacillating emotions in the speaker, which he would characterize as in the elegiac mode (147–48).

4. See Greenwald, Knox-Shaw, and Stevenson and Goldman.

5. Faulkner suffered fewer losses than Woolf, but his grandmother's death when he was ten—approximately the same age as his character the young Quentin Compson—offers a biographical source for the funeral in *The Sound and the Fury* (Bleikasten, *Ink* 367).

6. The available bibliographies of their libraries are, admittedly, incomplete. Nothing of Faulkner's appears in the *Catalogue of Books from the Library of Leonard and Virginia Woolf*, which includes the couple's books from Monk's House, Sussex, and 24 Victoria Square, London. The editors note that "the combined total of books in Monks House and Victoria Square at the time of Leonard's death was probably about

9,000 volumes. There is reason to believe however that at one time the library was considerably larger" (1), something in the range of fifteen thousand volumes. The most significant loss might be attributed to the bombing of their house at 37 Mecklenburg Square in 1941: "Leonard's account of the damage leaves little doubt that many books were destroyed and others damaged beyond repair" (2). Faulkner's library, as accounted for in *William Faulkner's Library: A Catalogue,* edited by Joseph Blotner, also holds no Woolf works. Faulkner's library is notably scarce on twentieth-century literature in general, particularly women writers. Significant exceptions to that tendency include nearly all of Joseph Conrad's oeuvre, Vita Sackville-West's *The Edwardians* (published by the Literary Guild of America rather than by the Woolfs' Hogarth Press), D. H. Lawrence's *Aaron's Rod,* James Joyce's *A Portrait of the Artist as a Young Man,* and Lytton Strachey's *Books and Characters.*

7. For her part, Woolf makes a single diary reference to "Faulkner" on the first of June, 1937: "By the way, I have been sharply abused in Scrutiny, wh., L. says, calls me a cheat in The Waves & The Years; most intelligently (& highly) praised by Faulkner in America—& thats all. I mean thats all I need I think write about reviews now" (*D* 5:91). Although she is widely assumed to be referring to William Faulkner, neither the editors of her diaries nor subsequent scholars have been able to trace the reference.

8. Sacks acknowledges in his epilogue, "To undertake a study of the American elegy would be to open yet another book" (312), and much recent work has sought to write just that book. Alexandra Socarides claims Emily Dickinson for that tradition, whereas Max Cavitch concludes his study of American elegy with Walt Whitman.

9. Both writers have, of course, since become closely identified with the height of literary modernism. The Bloomsbury Group, to which Woolf belonged, and the Hogarth Press, which she ran with her husband, Leonard, have become icons for literary establishment in the modernist period. She also had some experience at university, as Christine Kenyon Jones and Anna Snaith have recently discussed in "'Tilting at Universities': Woolf at King's College London." Likewise, Faulkner has emerged as the southern writer to beat, particularly for female authors. In the words of Flannery O'Connor: "The presence alone of Faulkner in our midst makes a great difference in what the writer can and cannot permit himself to do. Nobody wants his mule and wagon stalled on the same track the Dixie Limited is roaring down" (45). My point is simply that Faulkner and Woolf did, at times, regard themselves as outsiders, and this self-characterization influences their theories of perspective.

10. See Freud's "On Transience" (1916) for the beginning of such changes, and Clewell's "Mourning beyond Melancholia" for an analysis of this change (57–59). Clewell follows Freud through his "autodeconstructive" permutations (63), arguing that, in identifying subject formation in terms of the infant's loss of the mother, "Freud's text raises the possibility for thinking about mourning as an affirmative and loving internalization of the lost other" (64). Freud's "Mourning and Melancholia" was written in 1915, though it was not published until 1917. *The Ego and the Id* (1923)

and *Inhibitions, Symptoms and Anxiety* (1926) register the shift toward a conception of melancholia as an aid to ego formation.

11. Ramazani characterizes twentieth-century mourning as "melancholic mourning," drawing the line not between mourning and melancholia but between "different modes of mourning: the normative (i.e., restitutive, idealizing) and the melancholic (violent, recalcitrant)" (*Poetry* xi).

12. Clewell mentions the essay in her attempts to work beyond "Mourning and Melancholia," noting that in the later essay Freud registers a growing awareness of aggression, an element that plays a major role in his analysis of ego development in *The Ego and the Id* ("Mourning beyond Melancholia" 58–59).

13. Froula also reads this comment as an indication of Woolf's aesthetic project. In her reading of *Mrs. Dalloway*, she claims that Woolf creates "an elegiac act of imagination that intrinsically opposes violence" (*Virginia Woolf* 96).

14. Several contributions to the study of Faulkner's wars can be found in *Faulkner and War*, edited by Noel Polk and Ann J. Abadie.

15. Ramazani offers a great catalog of those who claim that genre has been abandoned in the modern era. He follows with a list of critics and theorists who recognize the turning away from genre as itself a genre-affirming activity. Ramazani's review concludes with the following quotation from Derrida: "Every text participates in one or several genres, there is no genreless text" (*Poetry* 25).

16. See in particular Edwards, Ryan, and Jaffe.

17. In *Black Sun: Depression and Melancholia*, Julia Kristeva has boldly addressed the violence that such mourning does to the other. In his own criticisms of Freud's "grief work," Jacques Derrida puts pressure on the implied "success" of Freud's formula and suggests that an alternative solution might be found in "virtual work," "a virtual space, of an *opus*, an *opus operatum*, that would accomplish the possible *as such* without effacing it or even enacting it in reality" (175).

1. Multiplying Mourners in *The Sound and the Fury*

1. André Bleikasten uses the term in his landmark *The Most Splendid Failure: Faulkner's "The Sound and the Fury"* and again in the revised volume, *The Ink of Melancholy*, a term that Bleikasten defines, "to borrow a phrase from Wallace Stevens—as a 'center on the horizon,' insofar as it represents at once the novel's origin and its *telos*" (*Ink* 46). Rachel of *The Voyage Out*, Donald Mahon of *Soldiers' Pay*, John Sartoris of *Flags in the Dust*, and, perhaps most intriguingly, Sutpen of *Absalom, Absalom!* have been suggested as characters who are significant but whose significance is derived from something other than their time "onscreen."

2. Competitive Elegy in *The Waves*

1. See also the first paragraph of Kennedy, the opening line of Froula's fourth chapter in *Virginia Woolf and the Bloomsbury Avant-Garde*, and the title of Stevenson and Goldman's article.

2. The growing body of work on Woolf and elegy includes Alex Zwerdling's "*Jacob's Room:* Woolf's Satiric Elegy," which earned a response from Karen Smythe, "Virginia Woolf's Elegiac Enterprise." See also Lisa Low's "Feminist Elegy / Feminist Prophecy: Lycidas, *The Waves,* Kristeva, Cixous"; Christine Froula's "*Mrs. Dalloway*'s Post-War Elegy: Women, War, and the Art of Mourning"; Tammy Clewell's "Consolation Refused: Virginia Woolf, The Great War, and Modernist Mourning"; and David Bradshaw's "'Vanished, Like Leaves': The Military, Elegy and Italy in *Mrs. Dalloway.*"

3. Although it becomes clear early in *The Waves* that the soliloquies by Jinny, Neville, Bernard, Rhoda, Susan, and Louis are not spoken aloud, each character's thoughts are prefaced by "*x* said." Critical convention thus has it that one refer to the words attributed to each character as if he or she had spoken aloud.

4. See Lee for an account of the textual transformation (628).

5. What she originally titled *The Pargiters* was later published as two separate works, *Three Guineas,* a series of critical essays, and the novel *The Years.*

6. Though Thoby Stephen was not an Apostle, his and Virginia's uncle was: James Fitzjames Stephen, father of J. K. Stephen (Q. Bell 8). Leonard Woolf also noticed the strong Apostle presence in the group: "Of the ten men of Old Bloomsbury only Clive, Adrian and Duncan were not Apostles" (*Beginning* 24).

7. In considering what would have happened had Thoby Stephen lived, Quentin Bell speculates that "if he had lived, he would have tended to strengthen rather than to weaken those barriers of speech and thought and custom which were soon to be overthrown amongst his friends. It was his death which began to work their destruction.... In her distress Virginia wanted to see no one save them ... Thoby's Cambridge friends.... As a result of Thoby's death Bloomsbury was refounded upon the solid base of deep mutual understanding" (118).

8. "I must record, heaven be praised, the end of The Waves.... I have been sitting these 15 minutes in a state of glory, & calm, & some tears, thinking of Thoby & if I could write Stephen 1881–1906 on the first page. I suppose not" (*D* 4:10). She did not, however, refrain from such commemoration when she finished *Jacob's Room,* nine years earlier.

9. Leonard has similar things to say of the anti-intellectual environment in British Empire outposts, like the one he manned in Ceylon: "The atmosphere was terribly masculine and public school" (*Growing* 135). It is perhaps not surprising that Percival, hero of the public-school yard in *The Waves,* is also the novel's link to the British presence in India.

10. For other work on Woolf's interest in, rather than criticism of, formal education, see Beer (140), Hollander (64), and Banfield, *passim.*

11. Frank Kermode cites Eliot's candle and looking glass as a representation of the author's balance between contingency and form, a means of answering the questions "How to do justice to a chaotic, viscously continent reality, and yet redeem it? How to justify the fictive beginnings, crises, ends; the atavism of character, which we cannot prevent from growing, in Yeats's figure, like ash on a burning stick?" (146).

12. James Naremore argues that Woolf's narrator lacks "that tone of certainty that one finds, for example, in George Eliot" (126). Richard Pearce responds that Woolf rather gains in the change, opening her novel to "the differences and conflicts among the different subjects, including the narrator, which makes the 'multipersonal subjectivity' truly multiple, heterogenous, polylogic" (134–35). My claim lies between the two: by denying the reader an authoritative narrative voice, Woolf preserves conflicting voices even as she reveals a different kind of unity in the group's shared desire for a central order.

13. As Gabrielle McIntire puts it, Bernard's dominance in the final section of the novel "performatively enacts heteroglossia's failure" (33).

14. In her description of the novel as a "cannibal" that eats up the other forms, one hears a precursor of Bakhtin's "Epic and Novel": "[The novel] sparks the renovation of all other genres, it infects them with its spirit of process and inconclusiveness. It draws them ineluctably into its orbit precisely because this orbit coincides with the basic direction of the development of literature as a whole" (7).

15. Celeste Schenck argues that "Women poets from the first refuse or rework the central symbolisms and procedures of elegy mainly, I think, because the genre itself excludes the feminine from its perimeter except as muse principle or attendant nymph" (13).

16. Jane Marcus attributes the incongruity of a poetic nature like Bernard's or Neville's or even Louis's celebrating a bully of both the schoolyard and the British Empire to the modern poet's "collusion in keeping alive the myth of individualism and selfhood that fuels English patriotism and nationalism" (137). Percival dies not in a valiant rush to defend the homeland but because his horse tripped while he kept up the British presence in India (*TW* 109).

17. Early feminist scholars of elegy claimed that women's elegies were set against those of male elegists, derived of different motivations and drawing on different sources, but recent feminist scholars, including Zeiger, have argued that some female elegists are very much in conversation with the male elegiac tradition (63).

18. Barbara Christian notes that Milton was also the favorite poet of Woolf's father, Leslie Stephen (174).

19. Hite also notices the resemblance between Rhoda's imagination and Vanessa Bell's paintings, and she reminds readers that among Bell's paintings of faceless subjects is a famous one of Virginia Woolf (*TW* 245n).

3. The Lively Response of the Dead in *As I Lay Dying* and *Jacob's Room*

1. Although in the published version Seabrook is a man of the outdoors, Woolf's early sketch aligns him with the interests of his son: he "had practised medicine, & trod the stage, & read many ~~Greek~~ books, & some said been in the East" (Bishop 6). The final version does much more to distance the son from the father, quite likely in order to shift the focus from familial responsibility for Jacob's death to a larger, social participation in the practices that led to the war.

2. See Trumpener and Booth for further details about Britain's burial policies during the First World War. Booth also notes Woolf's use of the traveling tombstones, reading in them a caution against using even Jacob's room as a fixed marker for his life, since it is being dismantled at the novel's conclusion.

3. Even the characters' different responses to the body's smell reflect changing cultural attitudes. As Victoria Bryan notes, the people in Jefferson meet the body in its greatest state of decay before burial, but they are also the most culturally removed from the practice of preparing the body for burial, as would still be common in rural Mississippi. Addie's rotting corpse attests to the backwardness of her family in a culture that increasingly turns to embalming before burial. Bryan also points to the people's shock when faced with a body that tumbles out of a casket in *Sanctuary*. As in *As I Lay Dying*, the corpse is on the move, disrupting modern attempts to hide away all signs of bodily decay. In a politically oriented reading, Tamara Slankard argues that for the southerner, modern-day burial practices are "yet another modern intrusion into the Southern home and pocketbook" (13). "Modern" here is synonymous with "Northern."

4. More disturbing than the ending, when Anse suddenly appears with a new wife, is its very predictability. As if she is reading through the lens of a literary genre, Vernon Tull's daughter, Kate, prophesies that, if Addie does indeed die, "he'll get another one before cotton-picking" (34).

5. Joseph W. Reed is a notable exception to this tendency; he concludes that the reader is encouraged to reject Addie's words.

6. When he was asked about the "villain" of *As I Lay Dying*, Faulkner replied, "If there is a villain in that story it's the convention in which people have to live, in which in that case insisted that because this woman had said, I want to be buried twenty miles away, that people would go to any trouble and anguish to get her there. The simplest thing would have been to bury her where she was in any pleasant place. If they wanted to be sentimental about it they could have buried her in some place that she would like to go and sit by herself for awhile. Or if they wanted to be practical they could have taken her out to the back yard and burned her. So if there was a villain it was the convention which gave them no out except to carry her through fire and flood twenty miles in order to follow the dying wish, which by that time to her meant nothing" (*FU* 112).

7. Some, such as David Sherman, are inclusive, as when he refers to "Addie's impossible chapter, narrated from beyond (or within, or toward) the grave" (135).

8. Lyn Frazier and Keith Rayner have written a series of papers on the "garden-path theory of sentence comprehension," studying the ways in which readers are forced to abandon an initial interpretation to form another when they have not yet finished a sentence. I find such theories remarkably similar to literary discussions of enjambment, such as in the works of John Milton.

9. Faulkner's desire appears to have some longevity; the character Gilligan in *Soldiers' Pay* (1926), Faulkner's first novel, claims, "I always thought I'd like to be a buzzard" (243). Earlier in that novel a different character expresses his admiration for them: "Regard the buzzard ... supported by air alone: what dignity! what singleness of purpose!" (47–48).

10. All but one of the Dickinson poems discussed here were included in the fourth section of Aiken's edition (*Selected Poems of Emily Dickinson*), which was euphemistically titled "Time and Eternity." Although in the text above I follow custom in numbering the poems according to Franklin's edition, the following numbers are the pages on which the poems can be found in Aiken's edition: "The Bustle in a House," 173; "Because I could not stop for Death," 175; "Ample Make this bed," 194; "The grave my little cottage is," 213; "I heard a fly buzz—when I died," 223; "'Twas just this time, last year, I died," 229.

11. Faulkner's short story "Beyond" features a male character, the Judge, who speaks to the conditions of life after death as he searches for his son, but in *As I Lay Dying* Faulkner gives readers a character who is simply not preoccupied with reporting back to the living the condition of life after death but instead with living it.

12. The tradition of the "corpse poem" is not exclusively an American one—one thinks of Hardy's 1912–13 elegies for his wife, in which she is often figured as the critical speaker—but it can be traced from Dickinson to Faulkner and on to Sylvia Plath. Jolene Hubbs sees correspondences between Addie's voice and Plath's "Daddy," particularly in their fixation on their fathers. Plath's marked-up copy of *As I Lay Dying* remains at Smith College, Plath's alma mater.

13. This Dickinson poem does not appear in Aiken's edition.

14. Raymond reads Dickinson's speaker through the lens of trauma theory and likewise concludes that the speaker "attends to the trauma of death not by coming through that trauma but rather by inhabiting it, making home by accepting homelessness" (129).

15. John was Dickinson's favorite New Testament author (Leiter 54).

16. Paul S. Nielsen also reads Addie's story as "a succession of pregnancies," though he does so in rosier terms than I propose here: "times when she grew round and full with life and meaning" (37); "Perhaps it is through childbirth, not words, that Addie attempts her first production of meaning and finds her most articulate mode of self-expression" (38). As Marc Hewson makes clear in his survey of the critical landscape, for some critics Addie has been significant in large part because of her maternal identity, but others have read that same quality in a negative light (551). Hewson argues that naming and language are expressions of patriarchy that Addie, with her emptying out of language and the focus on childbearing in her monologue, repudiates. Amy

Louise Wood argues that "Motherhood is not a 'duty' for Addie, but an experience for her pleasure and feeling, as she favors some children and rejects others" ("Feminine Rebellion" 103). Wood sets Addie's "My children were of me alone" as an answer to Cora's pious "I have bore what the Lord God sent me" (103).

17. For more on death as a kind of calculus, see also "I took one Draught of life—" (Fr 396), "For Death—or rather" (Fr 644), and "Some—Work for Immortality—" (Fr 536).

18. See Sacks (12–13) and Raymond (13) for more on the female body and elegy.

19. Zwerdling argues that one of Woolf's reasons for limiting Jacob's voice in the novel is her concern that internal access tends to produce sympathy, working against the satirical or critical intentions that Zwerdling reads as dominant in Woolf's narrative (*"Jacob's Room"*).

20. Little argues that Woolf works within something of a tradition, having read parodies of bildungsromans by Meredith, Wells, Richardson, and Huxley (106–7). Her argument dovetails nicely with one made by Alex Woloch in his study of narrative space and the minor character. If Woloch is right in characterizing the bildungsroman as facilitating the hero's progress through the help of delimited—often exaggerated or allegorized—minor characters (29), then a parody of such a structure might well be seen as an attempt to draw attention to the delimited minor characters Jacob finds so rudely "individual" here. *Jacob's Room* has garnered critical attention for its links to the elegy on a number of formal and thematic levels. See Froula, "War, Civilization"; Smythe; Wall; Walsh; and Zwerdling, *"Jacob's Room."* The majority of these articles read *Jacob's Room* as, at least in part, an elegy for Woolf's older brother, Thoby, and for the soldiers of the First World War. Kathleen Wall's work is notable in that she reads the novel as an elegy for literary techniques that are no longer appropriate; Woolf's narrator is, in her interpretation, something of "an elegiac gesture," a holdover from the dominance of omniscient narration in Victorian realist fiction: "It evokes an earlier, more authoritative and confident world view not imbued with loss and change" (312).

21. See Froula's "War, Civilization" for a detailed argument about the role of the myth of Greece in *Jacob's Room*. Froula argues that Woolf's narrator "points to the dangerous effects of myth and story—and especially of the classical heritage, the Greek myth—upon the modern world" (281).

22. Mrs. Norman wonders whether Jacob might be "nice, handsome, interesting, distinguished, well built, like her own boy" (*JR* 22). The word is taken up later, by the narrator, who echoes an earlier comment by a different character: "'Distinction'— Mrs. Durrant said that Jacob Flanders was 'distinguished-looking.' 'Extremely awkward,' she said, 'but so distinguished-looking.' Seeing him for the first time that no doubt is the word for him" (54–55). The adjective then reverberates in general gossip: "'That young man, Jacob Flanders,' they would say, 'so distinguished looking—and yet so awkward'" (124). Sandra Wentworth Williams comes to the same conclusion, independently, near the end of the novel: "'But he is very distinguished looking,' Sandra decided" (116).

23. In her annotations to Woolf's short fiction, Susan Dick notes that, in addition to the version of the story in the *Jacob's Room* holograph, there is an undated typescript of the story, with holograph revisions, that has the novel's title written at the top and then canceled out. Chapter and pagination on the typescript suggest that Woolf was, even at that later stage, still planning to use the short story in the novel (*CSF* 301).

24. Although most traces of Angela are removed from the novel, Woolf does include other explicit comparisons between men and women in the novel that suggest criticisms of the academy's insularity. When comparing Professor Erasmus Cowan with "old Miss Umphelby," Woolf makes a point of noting the ways in which the latter combines knowledge of Virgil with curiosity about the world around her. Although Professor Cowan attempts to emanate the essence of Virgil, turning ever inward in his scholarship and teaching, Miss Umphelby brings the knowledge of such figures into the modern world. But because the university culture favors the former, we are left, as occurs so often in Jacob's world, wondering about "the thing she might have said" if her voice had not been pushed to the margins and her lectures poorly attended (*JR* 31).

25. The brevity of battlefield description in *Jacob's Room* led early reviewers to ignore the role of the war in Woolf's novel; as Karen Levenback notes, it was not until Winifred Holtby's book in 1932, a full decade after the novel was published, that *Jacob's Room* was called a "war book" (*Great War* 44). But we might think of the narrative compression of the war as an echo of the violence that is being enacted upon the soldiers. As Alex Woloch observes of Achilles's sudden killing of a dozen nameless men in the *Iliad*, "The compression of so many figures into one line is crucial to our sense of the violence that Achilles is here enacting" (9). Such narrative violence, while perhaps underscoring the violence of the battlefield, is in stark contrast to the prolonged meditation on death that is the norm in elegiac literature.

26. It is worth noting that, although *As I Lay Dying*'s publication follows that of *The Sound and the Fury*, it does so only after Faulkner writes the first version of *Sanctuary*. His capacity for the grotesque got a thorough workout before he turned to Addie's novel.

27. In the manuscript Woolf wavers between "march" and "tramp," and initially writes that "they enter" before editing the text to the more martial "advance" (Bishop 27).

28. In her study of modernist poetic elegy, Gilbert reads the identity of those who suffer and those who share in the guilt as a significant shift in elegiac writing: "What gives special anguish to some of the antipastoral elegies that evolved out of the First World War is the paradoxical status of the mourner as *himself a murderer*" (190). Ruddick is particularly blunt when she reaches a similar conclusion about *Jacob's Room*: "Jacob is killed in a war which Woolf believed to be the effect of institutionalized hierarchies of class, sex and intelligence: he is himself in part a killer. As a child he catches a crab and lets it die in his bucket. As a grown boy he hunts butterflies" (192). The last activity is one to which Woolf and her brother Thoby were partial.

4. "A Host of Others" in *Mrs. Dalloway*

1. Molly Hite calls him a "second, shadow protagonist" ("Tonal Cues" 249).

2. See Joyes and Wang.

3. Even the act that gets Darl sent to the asylum—burning down a barn that contained his mother's coffin—aligns him with the whispered judgement of the community: it is simply disrespectful to let a corpse decompose aboveground for so long. Darl's consignment to the asylum is motivated as much by his sister's hatred and his family's economic interest as it is an assessment of his mind.

4. The allusion is striking, as Bradshaw notes: autumn leaves are rather conspicuous in a novel that takes place in June (113). The trope links Woolf's novel to a tradition in both classical (Homer, Virgil) and English (Shelley, Byron, Tennyson, Houseman, and Hardy) literature (Bradshaw 113–14).

5. Levenback writes of Rupert Brooke's influence on Woolf's war writing, arguing that it is overlooked by critics primarily because of Woolf's silence on his death—a silence Levenback attributes to a failure to come to terms with his death rather than a lack of influence (*Great War* 10). See also Levenback's "Virginia Woolf and Rupert Brooke."

6. See Hoff and Schlack for more about the classical allusions in *Mrs. Dalloway*. There is an additional reason for attending to the link between *Mrs. Dalloway* and Woolf's interest in classical literature: Rowena Fowler observes, "Because Woolf's reading notes on the Choephori of Aeschylus share a notebook with her working notes for *Mrs. Dalloway*, critics have paid special attention to the strands of vengeance and propitiation in the novel" (234).

7. Levenback claims Philip Woolf, Virginia's brother-in-law, as a model for Septimus (*Great War* 57). Hermione Lee argues for one of Woolf's former students, from her work at Morley College in 1907. The student, Cyril Zeldwyn, garners a mixed description in Woolf's remembrances, serving as both "my good working man" and "a socialist, of a kind, and a poet" (Lee 219).

8. In Schlack's work on Woolf's literary allusions she notes there is a clear divide in *Mrs. Dalloway* between those who are well read and those who are not: "The sympathetic characters read literature, or at the very least are respectful of its influence.... Unsympathetic characters are almost always presented as unsusceptible to literature" (57). In looking at Holmes and Bradshaw in particular, she draws attention to the way "these men of science are aggressively antiliterary. Dr. Holmes in a visit to Septimus 'opened Shakespeare—*Antony and Cleopatra;* pushed Shakespeare aside.' ... In Bradshaw the Philistinism is even more explicit: 'There was in Sir William, *who had never had time for reading,* a grudge, deeply buried, against cultivated people who ... intimated that doctors ... are not educated men'" (58; italics in original).

9. In her archival work for the Cambridge University Press edition of *Mrs. Dalloway*, Fernald notes that in the proofs of the novel, "there is only one page where Woolf crosses out a whole paragraph and substitutes a (significantly longer) typed

page. That single instance is the paragraph in which Septimus kills himself. Seventeen lines in proofs have been crossed out and two typed pages have been added, making the paragraph now twenty-eight lines long. In addition to many small changes, the chief addition here comes toward the beginning of the paragraph, with the addition of Septimus scanning the room for possible means of suicide before deciding to throw himself out the window" ("Textual Editing"). Fernald interprets such revisions as indicative of Septimus's significance to the novel: "To know that, at the very last minute, Woolf was rethinking the book's climax, giving it greater depth and a slower pace, is to know something about the centrality of Septimus to the novel." I would add that the addition of Septimus's contemplation of other means of suicide enhances the sense of theatricality of the event, the search for the right effect; this is not merely a question of the end but of his contribution to a larger scene.

10. See both articles by Guth. The US edition of the novel includes an additional line as Clarissa thinks of Septimus: "He made her feel the beauty; made her feel the fun" (Hite, "Tonal Cues" 252).

11. Froula argues that Woolf's original title for the novel, "The Hours," comes from Shelley's apostrophe to Keats's death (*Virginia Woolf* 92). Hoff, however, suggests that "The Hours" refers to Homer's *Odyssey* (188). When she makes her appearance in *The Voyage Out,* Clarissa Dalloway also quotes these lines from "Adonais." The sentiments of these lines from Shelley are echoed by many war writers, including Laurence Binyon in his "For the Fallen, 1914," which includes "They shall not grow old, as we that are left grow old: / Age shall not weary them, nor the years condemn" (qtd. in Parker 232). Parker also points out that Houseman expresses much the same in "A Shropshire Lad."

12. Woolf twice mentions Shelley's expulsion in her 1927 review of a biography of Shelley (*E* 4:466, 470).

13. See Sacks for a discussion of the two poets' views of the soul: "But whereas Shelley rejects the circumstantial world as contagious dross, Keats goes on to insist that an 'intelligence' should be immersed 'in the medium of a world like this' in order that it may advance to take on an 'identity.' Only this 'identity' can be called a soul. For Keats, this attainment of a soul adequately stained by the world and by the heart constitutes salvation—a far different idea from that of Shelley's celebration of the return of a disembodied purity to its source" (161).

14. Early titles for the book suggested this focus: "At Home" or "The Party," a book whose stories must "converge upon the party at the end" (qtd. in McNichol 8).

15. In this reading I differ from others who may see Clarissa's parties as a means of exerting complete order over a world, as opposed to the outside world, which remains chaotic. Chloe Wofford, better known as Toni Morrison, argues that Clarissa Dalloway "feels a need for some pattern of existence and transcends the chaos.... The pattern ... is expressed in her party-giving," through which she creates a "small but ideal world" (Morrison, "Virginia Woolf's and William Faulkner's" 6–7). Although Clarissa does hope to arrange things such that they will bear interpersonal fruit, she also acknowledges the limitations of her role in making that happen. She can organize the meeting, but she cannot control the relations that occur once it begins. This give

and take is an essential flexibility in the new protagonist that Woolf offers to the novel tradition.

16. For discussions of Woolf's political and social engagement, see Friedman, Cuddy-Keane, and Berman.

17. For further discussion of Bell's theory of civilization, as expressed in *On British Freedom* (1923) and *Civilization* (1928), as context for Woolf's 1925 *Mrs. Dalloway*, see Shaffer.

18. A handful of critics have investigated Clarissa's struggle with the Victorian understanding of identity as independent of society and stable through time. Shannon Forbes sees Clarissa's attempts to perform the role of the perfect hostess as a "substitute for what she refers to as her 'incompatible' self so that ... [she] may ... project to the outside world the image of one who possesses the much-coveted, Victorian conception of the self" (40). See also Wang. In my reading, however, Clarissa Dalloway is not a figure for stable Victorian identity or even a failed attempt at such a thing. Though critical emphasis has been on Clarissa's effort to collect "the whole of her at one point" (*MD* 37), as she looks into the mirror, the "self" she sees there is merely a public self and does not erase the other selves with which she lives.

19. Such attention to the effort that goes into parties may stem from the toll they took on Woolf even when she was only a guest. As Leonard reports of his wife, "She not only enjoyed society, the kaleidoscope of human beings, conversation, the excitement of parties, she was through and through a professional novelist, and all this was the raw material of her trade. This dual sensitivity to the most trivial meetings with her fellow human beings meant that society and parties were a great strain on her mental health and she herself was well aware of this" (*Downhill* 99). The two layers of which Leonard Woolf writes, that of pure enjoyment and that of purposeful material gathering, are interwoven throughout *Mrs. Dalloway*. The dominance of either one, of course, contributes to the value or devaluation of Clarissa Dalloway's role.

20. See Carroll, the opening paragraph of Levenback's *Virginia Woolf and the Great War*, and Brenda Silver's discussion of the critical response to Leonard Woolf (121).

5. "Unproductive" Grief in *Go Down, Moses*

1. Early reviews set the critical tone for decades. Malcolm Cowley, reviewing *Go Down, Moses* in the *New Republic*, called it "a hybrid: a loosely jointed but ambitious novel masquerading as a collection of short stories" ("Go Down to Faulkner's Land" 900), while Lionel Trilling, "after excepting the story called 'Pantaloon in Black,'" also called it "if not exactly a novel, then at least a narrative which begins, develops, and concludes" (632). More recently, after an extensive study of the shift from short stories to an integrated form, Joanne V. Creighton deemed it a "short story composite" (86). Thadious Davis has called the novel a "miscegenated text," perhaps the best description that has yet emerged from the critical discussion (11).

2. Even Susan Donaldson, whose general argument is that the stories unravel the master narrative of the McCaslin family, assumes that "Go Down, Moses" is a

concluding sign of hope. She sees in the final story "a moment of compassion, hope, and true community" (147).

3. In the introduction to his study of modern elegy, Jahan Ramazani underscores the rise of commercial interests in modern expressions of public mourning.

4. Melville Herskovits, in *The Myth of the Negro Past*, notes of West African practices that "as far as surviving relatives are concerned, two drives cause them to provide proper funeral rites. The positive urge derives from the prestige that accrues to a family that has provided a fine funeral for a dead member; negative considerations arise out of the belief that the resentment of a neglected dead person will rebound on the heads of surviving members of his family when neglect makes him a spirit of the kind more to be feared than any other—a discontented, restless, vengeful ghost" (qtd. in Suzanne Smith 20).

5. Godden and Polk share my doubt about this possibility, calling Stevens's conclusion "misguided and socially self-serving" (331).

6. In *Roll, Jordan, Roll*, Eugene Genovese compares slaves to the lower-class migrant workers of the nineteenth century who moved from country to city in England. A laborer who gave his child a pauper's funeral "would thereby pauperize himself—that is, would diminish his credibility as a 'respectable' working man—in the eyes of prospective employers. The laborers found themselves propelled by vicious economic pressures into spending much more than their strong sense of the right and the proper required.... But in the world they knew they dared not, if they could possibly avoid it, refuse to pay whatever it took to provide that decent respect for the dead which helps define respect for the living" (201–2). In his historical canvassing of antebellum American life, Genovese frequently links funerals to economic concerns, both the costs of the funeral itself and the social benefits to expressing the depth of one's human emotions through funeral spending.

7. Her characterization of Roth Edmonds leans on his familial responsibility, not his role as master. As in the biblical story, in which Benjamin and Joseph share a mother, unlike their brothers, so too Mollie is the link between Samuel and Roth in Faulkner's novel. Although neither man is actually Mollie's son, Samuel is raised by his grandmother (*GDM* 354), and she is "the only mother [Roth] ever knew" (97). Because of what Mollie perceives as Roth's betrayal, she is, as Jacob feared he would be, bereaved of both her sons. By speaking of Samuel in terms of Benjamin, Mollie implicitly prevails upon Roth to recognize Samuel as his brother rather than simply as his misbehaving tenant.

8. In the short story "Beyond," published in 1933, a black woman's wail marks her white employer's death, but there the "slow billows of soprano sound" are wordless, at least as recorded in the story (*Collected Stories* 782).

9. "Southern and northern black communities found a sorrowful ritual enacted at train stations whose box cars brought back the bodies of residents, bodies that retraced the journeys, back and forth, of migrating black families" (Holloway 143).

10. Faulkner also writes of Till's murder in his essay "On Fear," which was published in *Harper's* in June 1956: "If the facts as stated in the *Look* magazine account of the Till

affair are correct, this remains: two adults, armed, in the dark, kidnap a fourteen-year-old boy and take him away to frighten him. Instead of which, the fourteen-year-old boy not only refuses to be frightened, but, unarmed, alone, in the dark, so frightens the two armed adults that they must destroy him. What are we Mississippians afraid of?" (*ESPL* 100).

11. Mamie Till Bradley's involvement in the public eye continued long after her own son's funeral. After the 1998 murder of an African American man, James Byrd, in Texas, she not only spoke about the murder on a New York radio talk show but she also "held the hand of James Byrd's father at a Harlem memorial service" (Rushdy 76).

12. John Limon claims that *Go Down, Moses* "is either a collection of stories or a novel, depending on the success one has in integrating 'Pantaloon in Black' into it" ("Integration" 422). Limon continues, "The former custom was to regret the intrusion of this alien story into the novel. That being the former custom, the current one is to show how the story is not alien at all" (428). See Tick for an example of the former. The more successful critics of the "current custom," such as Robinson and Town, tend to read the narrative disunity as mirroring a social one: the racial tensions that persist after the Civil War. In "Pantaloon," there are a few connections to the McCaslin narrative: Rider rents his home from Roth Edmonds, and the story includes a brief mention of Lucas and Molly Beauchamp, but otherwise he has no explicit connections to either the Beauchamp or McCaslin families. When Malcolm Cowley asked Faulkner about the presence of Rider among the McCaslin stories, Faulkner replied, "Oh, you mean the story about Rider? . . . Rider was one of the McCaslin Negroes" (*Faulkner-Cowley File* 113). As Cowley puts it, "It was no use asking, 'Why didn't you say so?'" (113).

13. Thomas Hardy is the notable exception to this tendency; he is known for his 1912–13 elegies for his late wife.

14. In some parts of the antebellum South, not only African Americans but also white plantation owners took for granted that spirits roamed the earth in a state of unrest—due, one historian surmises, not only to the high ratio of blacks to whites in the region, but also to the effects of so many white children being raised by black "mammies" (Egerton 159).

15. In addition to the work of Genovese and Yalom, for more on West African burial practices, their ties to current African American culture, and interpretations of the objects' symbolic roles, see Montgomery (298), Holloway (210), and Suzanne Smith (23–25).

16. "The final act of burial, which was usually the shortest part of the ceremony, involved mourners dropping handfuls of dirt on the coffin or working together to shovel the dirt over the grave" (Suzanne Smith 29). Genovese traces this tradition further back: "The practice of throwing dirt into the grave has not been restricted to Africa and Afro-America and does not in itself prove cultural continuity; but there is no reason to doubt that the blacks of the eastern tidewater and low country brought it from Africa and made it largely their own in the New World. It was not unknown at white funerals. . . . However much European practice influenced American practice,

white southerners—Edward A. Pollard for one—referred to it as 'the negro custom'" (200).

17. See Godden and Sassoubre.

18. Richard Godden points out that the deputy later labels it "white-mule" whiskey, as in, "whiskey fit to keep a 'nigger' so 'bust-skull' that he will operate on weekdays as the white man's mule. Its purveyor knows its purpose, hence his unwillingness to sell more than a modicum on a working day" (93).

19. Faulkner's later essays reflect an acute awareness of the economic underpinnings of contemporary racial tensions. In "On Fear," in which he draws on the statement he issued after Emmett Till's murder, Faulkner argues, "Nor is the tragedy the fear so much as the tawdry quality of the fear—fear not of the Negro as an individual Negro nor even as a race, but as an economic class or stratum or factor, since what the Negro threatens is not the Southern white man's social system but the Southern white man's economic system—that economic system which the white man knows and dares not admit to himself is established on an obsolescence—the artificial inequality of man—and so is itself already obsolete and hence doomed"; "it is our southern white man's shame that in our present economy the Negro must not have economic equality; our double shame that we fear that giving him more social equality will jeopardise his present economic status" (*ESPL* 105).

20. For studies of elegy that manifest such Freudian tenets, see Sacks and Ramazani. Richard Godden's recent work on New Deal economic policies and Faulkner's late fiction makes brief reference to analyses of grief, but he relies on the work of psychoanalysts Nicholas Abraham and Maria Torok, who set up grief options along the usual Freudian dichotomy (Godden 107).

21. Faulkner included in his wide-ranging essay "Mississippi" a reference to "the lynching of Negroes not for the crimes they committed but because their skins were black" (*ESPL* 36–37).

22. Leanita McClain, who committed suicide in 1984, offered a succinct characterization of the black community's taboo of suicide: "We don't kill ourselves, we only kill each other" (Holloway 89).

23. This education is not, of course, limited to the African American community. As Robin Bernstein notes, "In 1902, an anonymous African American woman wrote in the *Independent*, 'I have seen very small white children hang their black dolls. It is not the child's fault, he is simply an apt pupil.' By couching that statement within a discussion of lynching, the anonymous author suggested that white children were 'pupil[s]' of an observed reality of antiblack mob violence, and that their doll play reflected this education. White children did witness the lynching of African Americans; indeed, white children actively participated in these murders. In the 1899 lynching of Richard Coleman in Maysville, Kentucky, for example, 'little children from six to ten years of age carried dried grass and kindling wood and kept the fire burning all during the afternoon.' The anonymous essayist in the *Independent* may have been correct, then, in her suggestion that some white 'pupil[s]' observed or participated in lynchings and then recapitulated that reality in their play" (210–11).

24. Faulkner read both *Native Son* and *Black Boy* and wrote to Wright about both works in 1945, with particular praise for the former (*SL* 201).

25. For an account of the ways that witnessing, photographs, and film played a role in both lynching and antilynching efforts, see Wood (*Lynching* 4–5).

26. Hans Skei also notes that it would be a mistake to read Rider's actions as simply "his means of escape," however much even those actions reveal skillful manipulation of the "Southern code": "some of his reactions clearly indicate that he wants to set other things right, too, in this unjust and unequal society" (128).

27. For more on Marsh's work as a whole and *This Is Her First Lynching* in particular, see Higginbotham.

28. For a reading of this sort as applied to Faulkner, see Matthews (213–15).

29. Indeed, as John Matthews observes, the fight between Lucas and Zack begins with Lucas standing over Zack's bed, holding a knife to the white man's throat (234).

30. This is not the only Faulkner novel in which Lucas appears. *Intruder in the Dust*, which features Lucas, was published in 1948. Although in it Lucas is falsely accused of murder, Philip M. Weinstein admits, "Perversely, I would like to envisage a Lucas at least capable of murder, one whose embroilment within the racism of the South were reciprocal, unpredictable, threatening.... To glimpse what such a Lucas might have been, we must go elsewhere, go backwards in Faulkner's career, and conceive a shadowy tripartite figure composed of Joe Christmas, Rider, and Samuel Worsham Beauchamp" (248). See Weinstein for a thorough analysis of Lucas Beauchamp's many appearances in Faulkner's fiction.

31. For more on the ways in which the mystique of white womanhood was used to ignite lynching fever, see Wood (*Lynching* 7).

32. It surprises no one that rape was part of the picture in only a minority of lynchings: "Nationwide, rape was alleged in only 19 percent of all lynchings; in Mississippi the figure was lower still, 12.7 percent" (McMillen and Polk 10). Timothy Pitts calls attention to a 1921 address given by Georgia governor Hugh M. Dorsey, in which Dorsey points out that "in only two of the 135 cases is the 'usual crime' against white women involved" (186). Even well after Faulkner's novel was published, the White Citizens Council, founded in 1954, had as its goal "'to bring economic pressure on the Negro to prevent him from voting and, later, to punish any Negro who worked toward the desegregation of the schools.' ... Within two short years, the WCC claimed over sixty thousand members in Mississippi alone" (Suzanne Smith 118).

33. After citing critical consensus on the matter, Creighton goes on to read Faulkner's emphasis on Ike as an important balance to the diffuseness of the other material, the individual that makes Faulkner's crowd compelling. She reads Faulkner as seeking "a form flexible enough to accommodate both the expansive panoramic across-the-generations look at a host of characters and incidents and an intensive examination of the moral consciousness of one individual, Isaac McCaslin" (86).

34. In this my reading resists Faulkner's own comments on the book, when he declared that "the central character in the book was a man named Isaac McCaslin" (*FU*

38). And yet Faulkner had his own reservations about Ike. When he was told that one interviewer's favorite character was Ike McCaslin, because Ike rejected his inheritance, Faulkner asks, "And do you think it's a good thing for a man to reject an inheritance? . . . Well, I think a man ought to do more than just repudiate. He should have been more affirmative instead of shunning people" (225).

35. James left, "shaking from his feet forever the very dust of the land where his white ancestor could acknowledge or repudiate him from one day to another, according to his whim, but where he dared not even repudiate the white ancestor save when it met the white man's humor of the moment. But Lucas remained" (*GDM* 102). Although the original legacy is one thousand dollars, Lucius McCaslin's sons later increase the amount so James, Fonsiba, and Lucas will each receive one thousand dollars (261). The increase indicates that all involved recognize one thousand dollars as the exchange rate for the failure to recognize paternity across racial lines.

36. Marvin Klotz notes this absence as well in his painstaking review of the "procrustean revisions" Faulkner made when turning the magazine articles into *Go Down, Moses* (11).

Works Cited

Abbott, H. Porter. "Character and Modernism: Reading Woolf Writing Woolf." *New Literary History* 24.2 (1993): 393–405.
Aiken, Conrad. Introduction. *Selected Poems of Emily Dickinson*. New York: Modern Library, 1948 [1924]. vii–xvi.
American Psychiatric Association. *Diagnostic and Statistical Manual of Mental Disorders*. 5th ed. Arlington, VA: American Psychiatric Publishing, 2013.
Aptheker, Herbert. *American Negro Slave Revolts*. New York: International Publishers, 1993.
Ariès, Philippe. *The Hour of Our Death: The Classic History of Western Attitudes toward Death over the Last One Thousand Years*. Translated by Helen Weaver. New York: Knopf, 1981.
Bakhtin, M. M. *The Dialogic Imagination: Four Essays by M. M. Bakhtin*. Edited by Michael Holquist. Translated by Caryl Emerson and Michael Holquist. Austin: U of Texas P, 1981.
Baldwin, James. "Faulkner and Desegregation." *James Baldwin: Collected Essays*. New York: Library of America, 1998.
———. "Going to Meet the Man." *Going to Meet the Man*. New York: Dial Press, 1965.
Banfield, Ann. *The Phantom Table: Woolf, Fry, Russell and the Epistemology of Modernism*. Cambridge: Cambridge University Press, 2000.
Barthes, Roland. *Mourning Diary: October 26, 1977–September 15, 1979*. Translated by Richard Howard. New York: Hill and Wang, 2010.
Beer, Gillian. "The Victorians in Virginia Woolf: 1832–1941." *Arguing with the Past: Essays in Narrative from Woolf to Sidney*. Routledge: London, 1989. 138–58.
Bell, Clive. *Civilization and Old Friends*. Chicago: U of Chicago P, 1973.
Bell, Quentin. *Virginia Woolf: A Biography*. New York: Harcourt, 1972.
Benjamin, Walter. "The Storyteller." *Illuminations*. New York: Schocken Books, 1968. 83–109.
Bergman, Jill. "'This Was the Answer to It': Sexuality and Maternity in *As I Lay Dying*." *Mississippi Quarterly* 49.3 (1999): 393–407.
Berman, Jessica. *Modernist Fiction, Cosmopolitanism, and the Politics of Community*. Cambridge: Cambridge UP, 2001.

Bernstein, Robin. *Racial Innocence: Performing American Childhood from Slavery to Civil Rights.* New York: NYUP, 2011.
Bérubé, Michael. "Disability and Narrative." *PMLA* 120.2 (March 2005): 568–76.
Bishop, Edward L. *Virginia Woolf's "Jacob's Room": The Holograph Draft.* New York: Pace UP, 1998.
Blaine, Diana York. "The Abjection of Addie and Other Myths of the Maternal in *As I Lay Dying.*" *Mississippi Quarterly* 47.3 (1994): 419–39.
Bleikasten, André. *The Ink of Melancholy: Faulkner's Novels, from "The Sound and the Fury" to "Light in August."* Bloomington: Indiana UP, 1990.
———. *The Most Splendid Failure: Faulkner's "The Sound and the Fury."* Bloomington: Indiana UP, 1976.
Bloomfield, Morton W. "The Elegy and the Elegiac Mode: Praise and Alienation." *Renaissance Genres: Essays on Theory, History, and Interpretation.* Edited by Barbara Kiefer Lewalski. Cambridge, MA: Harvard UP, 1986. 147–57.
Blotner, Joseph, ed. *William Faulkner's Library: A Catalogue.* Charlottesville: UP of Virginia, 1964.
Booth, Allyson. "Woolf, War, and Work." *Re: Reading, Re: Writing, Re: Teaching Virginia Woolf: Selected Papers from the Fourth Annual Conference on Virginia Woolf,* edited by Eileen Barrett and Patricia Cramer. New York: Pace UP, 1995. 65–72.
Bradshaw, David. "'Vanished, Like Leaves': The Military, Elegy and Italy in *Mrs. Dalloway.*" *Woolf Studies Annual* 8 (2002): 107–25.
Brogan, T. V. F., Peter Sacks, and Stephen F. Fogle. "Elegy." *The New Princeton Encyclopedia of Poetry and Poetics,* edited by Alex Preminger and T. V. F. Brogan. Princeton, NJ: Princeton UP, 1993. 322–25.
Brooke, Rupert. *The Letters of Rupert Brooke.* Edited by Geoffrey Keynes. London: Faber and Faber, 1968.
Bryan, Victoria M. "The Death Industry: Commodification and Dying in *As I Lay Dying, Sanctuary,* and 'Death Drag.'" Fifty Years after Faulkner: Faulkner and Yoknapatawpha Conference, 2012.
Bucknell, Brad. "The Sound of Silence in Two of Jacob's Rooms." *Modernism/modernity* 15.4 (2008): 761–81.
Carroll, Berenice. "'To Crush Him in Our Own Country': The Political Thought of Virginia Woolf." *Feminist Studies* 4.1 (1978): 99–132.
Catalogue of Books from the Library of Leonard and Virginia Woolf. Edited by Julia King and Laila Miletic-Vejzovic. Brighton: Holleyman and Treacher, 1975.
Cavitch, Max. *American Elegy: The Poetry of Mourning from the Puritans to Whitman.* Minneapolis: U of Minnesota P, 2006.
Christian, Barbara. "Layered Rhythms: Virginia Woolf and Toni Morrison." *Virginia Woolf: Emerging Perspectives,* edited by Mark Hussey and Vara Neverow. New York: Pace UP, 1994. 164–77.
Clewell, Tammy. "Consolation Refused: Virginia Woolf, The Great War, and Modernist Mourning." *Modern Fiction Studies* 50.1 (2004): 197–223.

———. "Mourning beyond Melancholia: Freud's Psychoanalysis of Loss." *Journal of the American Psychoanalytic Association* 52 (2004): 43–67.

———. *Mourning, Modernism, Postmodernism*. New York: Palgrave Macmillan, 2009.

Clough, Edward. "Violence and the Hearth: Lynching and Resistance in *Go Down, Moses*." *Mississippi Quarterly* 65.3 (Summer 2012): 391–412.

Colburn, Krystyna. "The Lesbian Intertext of Woolf's Short Fiction." *Trespassing Boundaries: Virginia Woolf's Short Fiction*, edited by Kathryn N. Benzel and Ruth Hoberman. New York: Palgrave Macmillan, 2004. 63–80.

Collins, Carvel. "Biographical Background for Faulkner's *Helen*." *"Helen: A Courtship" and "Mississippi Poems."* William Faulkner. Oxford, MS: Yoknapatawpha Press; New Orleans: Tulane University, 1981. 9–110.

Cowan, Laura. "The Elegy and Modernism." *Studies in the Humanities* 19 (1992): 43–57.

Cowley, Malcolm. *The Faulkner-Cowley File: Letters and Memories, 1944–1962*. New York: Viking, 1966.

———. "Go Down to Faulkner's Land." *New Republic*, 29 June 1942, 90.

Creighton, Joanne V. *William Faulkner's Craft of Revision: The Snopes Trilogy, "The Unvanquished," and "Go Down, Moses."* Detroit: Wayne State UP, 1977.

Cuddy-Keane, Melba. *Virginia Woolf, the Intellectual, and the Public Sphere*. Cambridge: Cambridge UP, 2003.

Davis, Thadious. *Games of Property: Law, Race, Gender, and Faulkner's "Go Down, Moses."* Durham, NC: Duke UP, 2003.

De Gay, Jane. *Virginia Woolf's Novels and the Literary Past*. Edinburgh: Edinburgh UP, 2006.

DeMeester, Karen. "Trauma, Post-Traumatic Stress Disorder, and Obstacles to Postwar Recovery in *Mrs. Dalloway*." *Virginia Woolf and Trauma: Embodied Texts*, edited by Suzette Henke and David Eberly. New York: Pace UP, 2007.

Derrida, Jacques. "By Force of Mourning." *Critical Inquiry* 22.2 (1996): 171–92.

Dick, Susan. "Introduction." *The Complete Shorter Fiction of Virginia Woolf*, 2nd ed. Orlando: Harvest, 1989.

Dickinson, Emily. *The Poems of Emily Dickinson: Reading Edition*. Edited by R. W. Franklin. Cambridge, MA: Belknap Press, 2005.

———. *Selected Poems of Emily Dickinson*. Edited by Conrad Aiken. New York: Modern Library, 1948 [1924].

Didion, Joan. *The Year of Magical Thinking*. New York: Knopf, 2005.

Donaldson, Susan V. "Contending Narratives: *Go Down, Moses* and the Short Story Cycle." *Faulkner and the Short Story: Faulkner and Yoknapatawpha, 1990*, edited by Evans Harrington and Ann J. Abadie. Jackson: UP of Mississippi, 1992. 128–48.

Du Bois, W. E. B. *Writings*. New York: Library of America, 1986.

Edwards, Erin. *The Modernist Corpse: Posthumanism and the Posthumous*. Minneapolis: U of Minnesota P, 2018.

Egerton, Douglas R. "A Peculiar Mark of Infamy: Dismemberment, Burial, and Rebelliousness in Slave Societies." *Mortal Remains: Death in Early America*, edited by Nancy Isenberg and Andrew Burstein. Philadelphia: U of Pennsylvania P, 2003. 149–60.

Egginton, William. "Intimacy and Anonymity, or How the Audience Became a Crowd." *Crowds*, edited by Jeffrey T. Schnapp and Matthew Tiews. Stanford, CA: Stanford UP, 2006. 97–110.

Eliot, George. *Middlemarch*. Edited by David Carroll. Oxford: Oxford UP, 1998.

Eliot, T. S. "Tradition and the Individual Talent." *Perspecta* 19 (1982): 36–42.

Eng, David L., and David Kazanjian. "Introduction: Mourning Remains." *Loss: The Politics of Mourning*, edited by David L. Eng and David Kazanjian. Berkeley: U of California P, 2003. 1–25.

Faulkner, William. *As I Lay Dying*. New York: Vintage, 1990.

——. *Collected Stories of William Faulkner*. New York: Vintage, 1995.

——. *Essays, Speeches, and Public Letters*. Edited by James B. Meriwether. London: Chatto and Windus, 1967.

——. *Faulkner in the University: Class Conferences at the University of Virginia, 1957–1958*. Edited by Frederick L. Gwynn and Joseph L. Blotner. New York: Vintage, 1959.

——. *Go Down, Moses*. New York: Vintage, 1990.

——. *A Green Bough*. New York: Harrison Smith and Robert Haas, 1933.

——. *If I Forget Thee, Jerusalem [The Wild Palms] Novels 1936–1940*. New York: Library of America, 1990. 495–726.

——. *Lion in the Garden: Interviews with William Faulkner, 1926–1962*. Edited by James. B. Meriwether and Michael Millgate. New York: Random House, 1962.

——. *Selected Letters of William Faulkner*. Edited by Joseph Blotner. New York: Random House, 1977.

——. *Soldiers' Pay. Novels 1926–1929*. New York: Library of America, 2006. 1–256.

——. *The Sound and the Fury*. 3rd ed. Edited by Michael Gorra. New York: Norton, 2014.

Fernald, Anne. "More on Textual Editing, More from the Lilly." 14 May 2007. http://fernham.blogspot.com/2007/05/more-on-textual-editing-more-from-lilly.html.

——. "Mourning in Greek." 6 December 2005. http://fernham.blogspot.com/2005/12/mourning-in-greek.html.

Forbes, Shannon. "Equating Performance with Identity: The Failure of Clarissa Dalloway's Victorian 'Self' in Virginia Woolf's *Mrs. Dalloway*." *Journal of the Midwest Modern Language Association* 38.1 (2005): 38–50.

Forster, E. M. *Two Cheers for Democracy*. London: Edward Arnold, 1951.

Forter, Greg. "Against Melancholia: Contemporary Mourning Theory, Fitzgerald's *The Great Gatsby*, and the Politics of Unfinished Grief." *Differences: A Journal of Feminist Cultural Studies* 14.2 (2003): 134–70.

Fowler, Rowena. "Moments and Metamorphoses: Virginia Woolf's Greece." *Comparative Literature* 51.3 (1999): 217–42.

Frazier, Lyn, and Keith Rayner. "Making and Correcting Errors during Sentence Comprehension: Eye Movements in the Analysis of Structurally Ambiguous Sentences." *Cognitive Psychology* 14 (1982): 178–210.
Freud, Sigmund. "Mourning and Melancholia." *The Standard Edition of the Complete Works of Sigmund Freud,* translated by James Strachey, vol. 14. London: Hogarth Press, 1963. 243–58.
———. "Thoughts for the Times on War and Death." *The Standard Edition of the Complete Works of Sigmund Freud,* translated by James Strachey, vol. 14. London: Hogarth Press, 1963. 273–300.
Friedman, Susan Stanford. *Mappings: Feminism and the Cultural Geographies of Encounter.* Princeton, NJ: Princeton UP, 1998.
Froula, Christine. "*Mrs. Dalloway*'s Post-War Elegy: Women, War, and the Art of Mourning." *Modernism/modernity* 9.1 (2002): 125–63.
———. *Virginia Woolf and the Bloomsbury Avant-Garde.* New York: Columbia UP, 2005.
———. "War, Civilization, and the Conscience of Modernity: Views from *Jacob's Room.*" *Virginia Woolf: Texts and Contexts: Selected Papers from the Fifth Annual Conference on Virginia Woolf,* edited by Beth Rigel Daughterty and Eileen Barrett. New York: Pace UP, 1996. 280–95.
Fuss, Diana. *Dying Modern: A Meditation on Elegy.* Durham, NC: Duke UP, 2013.
Fussell, Paul. *The Great War and Modern Memory.* Illustrated ed. New York: Sterling, 2009.
Genovese, Eugene D. *Roll, Jordan, Roll: The World the Slaves Made.* New York: Pantheon, 1972.
Gilbert, Sandra M. "'Rats' Alley': The Great War, Modernism, and the (Anti) Pastoral Elegy." *New Literary History* 30.1 (1999): 179–201.
Gilroy, Paul. "One Nation under a Groove: The Cultural Politics of 'Race' and Racism in Britain." *Anatomy of Racism,* edited by David Theo Goldberg. Minneapolis: U of Minnesota P, 1990. 263–82.
Glissant, Edouard. *Faulkner, Mississippi.* Translated by Barbara Lewis and Thomas C. Speak. New York: Farrar, Straus and Giroux, 1999.
Godden, Richard. *William Faulkner: An Economy of Complex Words.* Princeton, NJ: Princeton UP, 2007.
Godden, Richard, and Noel Polk. "Reading the Ledgers." *Mississippi Quarterly* 55.3 (2002): 301–59.
Greenwald, Elissa. "Casting Off from 'The Castaway': *To the Lighthouse* as Prose Elegy." *Genre* 19.1 (Spring 1986): 37–57.
Guth, Deborah. "Rituals of Self-Deception: Clarissa Dalloway's Final Moment of Vision." *Twentieth-Century Literature* 36.1 (1990): 35–42.
———. "'What a Lark! What a Plunge!': Fiction as Self-Evasion in *Mrs. Dalloway.*" *Modern Language Review* 84.1 (1989): 18–25.
Hackett, Robin. *Sapphic Primitivism: Productions of Race, Class, and Sexuality in Key Works of Modern Fiction.* New Brunswick, NJ: Rutgers UP, 2004.

Hays, Peter L. "Who Is Faulkner's Emily?" *Studies in American Fiction* 16.1 (1988): 105–10.
Henderson, Desiree. *Grief and Genre in American Literature, 1790–1870*. Farnham, Surrey: Ashgate, 2011.
Hewson, Marc. "'My Children Were of Me Alone': Maternal Influence in Faulkner's *As I Lay Dying*." *Mississippi Quarterly* 53.4 (2000): 551–67.
Higginbotham, Carmenita. *The Urban Scene: Race, Reginald Marsh, and American Art*. University Park: Pennsylvania State UP, 2015.
Higginson, Thomas Wentworth. "Emily Dickinson's Letters." *Atlantic Monthly* 68 (October 1891). https://www.theatlantic.com/magazine/archive/1891/10/emily-dickinsons-letters/306524/.
Hite, Molly. Introduction. *The Waves*, by Virginia Woolf. Orlando: Harcourt, 2006.
———. "Tonal Cues and Uncertain Values: Affect and Ethics in *Mrs. Dalloway*." *Narrative* 18.9 (October 2010): 249–75.
Hoff, Molly. "The Pseudo-Homeric World of *Mrs. Dalloway*." *Twentieth-Century Literature* 45.2 (1999): 186–209.
Hollander, Rachel. "Novel Ethics: Alterity and Form in *Jacob's Room*." *Twentieth-Century Literature* 53.1 (2007): 40–66.
Holloway, Karla F. C. *Passed On: African American Mourning Stories*. Durham, NC: Duke UP, 2003.
Holtby, Winifred. *Virginia Woolf*. London: Wishart, 1932.
Hubbs, Jolene. "William Faulkner's Rural Modernism." *Mississippi Quarterly* 61.3 (2008): 461–73.
The ICD-10 Classification of Mental and Behavioural Disorders: Clinical Descriptions and Diagnostic Guidelines. Geneva: World Health Organization, 1992.
Inge, M. Thomas, ed. *Conversations with William Faulkner*. Jackson: UP of Mississippi, 1999.
Jaffe, Aaron. "Introduction: Who's Afraid of the Inhuman Woolf?" *Modernism/modernity* 23.3 (2016): 491–513.
Jones, Christine Kenyon, and Anna Snaith. "'Tilting at Universities': Woolf at King's College London." *Woolf Studies Annual* 16 (2010): 1–44.
Joyce, James. *Ulysses*. Edited by Hans Walter Gabler. New York: Vintage, 1993.
Joyes, Kaley. "Failed Witnessing in Virginia Woolf's *Mrs. Dalloway*." *Woolf Studies Annual* 14 (2008): 69–89.
Kelley, Robin D. G. "'We Are Not What We Seem': Rethinking Black Working-Class Opposition in the Jim Crow South." *Journal of American History* 80.1 (1993): 75–112.
Kennedy, David. *Elegy*. London: Routledge, 2007.
Kenner, Hugh. "The Making of the Modernist Canon." *Chicago Review* 34.2 (1984): 49–61.
Kermode, Frank. *The Sense of an Ending: Studies in the Theory of Fiction*. New York: Oxford UP, 1967.
Klotz, Marvin. "Procrustean Revision in Faulkner's *Go Down, Moses*." *American Literature* 37.1 (1965): 1–16.

Knox-Shaw, Peter. "*To the Lighthouse:* The Novel as Elegy." *English Studies in Africa* 29.1 (1986): 31–52.
Kohler, Dayton. "William Faulkner and the Social Conscience." *College English* 11.3 (1949): 119–27.
Kristeva, Julia. *Black Sun: Depression and Melancholia.* Translated by L. S. Roudiez. New York: Columbia UP, 1989.
Lee, Hermione. *Virginia Woolf.* New York: Knopf, 1997.
Leiter, Sharon. *Critical Companion to Emily Dickinson: A Literary Reference to Her Life and Work.* New York: Facts on File, 2007.
A Letter from a merchant at Jamaica to a member of Parliament in London, touching the African trade. London, [1709]. *The Making Of The Modern World.*
Levenback, Karen. *Virginia Woolf and the Great War.* Syracuse, NY: Syracuse UP, 1999.
———. "Virginia Woolf and Rupert Brooke." *Virginia Woolf Miscellany* 33 (1989): 5–6.
Lilly, Paul R., Jr. "Caddy and Addie: Speakers of Faulkner's Impeccable Language." *Journal of Narrative Technique* 3.3 (1973): 170–82.
Limon, John. "Addie in No-Man's Land." *Faulkner and the War: Faulkner and Yoknapatawpha Conference, 2001,* edited by Noel Polk and Ann J. Abadie. Jackson: UP of Mississippi, 2004. 36–54.
———. "The Integration of Faulkner's *Go Down, Moses.*" *Critical Inquiry* 12 (1986): 422–38.
Little, Judy. "*Jacob's Room* as Comedy: Woolf's Parodic *Bildungsroman.*" *New Feminist Essays on Virginia Woolf,* edited by Jane Marcus. Lincoln: U of Nebraska P, 1981. 105–24.
Low, Lisa. "Feminist Elegy / Feminist Prophecy: *Lycidas, The Waves,* Kristeva, Cixous." *Woolf Studies Annual* 9 (2003): 221–42.
MacCarthy, Desmond. "J. K. Stephen." *Portraits.* London: MacGibbon and Kee, 1949. 248–54.
Mangan, J. A. "Grammar Schools and the Games Ethic in the Victorian and Edwardian Eras." *Albion* 15.4 (1983): 313–35.
Mao, Douglas, and Rebecca L. Walkowitz. "Introduction: Modernisms Bad and New." *Bad Modernisms,* edited by Douglas Mao and Rebecca L. Walkowitz. Durham, NC: Duke UP, 2006. 1–17.
Marcus, Jane. "Britannia Rules the Waves." *Decolonizing Tradition: New Views of Twentieth-Century "British" Literary Canons,* edited by Karen R. Lawrence. Urbana: U of Illinois P, 1992. 136–62.
Matthews, John T. *The Play of Faulkner's Language.* Ithaca, NY: Cornell UP, 1982.
McIntire, Gabrielle. "Heteroglossia, Monologism, and Fascism: Bernard Reads *The Waves.*" *Narrative* 13.1 (2005): 29–45.
McMillen, Neil R., and Noel Polk. "Faulkner on Lynching." *Faulkner Journal* 8.1 (Fall 1992): 3–14.
McNichol, Stella. Introduction. *Mrs. Dalloway's Party.* Orlando: Harcourt, 1979.

Millgate, Michael. "Faulkner on the Literature of the First World War." *Mississippi Quarterly* 26.3 (1973): 387–93.

Minter, David L. *William Faulkner: His Life and Work*. Baltimore: Johns Hopkins UP, 1980.

Monte, Steven. "Dickinson's Searching Philology." *Emily Dickinson Journal* 12.2 (2003): 21–51.

Montgomery, William E. *Under Their Own Vine and Fig Tree: The African-American Church in the South, 1865–1900*. Baton Rouge: Louisiana State UP, 1994.

Moretti, Franco. *Modern Epic: the World System from Goethe to García Márquez*. Translated by Quintin Hoare. New York: Verso, 1996.

Morrison, Toni. "Memory, Creation, and Writing." *The Anatomy of Memory: An Anthology*, edited by James McConkey. New York: Oxford UP, 1996. 212–18.

———[Wofford, Chloe Ardellia]. "Virginia Woolf's and William Faulkner's Treatment of the Alienated." Thesis. Cornell University, 1955.

Mortimer, Gail L. *Faulkner's Rhetoric of Loss*. Austin: U of Texas P, 1983.

Naremore, James. *The World without a Self: Virginia Woolf and the Novel*. New Haven, CT: Yale UP, 1973.

Nielsen, Paul S. "What Does Addie Bundren Mean, and How Does She Mean It?" *Southern Literary Journal* 25.1 (1992): 33–39.

O'Connor, Flannery. "Some Aspects of the Grotesque in Southern Fiction." *Mystery and Manners: Occasional Prose*, edited by Sally Fitzgerald and Robert Fitzgerald. New York: Farrar, Straus and Giroux, 1969. 36–50.

Parker, Peter. *The Old Lie: The Great War and the Public School Ethos*. London: Constable, 1987.

Pearce, Richard. *The Politics of Narration: James Joyce, William Faulkner, and Virginia Woolf*. New Brunswick, NJ: Rutgers UP, 1991.

Pitts, Timothy J. "Hugh M. Dorsey and 'The Negro in Georgia.'" *Georgia Historical Quarterly* 89.2 (Summer 2005): 185–86.

Phelan, James. *Narrative as Rhetoric: Technique, Audiences, Ethics, Ideology*. Columbus: Ohio State UP, 1996.

Polk, Noel, and Ann J. Abadie, eds. *Faulkner and War: Faulkner and Yoknapatawpha, 2001*. Jackson: UP of Mississippi, 2004.

Rae, Patricia, ed. *Modernism and Mourning*. Lewisburg, PA: Bucknell UP, 2007.

Ramazani, Jahan. "Afterword: 'When There Are So Many We Shall Have to Mourn." *Modernism and Mourning*, edited by Patricia Rae. Lewisburg, PA: Bucknell UP, 2007. 286–94.

———. *Poetry of Mourning: The Modern Elegy from Hardy to Heaney*. Chicago: Chicago UP, 1994.

Raymond, Claire. *The Posthumous Voice in Women's Writing from Mary Shelley to Sylvia Plath*. Burlington: Ashgate, 2006.

Reed, Joseph W. *Faulkner's Narrative*. New Haven, CT: Yale UP, 1973.

Reid, Joseph D., Jr. "White Land, Black Labor, and Agricultural Stagnation." *Explorations in Economic History* 16.1 (1979): 31–55.

Robinson, David W., and Caren J. Town. "'Who Dealt These Cards?': The Excluded Narrators of *Go Down, Moses.*" *Twentieth-Century Literature* 37.2 (1991): 192–206.
Rowley, Rebecca. "Dickinson, Emily." *A William Faulkner Encyclopedia*, edited by Robert W. Hamblin and Charles A. Peek. Westport, CT: Greenwood Press, 1999. 102.
Ruddick, Sara. "Private Brother, Public World." *New Feminist Essays on Virginia Woolf*, edited by Jane Marcus. Lincoln: U of Nebraska P, 1981. 185–215.
Rushdy, Ashraf. "Exquisite Corpse." *Transition* 83 (2000): 70–77.
Ryan, Derek. "Following Snakes and Moths: Modernist Ethics and Posthumanism." *Twentieth-Century Literature* 61.3 (2015): 287–304.
Sacks, Peter. *The English Elegy: Studies in the Genre from Spenser to Yeats*. Baltimore: Johns Hopkins UP, 1985.
Saint-Amour, Paul. "Weak Theory, Weak Modernism." *Modernism/modernity* 25.3 (2018): 437–59.
Sassoubre, Ticien Marie. "Avoiding Adjudication in William Faulkner's *Go Down, Moses* and *Intruder in the Dust.*" *Criticism* 49.2 (2007): 183–214.
Schenck, Celeste. "Feminism and Deconstruction: Re-Constructing the Elegy." *Tulsa Studies in Women's Literature* 5 (1986): 13–27.
Schlack, Beverly Ann. *Continuing Presences: Virginia Woolf's Use of Literary Allusion*. University Park: Pennsylvania State UP, 1979.
Sensibar, Judith L. *Faulkner and Love: The Women Who Shaped His Art*. New Haven, CT: Yale UP, 2009.
Shaffer, Brian W. "Civilization in Bloomsbury: Woolf's *Mrs. Dalloway* and Bell's 'Theory of Civilization.'" *Journal of Modern Literature* 19.1 (1994): 73–87.
Shakespeare, William. *Macbeth*. Walton-on-Thames: Arden Shakespeare, 2002.
Shelley, Percy Bysshe. *Percy Bysshe Shelley: The Major Works*. Edited by Zachary Leader and Michael O'Neill. Oxford: Oxford UP, 2003.
Sherman, David. *In a Strange Room: Modernism's Corpses and Mortal Obligation*. Oxford: Oxford UP, 2014.
Silver, Brenda R. *Virginia Woolf Icon*. Chicago: U of Chicago P, 1999.
Simmel, Georg. *The Sociology of Georg Simmel*. Translated and edited by Kurt H. Wolff. New York: Free Press, 1950.
Skei, Hans L. *Reading Faulkner's Best Short Stories*. Columbia: U of South Carolina P, 1999.
Slankard, Tamara. "'No Such Thing as Was': The Fetishized Corpse, Modernism, and *As I Lay Dying.*" *Faulkner Journal* 24.2 (2009): 7–28.
Smith, Susan Bennett. "Reinventing Grief Work: Virginia Woolf's Feminist Representations of Mourning in *Mrs. Dalloway* and *To the Lighthouse.*" *Twentieth-Century Literature* 41.4 (1995): 310–27.
Smith, Suzanne E. *To Serve the Living: Funeral Directors and the African American Way of Death*. Cambridge, MA: Belknap Press, 2010.
Smythe, Karen. "Virginia Woolf's Elegiac Enterprise." *NOVEL: A Forum on Fiction* 26.2 (1992): 64–79.

Socarides, Alexandra. *Dickinson Unbound: Paper, Process, Poetics.* New York: Oxford, 2012.
Spargo, R. Clifton. *The Ethics of Mourning: Grief and Responsibility in Elegiac Literature.* Baltimore: Johns Hopkins UP, 2004.
Spilka, Mark. *Virginia Woolf's Quarrel with Grieving.* Lincoln: U of Nebraska P, 1980.
Stevenson, Randall, and Jane Goldman. "'But What? Elegy?': Modernist Reading and the Death of Mrs. Ramsay." *Yearbook of English Studies* 26 (1996): 173–86.
Sundquist, Eric J. *Faulkner: The House Divided.* Baltimore: Johns Hopkins UP, 1983.
Taylor, Walter. "Faulkner's Pantaloon: The Negro Anomaly at the Heart of *Go Down, Moses.*" *American Literature* 44.3 (1972): 430–44.
Tick, Stanley. "The Unity of *Go Down, Moses.*" *Twentieth-Century Literature* 8 (1962): 67–73.
Trilling, Lionel. "The McCaslins of Mississippi." *Nation,* 30 May 1942, 632.
Trumpener, Katie. "Memories Carved in Granite: Great War Memorials and Everyday Life." *PMLA* 115.5 (2000): 1096–1103.
Tullberg, Rita McWilliams. *Women at Cambridge.* Cambridge: Cambridge UP, 1998.
Vickery, John B. *The Prose Elegy: An Exploration of Modern American and British Fiction.* Baton Rouge: Louisiana State UP, 2009.
Vickery, Olga. *The Novels of William Faulkner.* Baton Rouge: Louisiana State UP, 1959.
Walkowitz, Rebecca L. *Cosmopolitan Style: Modernism beyond the Nation.* New York: Columbia UP, 2006.
———. "Virginia Woolf's Evasion: Critical Cosmopolitanism and British Modernism." *Bad Modernisms,* edited by Douglas Mao and Rebecca L. Walkowitz. Durham, NC: Duke UP, 2006. 119–44.
Wall, Kathleen. "Significant Form in *Jacob's Room:* Ekphrasis and the Elegy." *Texas Studies in Literature and Language* 44.3 (2002): 302–23.
Walsh, Kelly S. "The Unbearable Openness of Death: Elegies of Rilke and Woolf." *Journal of Modern Literature* 32.4 (2009): 1–21.
Wang, Ban. "'I' on the Run: Crisis of Identity in *Mrs. Dalloway.*" *Modern Fiction Studies* 38.1 (1992): 177–91.
Watkin, William. *On Mourning: Theories of Loss in Modern Literature.* Edinburgh: Edinburgh UP, 2004.
Warren, Robert Penn. "The Snopes World." *Kenyon Review* 3.2 (1941): 253–57.
Weinstein, Philip M. "'He Come and Spoke for Me': Scripting Lucas Beauchamp's Three Lives." *Faulkner and the Short Story: Faulkner and Yoknapatawpha, 1990,* edited by Evans Harrington and Ann J. Abadie. Jackson: UP of Mississippi, 1992. 229–52.
Weinstock, Jeffrey. *Scare Tactics: Supernatural Fiction by American Women.* New York: Fordham University Press, 2008.
Wells, Ida B. *Southern Horrors: Lynch Law in All Its Phases.* New York: New York Age Print, 1892. 22–24. Reprinted in *Major Problems in African-American History,*

edited by Thomas C. Holt and Elsa Barkley Brown, vol. 2. Boston: Houghton Mifflin, 2000. 158–59.
Winter, Jay. *Sites of Memory, Sites of Mourning: The Great War in European Cultural History*. Cambridge: Cambridge UP, 1996.
Woloch, Alex. *The One vs. the Many: Minor Characters and the Space of the Protagonist in the Novel*. Princeton, NJ: Princeton UP, 2003.
Wood, Amy Louise. "Feminine Rebellion and Mimicry in Faulkner's *As I Lay Dying*." *Faulkner Journal* 9.1–2 (Fall 1993/Spring 1994): 99–112.
———. *Lynching and Spectacle: Witnessing Racial Violence in America, 1890–1940*. Chapel Hill: U of North Carolina P, 2009.
Woolf, Leonard. *Beginning Again: An Autobiography of the Years 1911–1918*. Hogarth: London, 1964.
———. *Downhill All the Way: An Autobiography of the Years 1919–1939*. London: Hogarth Press, 1967.
———. *Growing: An Autobiography of the Years 1904–1911*. London, Hogarth Press, 1961.
———. *Sowing: An Autobiography of the Years 1880–1904*. London: Hogarth Press, 1960.
Woolf, Virginia. *The Complete Shorter Fiction of Virginia Woolf*. Edited by Susan Dick. New York: Harcourt, 1989.
———. *The Diary of Virginia Woolf*. Edited by Anne Olivier Bell. 5 vols. New York: Harcourt Brace Jovanovich, 1977–84.
———. *The Essays of Virginia Woolf*. Edited by Andrew McNeillie and Stuart Clarke. 6 vols. New York: Harcourt Brace Jovanovich, 1986–2012.
———. *Jacob's Room*. Edited by Suzanne Raitt. New York: Norton, 2007.
———. *The Letters of Virginia Woolf*. Edited by Nigel Nicolson and Joanne Trautmann. 6 vols. New York: Harcourt Brace Jovanovich, 1975–80.
———. "The Mark on the Wall." *The Complete Shorter Fiction of Virginia Woolf*. Edited by Susan Dick. 2nd ed. Orlando: Harvest, 1985.
———. *Moments of Being*. Edited by Jeanne Schulkind. 2nd ed. San Diego: Harcourt, 1985.
———. *Mrs. Dalloway*. San Diego: Harvest, 1953.
———. *The Mrs. Dalloway Reader*. Edited by Francine Prose. Orlando: Harcourt, 2003.
———. "On Not Knowing Greek." *The Common Reader*. Orlando: Harcourt, 1925. 23–38.
———. *A Passionate Apprentice: The Early Journals, 1897–1909*. Edited by Mitchell A. Leaska. San Diego: HBJ, 1990.
———. *A Room of One's Own*. Orlando: Harcourt, 1981.
———. *Three Guineas*. Orlando: Harcourt, 1966.
———. *To the Lighthouse*. San Diego: Harcourt, 1981.
———. *The Voyage Out*. San Diego: Harvest, 1920.
———. *The Waves*. Edited by Molly Hite. Orlando: Harcourt, 2006.

———. *The Waves: The Two Holograph Drafts*. Transcribed and edited by J. W. Graham. Toronto: U of Toronto P, 1976.
———. *The Years*. Orlando: Harcourt, 1965.
Wright, Richard. *Black Boy: A Record of Childhood and Youth*. New York: Harper and Row, 1989.
———. *Native Son*. New York: Vintage, 1994.
Yalom, Marilyn. *The American Resting Place: Four Hundred Years of History through Our Cemeteries and Burial Grounds*. Boston: Houghton Mifflin, 2008.
Zeiger, Melissa F. *Beyond Consolation: Death, Sexuality, and the Changing Shapes of Elegy*. Ithaca, NY: Cornell UP, 1997.
Zwerdling, Alex. "*Jacob's Room:* Woolf's Satiric Elegy." *ELH* 48.4 (1981): 894–913.
———. *Virginia Woolf and the Real World*. Berkeley: U of California P, 1986.

Index

Abadie, Ann, 193n14
Abbott, H. Porter, 68
Abraham, Nicholas, 205n20
Aiken, Conrad, 91–93, 197n10, 197n13
animals, 23, 175; buzzard, 17, 40, 90–92, 100–101, 197n9; dead, 40–41
Apostles, Cambridge society, 46, 194n6
Aptheker, Herbert, 158, 163–64
Ariès, Philippe, 20, 127

Bakhtin, Mikhail, 17–18, 20, 62, 63, 195n14
Baldwin, James, 175, 177–79, 186
Banfield, Ann, 194n10
Barbusse, Henri, 14
Barr, Caroline, 155–56, 162
Barthes, Roland, 190
Beer, Gillian, 194n10
Benjamin, Walter, 13, 20
Bennett, Arnold, 21, 68
Bell, Clive, 141–42, 202n17
Bell, Quentin, 47, 48, 142, 194nn6–7
Bell, Vanessa, 46, 74, 195n19
Bergman, Jill, 100
Berman, Jessica, 3, 202n16
Bernstein, Robin, 205n23
Bérubé, Michael, 30
Bible, 15, 37, 96–97, 148, 152–53, 157, 160, 179, 197n15, 203n7
Binyon, Laurence, 201n11
Bishop, Edward, 105, 106, 196n1, 199n27
Bishop, Elizabeth, 29

Blaine, Diana, 100
Bleikasten, André, 4, 35–36, 40, 82, 85, 191n5, 193n1
Bloomfield, Morton, 191n3
Bloomsbury Group, 46–49, 192n9, 194nn6–7
Blotner, Joseph, 192n6
body, the, 15, 24, 57–58, 81, 83–84, 123, 127, 128–29, 151–54, 161, 167, 170, 173, 177, 184–85, 187–88, 196n3, 203n9
Booth, Allyson, 196n2
Bradshaw, David, 117, 194n2, 200n4
Brooke, Rupert, 14, 118–121, 133, 200n5
Bryan, Victoria, 196n3
Byrd, James, 204n11
Byron, George Gordon, Lord, 47, 53, 200n4

Carroll, Berenice, 202n20
Cather, Willa, 91
Cavitch, Max, 92, 192n8
character, fictional, 18–19, 20–22, 23, 29, 34, 35, 64–65, 67, 86–87, 102, 133; absent central figure, 4, 13, 20, 23, 34, 36, 39, 58–59, 61, 65, 73, 78–79, 82, 137–38; decentering, 138–39, 148, 182; Faulkner on, 20–21, 34, 36, 38; Woolf on, 21, 68
children: challenging mourning conventions, 22, 35–41; hide and seek, 41, 65–66, 68, 73, 76, 132; interracial friendship, 185–188

221

Christian, Barbara, 195n18
Churchill, Winston, 119
civil rights movement, 153, 164, 179
Civil War, American, 14, 15, 28, 29, 164, 180, 183, 204n12
Clewell, Tammy, 5, 9, 17, 87, 96, 111, 191n2, 192n10, 193n12, 194n2
Clough, Edward, 171
Colburn, Krystyna, 106
Coleman, Richard, 205n23
Collins, Carvel, 6
community, 3, 7, 13, 17–18, 32–33, 43, 45, 58, 61, 62, 75–76, 87–88, 90, 102, 116, 124, 128, 134, 139, 147–48, 150, 155, 157, 161, 162, 167, 169, 170–73, 181, 200n3, 202–3n2, 205nn22–23
Conrad, Joseph, 192n6
control and order, 31, 36, 38–39, 43, 44, 46, 51–58, 60–61, 65, 67, 69, 71, 75, 77, 86, 89, 100, 104–5, 127, 133, 157, 161, 163, 167, 171, 185, 201n15
corpse poem, 23, 92–93, 98, 100–101, 197n12. *See also* Diana Fuss
Cowan, Laura, 50
Cowley, Malcolm, 4, 178, 202n1, 204n12
Creighton, Joanne, 202n1, 206n33
crowd, 80–81, 115–17, 126–128, 130, 132, 142, 149–50, 158, 170–72, 189, 205n23, 206n33. *See also* party
Cuddy-Keane, Melba, 202n16
culture, 2–3, 8, 10, 29, 32, 39–41, 43, 45, 46, 49–50, 84, 96, 118, 120, 124, 144–45, 147–48, 155, 157, 160–61, 164, 170, 179, 185, 188, 190, 191n1, 196n3

Davis, Thadious, 41, 156, 182, 184, 202n1
death: burial, 84–86, 88, 149–54, 162, 164–66, 170, 172, 196nn2–3, 204n16; corpse, 23, 36, 81–85, 88–91, 93, 94, 101, 110, 133, 173, 196n3; decreasing presence in society, 20; funeral, 35–36, 38, 39–40, 43, 83, 85, 148, 149–61, 164–67, 170–71, 178, 191n5, 203n4, 204n16; homecoming, 150–54, 156, 172, 203n9; moment of, 84–86, 142; newspaper notice, 150–51, 153–54, 190; superstition, 160–62, 166, 204n14; tombstone, 82–83, 155, 196n2; violent response to, 158–59, 168–74, 179, 181, 186, 187–88, 206nn29–30
de Gay, Jane, 130
de la Mare, Walter, 73
DeMeester, Karen, 125
Derrida, Jacques, 4, 116, 139, 168, 193n15, 193n17
Dick, Susan, 199n23
Dickinson, Emily, 78, 91–101, 113, 192n8, 197n10, 197nn12–15, 198n17
Didion, Joan, 27, 31, 32, 189
disability, 29–31, 33
domestic space and care for the dead, 91, 95–96, 113, 145, 171
Donaldson, Susan, 163, 202n2
Dorsey, Hugh, 206n32
du Bois, W. E. B., 174, 179, 186–88

economics, 10, 106, 112, 148–51, 156, 164, 166–69, 173, 180–86, 88, 200n3, 203n6, 205nn19–20, 206n32, 207n35
education, 7, 47; critique of closed nature, 8, 18, 48–50, 69, 109–10, 194n9, 199n24; gender, 51–55, 62, 70, 72, 74, 96, 103–10; militarization of, 8, 43, 40, 51, 69, 111; outsider status, 7–8, 44, 47–49, 74, 139, 192n9; Woolf ties to, 46–49, 192n9, 194n10
Edwardian period, 44, 52, 139
Edwards, Erin, 193n16
Egerton, Douglas, 158, 171, 204n14
Egginton, William, 128
elegy: aesthetics, 50, 72; anti-consolatory, 2, 101, 120, 134, 145, 168; classical allusion, 7, 52, 54–55, 72, 119–22, 191n3, 198n21, 199n24, 200n4, 200n6; compensation for loss, 32, 99, 111, 127, 129, 133, 156–59,

172, 179; competition, 18, 22, 28, 44, 60–62, 65, 79, 113, 161, 163; consolation, 2, 23, 27, 32, 45, 79, 85–87, 93, 101, 134, 145, 149, 152–54, 157–58, 161, 168, 171–72, 178, 191n3; definition, 4, 7, 16; flowers, 7, 30, 74, 149–51; form, 2, 16, 21, 43, 58, 69, 74, 86, 191n3; inheritance, 44, 61–62, 74, 89, 96–98, 137, 182–83, 185, 207nn34–35; naming the dead, 31, 88–89, 197n16; occasion, 3, 25, 36, 38, 50, 66, 76, 115, 117, 129, 144; pastoral, 7, 50, 121; Romantic allusion, 72, 121, 133, 191n3; status, 7–8, 17, 75, 88, 133; tradition, 1, 7, 16, 75. *See also* corpse poem; death; mourning
Eliot, George, 55–57, 64, 128, 195nn11–12
Eliot, T. S., 14, 64, 73, 135
Eng, David, 10, 16
ethics, 10, 20, 59–60, 62, 74, 76, 87, 100–102, 105, 112, 146, 190
eulogy, 3, 8, 14, 23, 60, 79, 82, 101, 151, 155
exploitation, 17, 32, 76, 87–88, 155, 181

Faulkner, William: *Absalom, Absalom!*, 29, 147, 193n1; *As I Lay Dying*, 17, 18, 23, 30, 78–79, 81–103, 110–13, 116, 117, 118–19, 123, 159, 171; "Beyond," 197n11, 203n8; "Compson Appendix," 21, 30; "Dry September," 171; *A Fable*, 14; "On Fear," 203–4n10, 205n19; *Flags in the Dust*, 193n1; *Go Down, Moses*, 17–18, 24, 30, 80, 105, 116, 127, 146–88, 190; "Gold Is Not Always," 180; *The Green Bough*, 93; *"Helen: A Courtship"* and *"Mississippi Poems,"* 6; *If I Forget Thee, Jerusalem* [*The Wild Palms*], 15, 29; *Intruder in the Dust*, 80, 206n30; "Literature and War," 14; "Mississippi," 186, 205n21; as Mississippian, 14; as poet, 94; "A Point of Law," 180; "Red Leaves," 169; "A Rose for Emily," 93; *Requiem for a Nun*, 4; *Sanctuary*, 196n3, 199n26; as soldier, 14–16; *Soldiers' Pay*, 14–16, 85, 89, 122–123, 193n1, 197n9; *The Sound and the Fury*, 4, 5, 17–18, 21, 22, 24, 27–41, 43, 79, 87, 88, 147–48, 161, 171, 191n5, 199n26; *The Unvanquished*, 186; "The Wasteland," 14; *William Faulkner's Library: A Catalogue*, 192n6; on writing, 28, 30
feminism, 3, 50, 70, 75, 96, 195n15, 195n17. *See also* education: gender
Fernald, Anne, 120, 200–201n9
First World War: as constricting mourning of the dead, 4, 8, 76, 117; cultural effects, 70, 85–86, 109–11, 112–13, 115–16, 121, 142, 144–45, 159; French battlegrounds, 14; memorialization, 5–6, 68, 83; noncombatants, 11, 13, 16, 24, 119, 145; as perceived by Freud, 10–13, 119; school preparation for, 48–51, 111; shell shock, 18, 24, 117, 122, 124, 129, 132; war literature, 2, 13, 14, 16, 50, 66–67, 69, 79, 111, 120, 123, 134–35, 199n25, 199n28, 201n11
Forbes, Shannon, 202n18
Forster, E. M., 21, 63
Forter, Greg, 10
Fowler, Rowena, 121, 200n6
Fradenburg, Louise, 50
Frazier, Lyn, 197n8
Freud, Sigmund, 19, 24, 25, 28, 35, 86, 102, 147, 148, 158, 193n12, 193n17, 205n20; *Civilization and Its Discontents*, 10; *The Ego and the Id*, 9, 10, 192n10, 193n12; *Inhibitions, Symptoms and Anxiety*, 193n10; "Mourning and Melancholia," 1–2, 9–11, 22, 50, 116, 167–69, 172, 192n10, 193n12; "Thoughts for the Times on War and Death," 10–13, 66–67, 83, 119–20, 146, 190; "On Transience," 192n10
Friedman, Susan Stanford, 202n16
Froula, Christine, 5, 49, 117–18, 139, 193n13, 194nn1–2, 198nn20–21, 201n11

Fuss, Diana, 10, 23, 92–94, 101–2. *See also* corpse poem
Fussell, Paul, 2

Galsworthy, John, 49
gambling, 148, 168–69, 173–74, 179, 182
Genovese, Eugene, 155, 157–59, 161–62, 203n6, 204nn15–16
genre, 4, 8, 63–64, 147, 193n15
Gilbert, Sandra, 2, 191n2, 199n28
Gilroy, Paul, 169
Glissant, Edouard, 184–85
Godden, Richard, 159, 167, 181, 203n5, 205nn17–18, 205n20
Goldman, Jane, 191n4, 194n1
Gray, Thomas, 47
Greenwald, Elissa, 191n4
grief. *See* mourning
Guth, Deborah, 133, 201n10

Hackett, Robin, 51, 66, 70
Hallam, Arthur. *See* Tennyson, Alfred, Lord
Hardy, Thomas, 73, 135, 197n12, 200n4, 204n13
Hays, Peter, 93
Henderson, Desiree, 155–56, 158, 161, 165
Hentz, Caroline, 155–56
Herskovits, Melville, 203n4
Hewson, Marc, 197n16
Higginbotham, Carmenita, 206n27
Hite, Molly, 55, 72, 131, 195n19, 200n1, 201n10
Hoff, Molly, 200n6, 201n11
Hogarth Press, 192n6, 192n9
Hollander, Rachel, 194n10
Holloway, Karla, 151–54, 174, 203n9, 204n15, 205n22
Holtby, Winifred, 199n25
Homer, 200n4; *Iliad,* 17, 65, 199n25; *Odyssey,* 17, 86, 201n11
host or hostess, 115, 116, 137–44, 147, 202n18

Houseman, A. E., 200n4, 201n11
Hubbs, Jolene, 3, 197n12

idealization, 34–35; antebellum South, 18, 165; dead, 18–19, 22, 45, 59–60, 79, 83, 189; distinguished young man, 103; hero, 13, 14, 16, 22, 47, 58, 65, 68–69, 71, 119–120, 124, 132; nation, 21, 48–50, 58, 127, 128, 133, 195n16; prewar nostalgia, 9, 11, 29, 30, 31, 43–44, 47–49, 64, 66–67, 69, 142; school, 48–49, 59–60, 69; woman, 8, 34–35, 180

Jaffe, Aaron, 193n16
Jones, Christine, 192n9
Joyce, James, 84, 192n6
Joyes, Kaley, 200n2

Kazanjian, David, 10, 16
Keats, John, 50, 135–37, 201n11, 201n13
Kelley, Robin, 163–64, 169, 184
Kennedy, David, 73, 127, 194n1
Kenner, Hugh, 3
Kermode, Frank, 20, 195n11
Klotz, Marvin, 207n36
Knox-Shaw, Peter, 191n4
Kristeva, Julia, 193n17

labor, 24, 164–70, 172, 174, 180–81, 183–86, 203n6
Lawrence, D. H., 119, 192n6
Lee, Hermione, 5, 43, 67, 194n4, 200n7
leisure, 169–70, 184–185
Leiter, Sharon, 95, 97, 197n15
Levenback, Karen, 118, 119, 123, 199n25, 200n5, 200n7, 202n20
Lilly, Paul, 36–37, 90
Limon, John, 85, 204n12
Little, Judy, 103, 110, 198n20
Low, Lisa, 194n2
lynching, 24, 80, 155, 163, 166, 169–77, 179–81, 187, 205n21, 205n23, 206n25, 206n27, 206nn31–32

INDEX

MacCarthy, Desmond, 46–48, 60
Mangan, J. A., 52
Mao, Doug, 3
Marcus, Jane, 47, 195n16
marginalized figures, 7, 25, 29–30, 43, 44, 70–77, 105–7, 113, 116, 117, 156–57, 182, 188, 189–90, 199n24
Marsh, Reginald, 175–77, 206n27
mass death, 13, 45, 83, 110, 115–17, 125–26, 136, 170, 185
Matthews, John, 4–5, 32, 38, 156–57, 179, 206nn28–29
McClain, Leanita, 205n22
McIntire, Gabrielle, 195n13
McMillen, Neil, 180, 206n32
McNichol, Stella, 201n14
medicine, 85, 118–19, 123, 124, 125, 129–30, 133, 145, 190, 200n8
melancholia. *See* mourning
Millgate, Michael, 14, 15
Milton, John, 7, 50, 73, 121, 135, 195n18, 197n8
Minter, David, 93
modernism, 101, 112, 192n9; aesthetics, 2, 4, 43–44, 49, 65, 67–68, 74, 76, 138–39; cosmopolitanism, 3, 132, 139; new modernist studies, 3; politics, 2, 3, 50, 80, 129, 141–42, 144–45; weak modernism, 24–25
Monte, Steven, 97
Montgomery, William, 204n15
Moretti, Franco, 141
Morrison, Toni, 6, 67, 201n15
Mortimer, Gail, 4
Mottram, R. H., 14
mourning: denial of death, 41, 127, 148; distraction, 33, 39, 87–88, 184; hushing, 33, 37–41, 115, 148, 152, 160–61, 178, 188; mass memorial, 5–6, 59, 136; melancholia, 1, 2, 9–10, 11, 16, 22–23, 29, 31, 32, 35, 48, 50, 102, 120, 168–69, 172, 190, 193nn10–11; moaning, 31–33, 39, 40, 148–49, 203n8; productivity, 1, 22, 24, 35, 86, 92, 146–47, 158, 167–70, 172, 181, 193n17; professionalization, 149–50, 196n3; singing, 25, 39, 122, 148, 152, 162, 163, 177–79; spectacle and performance, 45, 127–30, 132, 140, 148, 154, 155–56, 164–65, 167, 177, 201n9; waves of grief, 27, 31, 42, 72–73
multiple perspectives, 5, 13, 17–20, 22–25, 27–31, 33, 44, 46, 62, 68, 75–76, 79–81, 96, 101–2, 113, 115–16, 126, 137, 140–43, 146–47, 157, 189, 195n12, 206n33

Naremore, James, 195n12
Nielsen, Paul, 197n16
novel form: critique of protagonist, 8, 23, 24, 53, 58, 61, 64–69, 82, 101, 103, 110, 116, 130–31, 137–39, 141–42, 182, 202n15, 206nn33–34; Faulkner characterization of, 86; incorporating culture and society, 2–3, 19, 70, 82, 90; indirection, 16–17; linking death with novel's conclusion, 20, 84; narrative space, 19, 58, 61–65, 70, 72, 76, 82, 86, 88–92, 99–100, 114, 116, 123, 125, 14–43, 147, 159, 189, 190; nineteenth-century novel, 44, 51, 64, 165; Woolf search for, 44, 63, 73–74, 76, 86, 115

O'Connor, Flannery, 192n9
Owen, Wilfred, 120, 134

Parker, Peter, 49–50, 70, 118, 201n11
party, 39–40, 56–58, 61, 81, 116, 126, 128–29, 138–44, 147–48, 159, 201nn14–15, 202n19
Pearce, Richard, 195n12
Phelan, James, 51
Pitts, Timothy, 206n32
Plath, Sylvia, 197n12
poetry, 2–3, 6, 8, 48–49, 54, 111, 118, 135; complicit in the war, 119–20; Faulkner on, 28, 93; lyric "I," 22, 62,

poetry (*continued*)
  68; Woolf on, 21, 63–64, 73, 121, 134. *See also* corpse poem; Dickinson, Emily; elegy
politics, 50–51, 74, 80, 129, 141–42, 144–45, 146, 160, 166, 179, 202n16
Polk, Noel, 159, 180, 193n14, 203n5, 206n32
posthumanism, 23
Prosser, Gabriel, 158
Prosser, Martin, 158
psychiatry, 1; depression, 1, 190, 191n1; *Diagnostic and Statistical Manual of Mental Disorders*, 1, 2, 42, 191n1; *International Classification of Diseases*, 191n1; mental health of Woolf, 118, 202n19

race, 8, 29, 39–40, 148–88
Rae, Patricia, 2
Ramazani, Jahan, 1–3, 9–10, 16, 29, 30–31, 44, 45–46, 50, 55, 70, 75, 135, 193n11, 193n15, 203n3, 205n20
Raymond, Claire, 82, 94, 197n14, 198n18
Rayner, Keith, 197n8
Reed, Joseph W., 196n5
Reid, Joseph, Jr., 185
religion, 22, 45, 49–50, 94–97, 100, 101, 102, 103–4, 109, 110, 133, 135–36, 148, 150, 152–53, 158, 160, 161–62, 166, 170–71, 178–79, 198n16, 204n14
Robinson, David, 204n12
Ruddick, Sara, 199n28
Rushdy, Ashraf, 204n11
Ryan, Derek, 193n16

Sacks, Peter, 1–2, 7, 9, 12, 16, 17, 31, 32, 46, 50, 61, 135, 159, 172, 182, 192n8, 198n18, 201n13, 205n20
Sackville-West, Vita, 192n6
Saint-Amour, Paul, 24–25
Sassoon, Siegfried, 14, 120, 134
Sassoubre, Ticien, 205n17

Schenck, Celeste, 195n15
Schlack, Beverly Ann, 200n6, 200n8
Sensibar, Judith, 155, 162
Shaffer, Brian, 202n17
Shakespeare, William, 94, 118, 119, 120, 121, 123; *Antony and Cleopatra*, 200n8; *Macbeth*, 87; *The Phoenix and the Turtle*, 6
Shelley, Percy Bysshe, 46, 50, 71–74, 94, 119, 134–37, 182, 200n4, 201nn11–13
Sherman, David, 87, 96, 102, 112, 196n7
Sidgwick, Henry, 107
Silver, Brenda, 202n20
Simmel, Georg, 140–41
Skei, Hans, 174, 206n26
Slankard, Tamara, 196n3
Smith, Susan Bennett, 126
Smith, Suzanne, 154, 160, 162, 170–71, 203n4, 204nn15–16, 206n32
Smythe, Karen, 194n2, 198n20
Snaith, Anna, 192n9
Socarides, Alexandra, 192n8
social justice, 24, 50, 145, 146–48, 150, 152–55, 157–59, 163–64, 167–70, 173, 177–78, 187, 190, 206n26
Spargo, Clifton, 20, 59–60, 74, 191n2
spectator, 13, 16, 25, 36–38, 40, 57, 90–91, 124, 127, 190
Spilka, Mark, 4–5, 134
Stephen, James Fitzjames, 194n6
Stephen, J. K., 46–47, 60, 194n6
Stephen, Leslie, 44, 195n18
Stephen, Thoby, 46–49, 194nn6–8, 198n20, 199n28
Stevens, Wallace, 193n1
Stevenson, Randall, 191n4, 194n1
Stowe, Harriet Beecher, 186
Strachey, Lytton, 192n6
Sundquist, Eric, 28, 36, 38, 91, 165
Swinburne, Charles Algernon, 73

Taylor, Walter, 174–75
Tennyson, Alfred, Lord, 17, 46–47, 125, 135, 200n4

Thompson, Robert Farris, 161
Tick, Stanley, 204n12
Till, Emmett, 153–55, 203–4n10, 205n19
Till Bradley, Mamie, 153–55, 157, 160, 190, 204n11
Tolstoy, Leo, 34
Torok, Maria, 205n20
Town, Caren, 204n12
Trilling, Lionel, 202n1
Trumpener, Katie, 123, 196n2
Tullberg, Rita McWilliams, 105, 107, 109
Turner, Nat, 158
Twain, Mark, 186

Vickery, John, 29
Vickery, Olga, 90
Victorian period, 44–46, 51, 55–56, 91, 120, 131, 136, 198n20, 202n18

Waley, Frank Raphael, 107–9
Walkowitz, Rebecca, 3, 5, 8, 132, 139
Wall, Kathleen, 198n20
Walsh, Kelly, 110, 198n20
Wang, Ban, 200n2, 202n18
Warren, Robert Penn, 17
Watkin, William, 191n2
Weinstein, Philip, 206n30
Weinstock, Jeffrey, 92
Wells, Ida B., 173–74
Whitman, Walt, 192n8
Winter, Jay, 2, 111, 123
Woloch, Alex, 19, 64–65, 68, 70, 76, 82, 123, 159, 198n20, 199n25
Wood, Amy Louise, 170, 198n16, 206n25, 206n31
Woolf, Leonard, 21, 46, 48, 86, 144–45, 191–92nn6–7, 192n9, 194n6, 194n9, 202nn19–20
Woolf, Philip, 200n7

Woolf, Virginia: biography and biographical criticism, 5, 42; *Catalogue of Books from the Library of Leonard and Virginia Woolf,* 191n6; *The Complete Shorter Fiction,* 106, 134, 199n23; *Jacob's Room,* 7, 21, 23, 42, 49, 69, 78–79, 81–87, 103–6, 109–14, 116, 120, 131, 132, 136, 159, 190, 194n2, 194n8; "The Mark on the Wall," 8, 34–35; *Moments of Being,* 18, 45, 134; "Mr. Bennett and Mrs. Brown," 21, 68, 138; *Mrs. Dalloway,* 17–18, 21, 24, 42, 105, 112, 115–45, 147, 159, 162–63, 170, 181–82, 193n13; "Mrs. Dalloway in Bond Street," 134, 137; "The Narrow Bridge of Art," 2, 16, 63–64, 115, 116–17; *Orlando,* 6; *The Pargiters,* 4, 45, 194n5; *A Room of One's Own,* 7, 55, 109; "A Sketch of the Past," 134; *Three Guineas,* 7, 44, 48, 109, 139, 194n5; *To the Lighthouse,* 1, 5, 42, 62, 136; *The Voyage Out,* 49, 134, 193n1, 201n11; *The Waves,* 4, 17, 18, 21, 22, 27–28, 41, 42–77, 78–79, 81, 86, 87, 88, 105, 116, 123, 127, 132, 138, 147, 157, 192n7, 194n3, 194nn8–9, 195n16, 195n19; "A Woman's College from Outside," 106; *The Years,* 4, 45–46, 62, 192n7, 194n5
World War I. *See* First World War
Wright, Richard, 173, 175, 206n24
Wylie, Elinor, 91

Yalom, Marilyn, 161–62, 204n15
Yeats, W. B., 73, 195n11

Zeiger, Melissa, 50, 70, 75, 159, 191n2, 195n17
Zeldwyn, Cyril, 200n7
Zwerdling, Alex, 103, 129, 133, 194n2, 198nn19–20

www.ingramcontent.com/pod-product-compliance
Lightning Source LLC
Chambersburg PA
CBHW030825230426
43667CB00008B/1373